LIEUT. BARTON AND CAPTAIN GARDNER.

Page 57.

THE
QUAKER PARTISANS.

A Story of the Revolution.

BY THE AUTHOR OF "THE SCOUT."

WITH ILLUSTRATIONS.

PHILADELPHIA:
J. B. LIPPINCOTT & CO.
1869.

Entered, according to Act of Congress, in the year 1869, by
J. B. LIPPINCOTT & CO.,
In the Clerk's Office of the District Court of the United States for the Eastern District of Pennsylvania.

PREFATORY.

My apology for intruding upon the public with a book connected with a subject so pitilessly be-storied as the Revolution is, simply, that its route is mainly over ground hitherto untraveled.

The deep feeling that pervaded the community in the early part of the War of Independence showed no more striking and wonderful manifestation than appeared in the fact that members of the Society of Friends in Philadelphia, still claiming to be "Friends," actually withdrew themselves from the great body of the Society, and organized troops, composed of their own members, to assist in the great struggle.

In all respects, except taking up "carnal weapons," —and making good and vigorous use of them too,—I believe they maintained all the religious usages of the Society, and, after the war, they built the church described in the following pages, in which they met for worship under the title of " Free Quakers."

The Society, in its distinctive character, died out

many years ago; but there seemed to me to be an element of romance in this feature of the great war, that was worth preserving.

I lament that, since the story was written, the quaint little old house of Thomas Sanford has been so deplorably modernized and improved that no one would recognize it.

The story has no particular plot, being intended only to tell what certain very irregular people did, under the pressure of varying circumstances, long ago, and having no reference to what regular and sedate people ought to do now.

PHILADELPHIA, March 1, 1869.

THE QUAKER PARTISANS.

CHAPTER I.

THERE are not many scenes this side the "Delectable Mountains," more beautiful, after their kind, than the Brandywine Hills. There is nothing grand, nor sublime, nor magnificent, in them; there is no stern or rugged feature, except one of which I will speak in a moment, to be seen, as far as the eye can reach, in that part of them among which my story begins; but the hills roll back in long gentle slopes east and west from the little river; low, exquisitely rounded hills, rolling back and back like waves, with sweet valleys sleeping between them, through which flow small streams, sometimes silently, sometimes gurgling over stones and against sharp turns in the banks, into the river. It is the beauty of tenderness and repose. Soft shadows slumber on the hill-sides and in the valleys, and nestle among the masses of foliage in the woods which still overspread the country.

In the cool gray of the dawning, in the shimmering blaze of a July noon, bathed in the golden splendor of the sunset, or sweeping their wavy outline in strong, sharp relief against the night sky, they are alike beautiful with a solemn, tender loveliness, the recollection of which never fades out from the hearts of any who have lived among them.

The one rugged feature of which I spoke—and that is not visible at a distance which takes in the whole sweep of the landscape—is a rock which stands upon the right bank of the river, about two or three hundred yards below the bridge over which the Strasburg road crosses it, and about two miles from the borough of West Chester, now one of the prettiest towns in Eastern Pennsylvania,—though at the time of which I am writing, consisting as it did of a single tavern, known then, and indeed ever since, with the exception of a year or two during which it was occupied as a girls' boarding-school, as "The Turk's Head," its beauty may be said to have been in an undeveloped and inchoate state. There may have been a blacksmith's shop and a country store, also; I presume those concomitants were not wanting; but, having no historical evidence thereof, and wishing to be as exact as circumstances will admit of, I had rather not say positively.

This rock rises perpendicularly from the water's edge to the height of about forty or fifty feet, having near its southern extremity a mass of stone projecting some six or eight feet from the rough, craggy face, over the water, at perhaps three or four feet above the ordinary surface-level, and perfectly flat on the under side, thus forming a capital shade from sun or shelter from rain for that most patient class of men yclept anglers; albeit the stream at this day furnishes but little to reward their patience.

On the south side the rock, covered there, as indeed everywhere except on its perpendicular face, with green sod, rises with a steep ascent to the top, while backwards it slopes by a gradual descent to the level of the country behind; from the top northward runs a rather steep bluff for some distance up the stream, and parallel with its course.

At present there are a few trees scattered over its sides and top, while a number of others, some large and some small, grow in front of it, on the strip of ground between it and the stream which flows placidly on below. At the summit, the ground is covered with scattered boulders, some loose, but mostly only cropping out above the surface, which, near the front, is much broken; the highest part humps up, as it were, into a ridge, leaving a rugged, irregular terrace on each side, that on the south falling away rather precipitately, and that on the north stretching away up the stream, as I have mentioned, in a steep bluff, almost resembling an artificial embankment.

The ridge above is not more than thirty or forty feet wide where it begins, running back, and gradually widening as it goes, to the distance of perhaps five hundred yards, before it is lost in the level of the ground in the rear; rough near the face of the rock, but growing smoother as you recede from it.

Below the rock, for some distance down the stream, and extending two or three hundred yards on each side of it, the ground consists of low and level meadow, rich and fertile, as indeed is all the land in this part of Chester county.

About a quarter of a mile before you reach the bridge, which steps on its solid stone piers across the Brandywine, a road turns off to the left from the Strasburg road, nearly at right angles with it, and runs parallel with the stream at about the same distance, till it reaches what is known as the "Factory" (which for a good many years went periodically into a state of suspension for want of funds), where the stream sweeps to the eastward, so as to bring itself close to the road; thence they run cosily side by side to Jefferis' Ford, and thence, the road, leaving the stream, goes across the country, past Strode's Mill (both of them points connected with Chester county's share of Revolutionary history), to Birmingham, which is as far as we need to follow it. On the east side of this road, about two or three hundred yards below the main road, and in full view of the rock, stands a quaint little old brick house with a steep roof, which, though modernized in some respects, still retains one of the narrow windows, glazed with small lozenge-shaped lights set in lead, which was brought from England when the house was built. Nobody knows how old the quaint little building is, nor who built it; but there it stands, facing the old rock, a relic of the good old times, the only thing there, with which man's meddlesome hands have had anything to do, that saw the time when Chester county was part of " ye pprovince of Pennsilvania,"—at whose door, for aught I know, William Penn himself may have sat on some summer evening, with his plain cocked hat laid off to allow the cool evening wind to play on his brow, while he looked abroad through the curling smoke of his pipe over the goodly land which the munificent Charles II. had allowed him to buy from the red owners of the soil and thus cancel a bad debt the monarch owed to William Penn the elder.

Verily, William the younger found it an exceedingly bad debt before he had done with it.

At the door of this house, on a pleasant evening in the beginning of July, 1777, resting after his day of labor, sat an old man, quietly enjoying the evening air, as it came cool and moist from the creek, laden with the fresh smell of the sedge upon its banks. The sun was sinking behind the trees, and the mist was beginning to settle down along the course of the stream, while the light grew fainter and fainter as the night came on.

The old man had been sitting silently, his eyes wandering carelessly over the scene before him, when something in the by-road on which the house stood, attracted his attention. Turning partly around in his chair toward the door, he called,—

"Jenny!"

"What is it, father?" answered a low, very pleasant voice within the house.

"Come here and tell me what this is comin' up the mill-road. I can't make out whether it's a steer, or a man on horseback."

"Why, father, it's a man on horseback," said Jenny, coming beside him. "I can see him plain."

"Yes, yes; young eyes are better than old ones! to me it looks like nothing but a big black spot movin' along. Can thee see who it is?"

"No," said Jenny, "I can't make out yet: if I do know him, it's too dark, and he's most too far off."

Jenny stood by her father, scrutinizing the stranger, until the latter, having arrived opposite the door, reined up his horse and stopped, looking inquiringly for a few moments alternately at the old man and at Jenny, after the usual greetings had been exchanged.

He was a well-built man, about five feet ten inches

high, rather slender, but muscular-looking, and clad in an ordinary citizen's dress. At last he spoke.

"Can you tell me where a person lives named Thomas Sanford, somewhere in this neighborhood?"

"That's my name," said the farmer. "What does thee wish with me?"

"You are the man I'm looking for, then," said the stranger, with a frank smile. "I judge so from what you say, as well as from the location, which answers the description pretty well, and—and—from some other things which Frank told me," he added, with a glance at Jenny.

"Frank!" exclaimed the old man; "then thee comes from—where *does* thee come from, and who is the Frank thee speaks of?"

"I come from Philadelphia," said the stranger, "and the Frank I speak of is the man to whom you lent this purse, with instructions to send it back by the right man"—laying a slight emphasis on the last words, and holding out an ordinary wallet purse with very gaunt-looking sides.

"Thee comes from Frank Lightfoot, sure," said the old man, getting up and taking the purse from the other's hand; "he's sent back the purse leaner than he took it; but light down, light down, and come into the house; thee's hungry, and so's thy beast, I know. Jenny, get something for this friend to eat—I forgot to ask thee thy name——"

"Bettle—William Bettle," answered the other, dismounting; "but it would be as well, for several reasons, that my name should be kept as quiet as possible. Just call me William; nothing more."

"I understand," said the old farmer; "calling names

does no good. Here, Mike," he added, addressing the
hired man, who had just made his appearance; "take
this critter to the stable and give him a feed and some
water, and rub him down, and put some straw in the
stall for him."

"Yis, sur," said Mike, springing into the saddle with
a "whoop, git 'lang now!" and kicking his heels into
the spirited beast's sides as he lit.

Showing off one's agility on strange horses is sometimes unsatisfactory in its results. The fiery animal,
as he felt the heels touch him, sprang from all fours
into the air, whirling half round as he did so, and suddenly humping his back in a way that shot Mike up as
if from a spring, and landed him in a very crumpled
state in the fence-corner on the opposite side of the
road, while the horse stood looking at him as quietly
as if nothing had occurred.

"Roland don't fancy strange heels in his ribs," said
Bettle, dryly, as he crossed the road to the assistance of the discomfited Mike. "Any bones cracked,
neck put out of joint, or any little matter of the
kind?"

Mike slowly raised himself, feeling his limbs, and
carefully moving his joints one by one, looking first at
the horse and then at his questioner, in a kind of ireful
bewilderment, without speaking.

"All right, I see," said Bettle; "nothing's out of
joint but the nose, this time. I think you'll find it quite
as comfortable an arrangement to *lead* him to the
stable:" which Mike immediately did, with a rather
crest-fallen air.

"That's rather a 'ree' critter o' thine," said the
farmer, as Mike led the horse away. "As Mike's not

hurt, I'm not sorry to see his comb cut a little, he's so fond of braggin' about his ridin', and sayin' there are no horses here fit for a 'gintleman' to ride."

"Roland is an Irish hunter, and therefore a sort of cousin to Mike: he'd have been more neighborly if Mike hadn't introduced himself quite so uproariously. But what's up now?" exclaimed Bettle, suddenly, as a fierce, ringing neigh, followed by the sound of a lash or two, then a sudden rush of the horse and a crashing blow of his feet upon what seemed to be some boards, came from the barnyard. "The fool is beating him! He'd better have grappled with a mad bull."

So saying, Bettle rushed to the stable just in time to see Mike standing behind the pump, his teeth chattering and hair standing on end with fright, while the horse, with his ears laid flat back upon his head, and the foam flying from his distended nostrils, leaped open-mouthed at him, right over the well-curb and the trough that stood upon it, snapping at him savagely as he passed.

"Och, git out, ye divil!" exclaimed Mike, dodging around the pump again, so as to have it between him and the furious brute; "ye're no horse at all; ye're——"

"Run, you fool! Run for your life!" shouted Bettle, darting into the yard. "The horse'll kill you! Run, I say!"

It was high time; for the beast, finding that he had missed his aim, had turned again, after making a short circuit, and was crouching for another spring.

Mike ran with a speed he never accomplished before nor afterward, never stopping till he was safe in the house, with the door bolted.

As he shot past Bettle, who was standing about

half-way between the gate and the pump, the horse came flying over the well-curb again, after him; but, as he lit, Bettle, who had stepped directly in his track, threw up his hand, saying, calmly enough, "Halt! Roland;" and the horse, in the heat of his mad fury, stopped as if he had been struck dead.

"Thee has the beast under tolerable good command," said Thomas Sanford, from the gate, whither he had hurried, though not quite so fast as the younger man. "I don't think a farm-horse would have understood that 'Halt!' as well as thine did. I reckon he's smelt powder before now; and there's something about thee that looks as if it would be more at home under the blue coat than the drab one thee wears."

Bettle smiled, and answered,—

"I suppose there's no use in denying that I'm a soldier, or that Roland has been trained to something besides road-service. I'll tell you more when we get to the house. In the mean while, I had better take him to the stable myself, as I don't suppose Mike will want to have much to do with him. Where shall I put him?"

The farmer accompanied Bettle to the stable, the horse following as quietly as a dog, and indicated the place he was to occupy, where Roland in a few minutes was standing at his ease, munching the fragrant hay with which the rack was filled.

They then returned to the house, where they found supper ready, with Jenny at the head of the table, her mother sitting at a little distance from it, knitting, and Mike in the chimney-corner, recovering, as well as he could, from his fright. He was not naturally timid, but he had never come in contact with anything in the shape of horseflesh possessing the peculiar traits of character with which Roland had so unceremoniously made him acquainted; and let me tell you, you who are incredulous, that there is no more dangerous wild beast on this earth than an enraged stallion; and a braver man than Mike ever claimed to be might well be excused for letting his discretion get the better of his valor, under the circumstances. Besides, he was firmly persuaded in his own mind that the horse was possessed of an evil spirit, and, as soon as the two men entered, he exclaimed, eagerly,—

"Did ye ixercise the divil out iv 'im, misther? Sure I niver was so frekened in my life."

"There was no devil in him to be exorcised," said Bettle, quietly; "but he don't like the whip, and I'd recommend you not to try it on him again."

"Sure an' I'm not goin' within rache iv his ugly mouth agin, nor thim hales o' his, aither. Bedad, whin he sthruck at me wid his fore faate, they splut the well-curb like an axe." So saying, Mike, whose bones were a little sore, betook himself to bed.

The supper was soon over, Bettle being the sole performer, as the family had finished their meal an hour before. He then entered into an explanation of the meaning of his visit.

Frank Lightfoot, he said, had directed him to Thomas Sanford, as a stanch Whig, and one who could tell him where to find fifteen or twenty bold, active young farmers of Frank's acquaintance, who were ready and willing to fight, if they had anybody to lead them. Did Thomas know of such, and would he give him the assistance Frank had promised?

"Yes," answered the farmer, "I do know, I s'pose,

hat many idle young vagabonds who are ready for anything but useful work. But it was strange for Frank to send thee to *me* on such an errand. He knew well enough, as I s'pose *thee* knows by this time, that I am a Friend, and——"

"So am I," said Bettle, quietly, "and have had none but Friends in my family since William Penn came over."

"And a soldier?" said Mrs. Sanford, who was a stout, comfortable, motherly old lady, such as most farmers' wives become. "How's that? Haven't they dealt with thee?"

"No," answered Bettle, smiling; "I'm in good standing in the meeting to which I belong. Did you never hear of the Free Quakers?"

"Yes," said Thomas, "I have heard tell of them, but never knew much about them. I s'pose thee's one, of course?"

"Yes, I am."

"Have they all dropped the plain language as completely as thee has?" inquired Jenny, mischievously.

"Well, no," answered Bettle, coloring slightly; "the fact is, I've been so much in bad company, as regards that, for a year or two past, that I've got out of the way of using it, almost without knowing it."

"Never mind that, Jenny," said her father; "I want Friend William to tell me more about the people called Free Quakers."

Bettle proceeded to give the history of the schism, in substance as I shall describe it in a future chapter, having no room for it here, and contrived to interest the old farmer so much, and so far to enlist his sympathy in the movement, as to induce him to say,—

"Well, if thee chooses to go among the boys and talk the matter over with them, and Mike chooses to tell thee where to find them, I don't know as I can help it, though I may not feel exactly free to tell thee myself. It's hard to know exactly what *is* right. I'll tell thee this much, though: most of the people in this region are Friends and Loyalists—what thee calls Tories—and I must keep quiet on the subject, if possible, so as to keep out of trouble with the meeting and with them. Thee will stay here, as a visitor, as long as thee sees proper, and I shall ask no questions about matters that are none of my business. Thee understands?"

"Perfectly," said Bettle; "and I'll take care not to compromise thee."

He was gradually drifting back into his old style of language, partly from the force of present associations, and partly because he had an idea that it would please Jenny better.

And this reminds me that I have omitted a very important matter, that should have been attended to earlier. Here have I been talking, through the larger part of a chapter, about a young lady, without giving any idea of her personal appearance.

The fact is, there was nothing very extraordinary about her to describe. She was not one of your impossible beauties, but she had a face that was pretty enough, though not handsome in what I conceive to be the strict acceptation of the term; that is, she had no features that were aristocratic or classical (whatever those terms may mean), but simply a sweet, rather childish face, shaded by chestnut-brown hair, which *would* run waving across her forehead and cheeks in spite of all her efforts to coax and smooth such vanities out of it. Her complexion was of a clear red and white, which contrasted well with large hazel eyes, that in repose had something in kind, though not in degree, of the sad, dreamy look of Faed's Evangeline, if you ever saw the engraving; it is the most touching face, in its depth of desolate woe, that ever artist's pencil drew or engraver's burin traced.

I love to see a broad, well-opened eye, in either man or woman; one into which your own glance sinks, as it were, sounding unfathomable depths of clear light. When Jenny was aroused by conversation, or her attention was attracted in any way, she had a frank, earnest look, straight and steady, into the eyes of the one to whom she spoke or listened; an expression of simple, straightforward sincerity and faith, that showed a nature utterly free from guile in itself or suspicion of it in others. There was something in this look of hers, joined to her low, clear voice, that attracted Bettle as he had never been attracted before.

He was a good-looking fellow himself, moderately tall, broad-shouldered and narrow-hipped, with well-developed muscles, and a rather small head, surmounted by light curly hair, and with bluish-gray eyes, in which, though their expression usually was mild and quiet, there shone now and then, as he talked of the war and its events, a light, quick and flashing, that showed that there was a world of reckless daring beneath that quiet exterior. He was about twenty-three years of age, and had satisfied himself, or rather the thought had slid into his mind almost insensibly, that Jenny must be somewhere from eighteen to twenty. I am afraid that something else was sliding into his mind—or his heart—along with this calculation, quite as insensibly, and taking a good deal firmer hold of it. At any rate, unconsciously to himself, his conversation was soon directed almost exclusively to Jenny, who sat opposite him, looking into his eyes with that earnest look I have mentioned, which seemed, without any design on her part, to read what he was saying, even before he had uttered the words.

What feelings occupied her mind I will not undertake to say, or whether any but the curiosity and interest a maiden might naturally feel in listening to and conversing with a young and good-looking stranger who was talking upon subjects in which she felt a great interest.

Women do not fall in love as promptly as men do. Sophisticated or unsophisticated, trained in the ménage of society or growing up artless and unsuspecting in the seclusion of home, they keep a better guard upon their feelings, acting unconsciously from the instinct of danger,—a faculty entirely apart from reasoning or judgment, working independently of both, and always on the alert in the weak when thrown into collision with natures stronger and more aggressive than their own.

It was so with Jenny Sanford. She was interested in Bettle; she could not help admiring him, and contrasting the gentleness and courtesy of his manner, not only toward herself, but toward her aged parents, with the hearty but frequently uncouth demonstrations of the young men of the neighborhood, who, up to this time, were all she had seen of male society.

Women do not like feminine men, though they frequently make them useful; but they do like gentle ones, who treat them as reasonable creatures, and not as children or playthings; who show them a manly deference and respect, instead of obsequious servility on the one hand, or a coarse assumption of superiority on the other.

I said that Jenny was interested in Bettle; and, after the group had separated for the night, she found herself recalling his look and voice with a vague, indefinite kind of pleasure, such as she had never before experienced, and which she neither understood nor thought of analyzing. Even had she possessed experience enough to do so, she would at this stage, with her Quaker feelings, and principles even more powerful, have shrunk from the thought of becoming attached to a soldier, and one whose sole errand in the neighborhood was to procure men for a purpose which she had always been taught to abhor as unrighteous and abominable.

No, Jenny was not in love, *yet;* but the soldier had a share in her dreams, nevertheless.

CHAPTER II.

The family were stirring next morning by sunrise; a good old country fashion, which we in the city have pretty thoroughly got rid of. In fact, here, unless your business calls you up early,—and when you have enough of it for that in the city it is very apt to keep you up *late* too, thus cutting off your sleep at both ends,—I really can't see any sound reason for getting up much before breakfast-time.

In the country, had we been with Bettle, as he walked slowly along the road toward a little bridge which he had crossed the evening before, just before reaching the house, we might have seen what he did: the thin morning clouds floating tranquilly over the horizon, in the glowing light, golden-edged below and rose-tinted above, relieved against the pale blue of the eastern sky; the wide sky itself, with no bound but the distant horizon, to which his gaze traveled over rolling hills, crowned with solemn old woods; over quiet valleys, dotted with trees in little groves, or standing in lonely majesty; over the calmly flowing Brandywine and its tributary streams, flashing where the rising light glanced from them, like mirrors held toward the sun. We might have seen old Deborah's Rock, with its seamed and rugged face all aglow with the flood of sunlight which poured directly upon it, lighting up even the dusk and gloom beneath the pent-ouse crag that projected over the water from its foot. We might have heard the wild birds singing by the thousand among the orchard-trees, in the chestnut groves, and the bushes which fringed the banks of the little river; all warbling at once, each in his own time and at his own pitch, but all, somehow, blending in a wonderful harmony; and the chattering of the blackbirds from the willows that fringed the run, on whose edge he stood listening to the musical murmur of the water; while from the topmost sprig of the solitary hickory-tree, where he sat with his head knowingly sewed half around, watching Bettle's motions out of one bright eye, the crow shouted hoarsely his uncouth welcome to the sunrise; from the meadow below rose the lark's long, liquid whistle, and from every farm the cock's harsh, rasping call.

If we get up by sunrise in the city, what have we? The sun does not rise on the city at all. He only gets up from behind the houses or the end of the long street, a mile or two off. We have no crisp, dewy air full of the fresh, sweet scent of new-mown hay and clover-blossoms; but, instead, a smoky atmosphere, with a chilly dampness, impregnated with villainous coal-gas, and heavy with a vague, sooty smell, as though it had been cooked over-night and been slightly scorched in the process.

For the song of birds, the lowing of cattle, and the booming of the musical cow-bells, we have the rumbling of bakers' carts, the rattling of milk- and market-wagons over the cobble-stones, and the rumble of street-cars, enlivened by the infernal howl of the factory steam-whistles pealing and echoing all around. Decidedly, getting up early in the city, merely for the sake of getting up, don't pay; and that, after all, where business is king, is the ultimatum in all questions.

Bettle sat upon the rail of the bridge, watching the glancing water as it shot away beneath him, and abandoned himself passively to the influence of the scene around him. Many thoughts passed through his mind. Old recollections of childhood crowded back upon him, some quaint and grotesque, bringing a faint smile upon his face as they trooped fantastically before him; some tender and solemn, full of that indefinite sadness which is not sorrow nor regret, but resembles them only

"As the mist resembles rain."

In all these thoughts, Jenny Sanford somehow was present in some incomprehensible, though seemingly natural, connection. From some power of association and sympathy, he felt as though he had always known her. She was the embodiment of many a boyish vision and romantic day-dream.

She it was, he knew now, whom, under Protean shapes, he had defended and saved in all manner of imminent perils, in his dreams. She it was whom he had rescued, single-handed, from a troop of banditti, in a horrible, dark, lonely forest—whom he had carried from the burning house, where the fire was raging beneath him, and the charred beams bent and cracked beneath his tread, and the reeling walls gaped open, and the red flame licked out through the fissures as he sprang over the fallen door into the street and bore her off triumphantly amid the clanking of the engines and the shouts of the toiling firemen. She it was for whose sake——At this moment his reveries were cut short by the horn blowing for breakfast. The sound recalled him at once from the delicious dream-land in which he had been wandering, and he walked slowly back to the house, where he found the meal prepared and the family seated at the table, including Mike, who had pretty well recovered from his last evening's fright, and two young men, one apparently about his own age, the other about sixteen, whom Jenny introduced as her brothers; explaining their absence the evening before by saying that they had been helping a neighbor get in his harvest, and had stayed overnight.

Jenny looked as fresh as the morning itself, and blushed just a little as Bettle greeted her, for she recollected something of her dreams, in which the young soldier had figured somewhat prominently.

Bettle had recovered his faculties, and with them his cool ease of manner; and no one would have suspected that the frank, off-hand, careless man had in his nature the capability of such a reverie as the breakfast-horn had roused him from. He talked to the old people about the harvest and the prospect of crops, told the young men anecdotes of the war and its stirring incidents, talked with Jenny of the beauty of the country around, inquired of Mike concerning his bones, and offered to introduce him to Roland,—an offer which Mike declined with a grimace,—and, by the time the meal was over, had the whole family as completely at home with him as though they had known him for years.

After breakfast, he went to the stable and curried and rubbed down his horse,—a thing which every

American officer in those days was expected to be able to do as well as his men, or better,—while the two sons stood by, watching with admiration the beauty of the animal, and the skill with which his master groomed him; and Mike stood at a more respectful distance, eyeing the horse rather nervously, especially as the latter, though he stood perfectly still, once or twice turned his eyes toward him, and laid his ears back.

"You had better keep out of his sight for a day or two, Mike," said Bettle; "he hasn't forgotten last night's work yet, and he may attack you some time when I'm not near."

"Why, what's the matter with Mike and the beast?" inquired Mahlon, the younger son.

"Oh, nothing much. Mike undertook to lash him last evening; Roland didn't like it altogether, and Mike had to run for it," said Bettle, throwing the saddle upon the horse's back and fastening the girths. "I would like to go to that large rock yonder; can you tell me where I can ford the stream?"

"Yes," said John, the elder brother; "there's a ford where the Lancaster road yonder crosses the creek; but Mahlon, here, will go with thee, if thee would like company, and show thee wherever thee wants to go."

"Nothing could be better," said Bettle, "if you would like to go," turning to Mahlon, who he saw was eager to go.

"Oh, yes, I'd like to go, right well," said the boy; "I'm ready for anything; father says, anything but work; but I'm always ready for that, too, when there's nothing better on hand. Anyhow, I can push John, here, in the wheat-field, if I can't cut as wide a swath. Just wait till I saddle my horse, and we'll be off."

In a few minutes more Bettle and his companion were cantering briskly along the hard, level road, which skirts the foot of a steep wooded hill, the long shadows capering fantastically before them on its beaten surface.

Entering the stream a rod or two above the point where Buffington's bridge now stretches its solid stone bulk across, they reached the other side, stepping on shore, not, as now, into a nest of workshops, the rattle of whose cranks and wheels, enlivened by the monotonous "bumpety-bang" of a tilt-hammer, scares all the peace from the beautiful river, but into the quiet road again, which, however, they soon left for a bridle-path which led off to the left, through the woods, toward the rock.

Leaving their horses at the back of the rock, tied to a sapling, the two companions proceeded along the slope until they reached the top, where Bettle's observant eye noticed at once the peculiar formation of the top, and the facilities for holding it against an enemy by posting thirty or forty men among the scattered rocks and behind the inequalities of the ground; also that it commanded a good view of a considerable stretch of road to the eastward.

"This will do," said Bettle; "we could hold this place against an army. Do the people in the neighborhood often come up here?" he inquired, turning to Mahlon.

"No," said the boy; "I don't think anybody comes here once a month. They never come if they can help it, and never stay long when they do."

"Why?" said Bettle.

"'Cause they're afeard of Deborah's ghost. They say it lives under the big rock that sticks out over the water."

"She must find it rather damp," said Bettle, quietly. The boy glanced at him with a half-quizzical look.

"Then thee don't believe in ghosts?"

"Not much," said Bettle, coolly. "I'll wait till I see one that I can't show to be something else. But who was this Deborah, and what brings her ghost here?"

"Oh, it was in the old times, when the Injins was about here; she jumped off the edge of the rock one day, 'cause the fellow she wanted wouldn't marry her, I b'lieve."

"Well," said Bettle, "when I see her, I'll ask her how it happened. Is there any path by which horses can be got up here?"

"Not easy, unless you go back and come up the ridge; it's too steep, and the trees are too thick. But what would thee want to bring horses up for? does thee think of makin' a randyvoo of the old rock?"

"I want to see if it would do for that," said Bettle. "If there was any way for horses to travel up and down, and no danger of the place being visited, it might do for that purpose sometimes. At any rate," he added, half soliloquizing, "it would be a capital place to retreat to if we were hard pushed."

After a little more examination of the ground, Bettle came to the conclusion that it was practicable for horses, even, on an emergency, up the side of the hill, though it was a thing to be done only in utter desperation.

Descending, they remounted their horses, and rod to the house of another farmer, about two miles off, where Mahlon assured his companion that he would find at least three able-bodied men who were ready to enlist.

"How do?" said the farmer, as they rode up to the barn, where all hands were busy unloading a hay-wagon. "How do, Mahlon? How's the folks? Got through hayin'?"

"Yes," answered the boy, "all in the mow."

"Who's this friend with thee?" inquired the old man, who, though not a Quaker, either in principle or practice, had, from long association, insensibly adopted their phraseology.

Mahlon whispered in the farmer's ear, when the latter, seizing Bettle's hand, shook it warmly, exclaiming,—

"That's right, that's right! Thee's come to the very place. I s'pose I'm too old for service, ain't I? what does thee think?"

"Not too old to do good service, yet; but ours is of a kind I should be sorry to put an old man at. It is too rough and helter-skelter a life for any but young men who have some spare strength and vitality to draw upon."

"Well, may-be I'd better stay home and look after the old woman and the gals, for they're gettin' a little skeary with all this war news; but I've got three boys here that I know 'ud ruther be handlin' a bagnet than a pitchfork, or swingin' a broadsword than a scythe."

"Are they good riders?" inquired Bettle, glancing up at the door of the hay-mow, in which the "boys" were busily engaged in tramping down the hay as it was thrown in. " Can they stick on a horse wherever they touch him, right side or wrong side up? We'll have wild riding to do."

"I'll warn't 'em. I'll war'nt 'em," said the old man. "They've all three 'most growed up on horseback. Boys, come down here; I want ye."

The three young men leaped out of the window upon the load, and slid thence to the ground, light, active forms, with the broad, square shoulders which a life of work gives to men, and gathered around their father and Bettle, answering his pleasant "good-morning" cordially enough.

"Now, look here, boys," said the father; "here's the chance you've all been wishing for. This—what did thee say was thy name?"

"I didn't say anything was," said Bettle, smiling; "you didn't give me a chance. My name is William Bettle. I am one of the lieutenants of a troop of irregular cavalry under the command of Captain Ellis Clayton, a worthy member, like myself and a good many others of the troop, of the Society of Friends."

"A Quaker!" exclaimed father and sons together. "A Quaker officer of a Quaker troop! That's somethin' new. Does Tommy Sanford know that?" added the old man.

"Yes," answered Bettle; and then gave them a short description of the separation, as he had done to Thomas Sanford.

"That's a fine beast of thine," said one of the sons. "Are all the horses in the troop equal to him?"

"Not quite; but all that we have are good. We couldn't get along with second-rate horses."

"The boys have good beasts," said the farmer; "they are all three-parts blooded, and as sure-footed and active as cats."

"That's just what we want," said Bettle. "Now, let us understand each other exactly: we want just the kind of men I take you to be,—strong, active, fearless, ready for anything, and willing, if they join us at all, to join for the war, whether it be long or short. For pay, I'm afraid I must promise you more hard knocks than hard dollars; they are a good deal more plentiful. So far, all who are in the troop have equipped themselves at their own expense, and are able and willing to take their chance of pay when they can get it. Now, I have been perfectly frank with you. What do you say?"

"Why, I say," said the old man, "that I'll undertake to equip 'em, and keep 'em equipped, if they can't do it themselves, just as long as they choose to stay."

"Well, gentlemen," said Bettle, "may I calculate upon you?"

"We are willin', if we can go under thy orders," said the eldest brother.

"Of course, if you would rather," said Bettle; "each lieutenant has a division under his separate command, though all are subject to the captain's orders. You can come into mine, if you wish, as it isn't full; but you will have the hardest and most dangerous service to perform, along with the rest of us."

"That's just what we're ready for," said the brother who acted as spokesman. "I reckon thee won't find us far behind the rest."

"Very well; I'll depend upon you," said Bettle. "Now, if you can persuade any other good, hearty fellows—you know about what I want—to join you, you can help me as well as your country. But I must go; I have several more I want to see to-day."

So saying, Bettle bade them good-morning, and cantered away with his young companion, while the farmer and his sons stood looking at the light, springy movements of Roland, with an admiration which was mingled, in the minds of the young men, with a slight degree of bewilderment at the suddenness with which they found themselves enlisted for a war of very uncertain length and sufficiently doubtful result.

"Well, father, what's thee think?" inquired one of the sons.

"A Quaker troop of horse, with a Quaker captain. Well, I never!" said the old man. "What do I think? Why, I think the cause that has made that sort of fightin' men is a good one, and *must* succeed."

The men returned to their work for the present, while Bettle and Mahlon pursued their journey, visiting a number of persons in the course of the day, with varying but, on the whole, tolerable success. At any rate, he succeeded in getting the promise of two more to join the troop, and returned to Thomas Sanford's in the afternoon, pretty well satisfied with his day's work.

He found it quite refreshing after his warm ride to meet Jenny again, looking as fresh as she had done in the morning, and with the faintest possible little blush upon her face as she asked him "how many soldiers he had caught?"

"Only five," he answered, laughing. "If I had a

tempting bait, I might have done better; but I have to fish with a bare hook."

"How does thee mean?"

"Only, that I don't want to deceive anybody and be told of it afterward; so I tell them all just what they have to expect, and then let them decide."

"That's right," said Martha, her mother; "I like that in thee. But thee's not going to persuade my boys to go, is thee? I don't feel as if it would be right."

"Not on any account, unless thee and——" he glanced at Jenny, who was looking eagerly at him, "not unless you are all willing."

"Oh, no, I can't spare my boys; thee mustn't think of them; it would kill me to lose them."

"Many a mother has lost her boys in this sad war, Martha," said the old man, solemnly, "and many another will lose 'em before it's over. Why should we keep back ours if they're needed for the work?"

"It's no use talking, Tommy," said she; "I can't consent. Thee won't take them, will thee?" she added, imploringly, to Bettle.

"Make thyself easy," said Bettle: "no word of mine shall lead them off; and if they should go without thy free consent, it will be because I can't persuade them to stay at home; I've no wish to leave hard thoughts or sorrow behind me, where I have been so kindly met as I have been here."

There was a very eloquent look of gratitude on Jenny's face, as she turned it toward the speaker, which said a great deal, though her lips said nothing; and perhaps Bettle understood it quite as well.

This point being disposed of, and Martha's mind at

rest, the evening was spent very much as the previous one had been.

The next morning was a repetition of the one I have already described, with the exception of the reverie on the bridge, which was *not* repeated.

Bettle remained in the neighborhood about two weeks; not spending all the time, however, at Thomas Sanford's; old Azariah Woodward,—better known, both to himself and his neighbors, as " 'Riah Wood'r't," —the farmer who had so unceremoniously turned his three sons over to Bettle to be made troopers of, having insisted upon keeping him as a guest for several days, effectually backing his arguments in favor thereof, at the beginning, by coolly locking Roland in the stable one afternoon, and sending his man to Sanford's after his rider's portmanteau. Most evenings, however, found Bettle at Sanford's. He spent the two weeks in diligently gathering recruits, and training them in the peculiar discipline of the troop, of which he, as indeed were all the lieutenants, was as perfect a master as the captain himself.

He met all sorts of people in his researches; Tories, with whom he argued good-humoredly, whenever they would let him; though he had felt it incumbent upon him, on one occasion, at a raising, where, without any special intention of the kind when he began, he found himself making a regular speech, to take one of this class by the waistband of his breeches and the slack of his shirt, and pitch him into the Brandywine, for calling him "a bloody cantankerous rebelizin' varmint." The fellow, who was full twenty pounds heavier than himself, and had been the bully of all gatherings of the kind, scrambled out of the water, shook himself, and,

mply remarking, "Mister, you're not a bad hand at
hyst," betook himself to another part of the ground,
nid the uproarious laughter of the crowd. He found
en who were anxious to enlist, only they didn't ex-
tly like that particular kind of service; men who
ade it a simple question of pay; men who were well
ough satisfied with King George, though they would
ave no objection to this independence if somebody
se would take the trouble to get it for them; men
ho were "on the fence;" who "didn't know 'zactly
hat to say; hadn't thunk much about it; reckoned
ings 'ud come round about right, anyhow, after bit;
d see 'bout it," etc. He found, however, in addition
those he had procured the first day, half a dozen (of
hom the ducking-episode at the raising had procured
m four, on the spot) of just that restless, adventurous
mperament to which the irregular service he promised
em was especially adapted.

He had now eleven able-bodied young men, all well
ounted—this he made a *sine qua non*—and armed,
me with rifles, some with fowling-pieces.

Satisfied, by this time, that he had possession of all
e patriotism of the neighborhood,—all that was likely
be demonstrative, at least,—he prepared to return to
hiladelphia with his small force.

As I said before, he had found himself somehow in
nny Sanford's company almost every evening; and,
hatever he may have thought at first, when he was
out to leave her for an indefinite time he had no
ubt whatever as to the nature of his feelings. He
ved Jenny Sanford. There was no mistake about
; and he felt pretty well satisfied that she knew it as

C

well as he did. He felt as little doubt that his love was frankly and freely returned.

True, no such word had passed between them; but words are not necessary to an understanding between hearts that feel and answer each other's mute yearnings for sympathy.

Sudden! did you say? Love is always sudden, lady. I said before that women do not fall in love as promptly as men do; but when you first discovered that you loved your husband that is, or is to be, I care not which, were you not conscious of a feeling in your heart that was never there before? Something new and strange, and of a wondrous power, to which you had been, up to that moment, a stranger?

Well, the day came. The new recruits were waiting on the Lancaster road, and Bettle stood with Jenny at the gate of the old farm-house to say farewell. His voice shook, in spite of himself, and his hand trembled as he held Jenny's in his grasp, and spoke the parting word. As he galloped to the great road, and the party moved along toward the city, she stood, with the family, watching him until her eyes were dim with the tears that *would* come; and she hurried into the house, and to her own room, to hide them.

CHAPTER III.

WHILE Bettle and his men are on their way to the city, I may as well go back, according to promise, to give some account of the Free Quakers, and how there happened to be such a thing as a Quaker troop, at least so far as regarded a good many of its members, under a captain and lieutenants all of the same peaceful persuasion.

Well, in the latter part of "First Month" in the year 1775, there was division in the council of Friends, and the Yearly Meeting, then in session at Philadelphia, was *un*peaceful, with a spirit of dissension, and *un*quiet, with discussions often protracted into the night, as to the course the society should take in the war that had already begun.

Most of the members, particularly the elder portion, were inclined to oppose the course matters were taking, not only in obedience to their abstract peace principles, but because they were, in reality, in favor of the established government, believing that, bad as it was, it was better than rebellion and the anarchy which, there was reason to fear, would follow it.

At the beginning of the excitement, while the action of the Colonies was confined to respectful petition and remonstrance, they had been almost unanimously upon their side; but now, when men were beginning to talk boldly of armed resistance, of throwing off at once and forever the authority of the mother-country, the case assumed a different aspect.

The most perplexing part of the business was, that the idea of fighting had actually found its way into the society itself, and the echoes of the popular voice were making themselves heard within the walls of the quiet Quaker meeting from the lips of the younger and more hot-blooded members, in tones which startled the grave conservative elders.

There was a most unmistakable disposition on the part of some of these younger men to side with the stirring proclamation which had been recently issued by the Convention; and a lamentable want of reverence for the principles laid down in the "Discipline" was manifested in the remarks which they took upon themselves to make concerning the duty of "Friends" in the present crisis. The Discipline, however, prevailed, and on the 24th of the same month a "Testimony" upon the subject was prepared and published, urging members to "discountenance and avoid every measure tending to excite disaffection to the king, as supreme magistrate, or to the legal authority of his government," and publicly declaring "against every usurpation of power and authority in opposition to the laws and government, and against all combinations, insurrections, and illegal assemblies."

This gave such offense to the minority, that they at once issued *their* Testimony in a very practical way, by summarily withdrawing from all connection with the meeting: they still retained the title of Friends, as a general designation, but, by way of distinction, assumed, or had put upon them,—it is uncertain, at this distance of time, which,—the title of "Free Quakers."

However this may be, they afterward adopted it, and so designated themselves on the tablet which still remains in the pediment of the meeting-house they built for themselves at the southwest corner of Fifth and Arch Streets, and which is now occupied by the Apprentices' Library.

A number of them afterward gave a still more practical evidence of their sincerity by forming themselves into a military company, which was known by the name of the "Quaker Blues." Whether they were drilled in "plain" language, or whether their drill-master ever indulged himself in swearing at them while they remained an "awkward squad," as drill-masters have a bad habit of doing, I am not able to say. With these, however, we have nothing to do.

In addition to this company, many individuals employed themselves actively in the contest, according to their various gifts; some in gathering and carrying intelligence, some furnishing clothing and supplies to the troops, some contenting themselves with busily talking treason in a general way, while others acted it out boldly by doing a very fair share of hard fighting whenever occasion offered.

Among the most active and energetic of those who had thus abandoned their peaceful professions, and had lent their voice and example to the spirit of strife and resistance, were Bettle and his cousin, Ellis Clayton, the captain of the troop, whom I have already mentioned. Both had been born and trained in the tenets of the society, after its straitest manner. Bettle's natural disposition, however, was headlong and reckless, though under tolerable control when not too far roused; but Clayton, though utterly fearless, and never recognizing danger to himself or his troop as an obstacle to anything that his judgment told him should be done, had none of the headlong, restless bravery which delighted in and sought danger for its own sake. The grand elements in his character were, unshaken calmness under all circumstances, a presence of mind which there was no confusing, backed by a sober determination and an iron will that held their ground with a dogged composure against which furious attack and steady pressure alike spent themselves in vain.

His life-long training in self-command, acting upon a nature like this, had eminently qualified him for such a command as he now held. He had not accepted it rashly, nor without due consideration; but, after calmly weighing the matter, had come to the conclusion that it was *his* duty to fight, and he straightway went about performing his duty. He was at this time about twenty-eight years of age, but with the staid, grave manner of a man much older.

Among his most intimate companions were Bettle and four others,—all younger than himself, and all belonging to the same society. These five men organized themselves into a troop consisting at first entirely of officers,—Clayton having first been unanimously chosen captain, and having in turn appointed the others his lieutenants: this done, all immediately began the work of raising the troop in earnest.

This was a work of time, not only from the severity of the requirements as to qualification, for Clayton had set out from the first with the determination to make his troop one of picked men, who should all come fully up to his standard, not for the purpose of making a fine display, but that it should be thoroughly

THE QUAKER PARTISANS. 39

ffective; but also, most of all, for the reason that it was to be made up of volunteers, who, as Bettle, in the preceding chapter, explained to his recruits, should quip at their own expense, and take their chance of pay. They were carefully trained by Clayton himself, ach new recruit, as he came in, having the advanige of the example of the older hands, so that, after aving got enough together to form a kind of nucleus f discipline, he had comparatively little trouble in raining them.

This training, of both men and horses, was directed) making them as effective as possible for both regu-ır and irregular service,—for fighting, either alone or)gether, as detached skirmishers, or, when desirable, s a part of the regular line. For this latter service, owever, Clayton, who, grave and sober as he was, referred to be his own master, had little affection, nd never subjected himself to it long at a time.

It was just such bands as this (for Clayton was by o means the only partisan leader in the war) that erformed some of the most brilliant exploits in the rar of Independence.

They have found no place in history beyond mere ursory allusions, from the fact that they led to no reat or decisive results affecting the ultimate issue of ne contest, and therefore had no claim to room upon s pages.

Their service was of a rambling, desultory character, ıvolving a great deal of hard fighting, a rough and xposed life, and calling for an unceasing exercise of hat is familiarly known as "mother wit"—that valuble faculty which tells men what to do, in an emerency, just when the emergency comes—in managing or guarding against surprises, and in eluding or diverting pursuit where fighting was not deemed advisable.

These parties, when not actually attached to the main body, amused themselves by various irregular escapades, such as beating up the enemy's quarters at divers untimely and unseasonable hours between midnight and dawn, setting the whole camp in turmoil with firing and running in of sentries, rattling of drums, yelling of bugles, officers shouting all manner of unintelligible orders, half-dressed men hurrying to their stations, horses neighing and plunging, while in the midst of the hurly-burly a body of twenty or thirty horsemen shouting like a hundred, and magnified by the darkness and confusion into twice as many, would skirr through the camp, slashing, shooting, and trampling down all who stood in their way, and before anything like order could be restored or any effectual resistance offered, would be out of sight and reach, the fierce clatter of hoofs and steel scabbards gradually dying away in the gloom, leaving the discomfited enemy to turn in again, sending a storm of unsavory blessings after the uneasy Yankees who couldn't let tired men enjoy their sleep in peace.

When nothing better was on hand, they were ranging the country, intercepting supplies intended for the British, cutting off foraging-parties, at times quartering themselves on the Tory farmers and doing a little foraging among them on their own account; at others, bivouacking in the woods; now here, now there; in their movements as rapid and unreliable as swallows, as silent and unseen as the terrible copperhead, and with a stroke as deadly.

During all the spring and part of the summer of

1777, Philadelphia had been in a state of anxious excitement in view of the evident intention of the British general, who was then stationed with his army in New York, to possess himself of the city.

Washington was holding northern New Jersey, doing little in the way of active service, but warily watching Sir William Howe's motions, baffling every attempt of the latter either to draw him into a battle or to deceive him into withdrawing his forces from the post they occupied and thus give him a clear passage across New Jersey.

Sham deserters from the enemy came into Washington's camp, bringing cunningly devised fables about northern marches of the British; his own scouts and spies lent themselves, wittingly or unwittingly, to these attempts; and letters were sent by messengers who were instructed to get themselves intercepted, containing false intelligence of intended movements.

Washington held his ground, satisfied that Philadelphia, and Philadelphia only, was the point to be protected.

During all this excitement, Clayton was busily engaged in filling up his troop and preparing them for service. All his lieutenants were out in different directions; though, as Bettle is more intimately connected with my story, he is the only one whom I have followed. At the time he left Thomas Sanford's, however, the others had all got in with their recruits, and the troop was nearly full. From the time of his arrival with his eleven men, who just made up the hundred to which Clayton had limited his force, the work of training men and horses—and severe training it was—was diligently pursued, until the early part of August.

4*

At this time Washington received unquestionable information that the British had embarked, and that on the 23d of July the fleet had left Sandy Hook and was moving southward: he immediately marched in the same direction, keeping out reconnoitering parties in advance to watch the coast, until he was informed that the fleet was off the capes of Chesapeake Bay. Upon receiving this intelligence, he marched at once for Chester by way of Philadelphia, reaching the latter on the morning of the 24th of August, marching with his whole force through the city in order to encourage the Whigs with a display of his strength, and then moving directly to Chester, where he arrived the same evening. And while the doomed army of eleven thousand men, half of them raw militia, was marching southward on that peaceful Sabbath morning, the farmers of Turkey Point, together with some fifteen hundred of the Pennsylvania and Delaware militia, were watching the debarkation of seventeen thousand trained veterans under Cornwallis and Knyphausen.

The American army entered Philadelphia at the upper end of Front Street, and marched down to Chestnut, up which they turned and proceeded westward. As they passed the State-House, a company of about a hundred horsemen, which was drawn up in the meadow on the north side of the street, was put in motion, and, wheeling in solid column into the street in the rear, fell into the line of march in a grave silence which contrasted strongly with the vociferous cheering all around them, through which was heard the loud clanging of the old Liberty Bell in the steeple.

They were all young men, ranging apparently from

twenty to thirty-five years of age, splendidly mounted, and sitting in their saddles with that easy, at-home look which is only acquired by a life-long practice in riding. As they wheeled into the line, a new hurrah broke forth from the crowd, and a boy's shrill voice yelled,—
"Hooray for the fightin' Quakers!"

The words caught the ear of Washington, who was riding with his staff a short distance in the rear of the army, and he sent forward an aid to inquire into the meaning of it and ascertain who these silent volunteers were. The officer accordingly rode to the head of the company, and asked,—

"Who commands this troop?"

"Ellis Clayton," was the answer given by the person addressed, who was a young man in a drab coat, such as Quakers wore then, not differing materially in shape from that of the officer himself, but destitute of any ornament whatever. The principal officers of the troop wore similar coats, and the ordinary felt hats of the time, looped up at the sides, and, as well as their leader, were manifestly Quakers. The only thing about the leader's dress to distinguish him from these was a blue silk sash which he wore about his waist, while his officers wore only plain black belts. The rest of the troop wore an indescribable variety of costumes.

"Well," said the officer, "who may Ellis Clayton be?"

"The captain of this troop," was the laconic answer.

"So I suppose," said he, dryly; "and what regiment may the troop belong to?"

"None; the troop is its own regiment."

"You are pleased to speak in riddles, sir," said the

officer. "Will you do me the favor to explain yourself?"

"The explanation is very simple; we are here to fight, but we must fight in our own way, under our own orders, without being in any way attached to the regular line, except at our own discretion."

"I doubt if that will be permitted; his excellency is not fond of anybody's discretion but his own, and will require you to join some regiment."

"Thee may tell the general that we are ready to withdraw at any moment from the line if he is not satisfied with our terms; if we fight, we do so without being hampered by camp regulations or general orders, except when we see fit to subject ourselves to them temporarily."

"You are tolerably independent," said the officer, "and a model of conciseness. Will you ride back with me and explain yourself to the commander?"

"Willingly," said Clayton.

So they rode back to the commander, and the aide-de-camp reported substantially what he had learned.

"How many men have you?" inquired Washington.

"One hundred," was the answer.

"And I'll say this for them, your excellency," exclaimed the aid, "that I never saw a hundred men together that looked more like doing service; and the horses"—he had been eyeing the whole troop critically while talking to Ellis Clayton—"the worst of them would be a fitting mount for a general."

"As you are not willing to join the line, sir, what kind of service do you propose to undertake?" asked the general.

"We propose, with thy permission,"—a grave smile

itted across Washington's face at the word "thy,"— we propose, with thy permission, to act as irregular avalry; as scouts; as outliers, free to come and go as we please."

"You are asking a dangerous license; what guarantee have I that you will not carry intelligence of my movements to the enemy, or act against me in some other way?"

"I don't think thee would ask any guarantee after the first battle; but I have prepared myself for this objection."

He handed an unsealed note to Washington, who opened it and read as follows:

"The bearer, Captain Ellis Clayton, is a true and stanch patriot, as I know from long personal acquaintance with him. His own fidelity, and that of those for whom he vouches, may be relied upon.

"JOHN JAY."

"I am satisfied, sir," said Washington, handing him back the note, "and am willing to accept your service on your conditions; and if you and your men are active and faithful, you may be of great value. You shall be free to come and go as you please, understanding, however, that while you may be in camp, or within the lines, you will be subject to my orders."

The captain looked doubtful.

"Outside the camp, your movements will not be interfered with, nor controlled in any way (except, always, when you may have been *sent* out by the officer in command for the time being), unless I hear that your men have been guilty of some unwarrantable excess: in that case they will be controlled very promptly and very much to the purpose. Now, sir, we understand each other: if you are content, join your troop; if not, there is time to withdraw."

"I am content," said Captain Clayton; and, touching his hat a little awkwardly, as if unused to such motions, he galloped back to the head of his troop.

"This is a curious addition to our forces," said Washington, turning to General Greene, who was riding beside him. "What do you think of them?"

"Whatever a Quaker feels 'a call' to do," answered Greene, who was of Quaker stock himself, "he is very apt to do thoroughly. Your excellency may depend upon it, there will be hard fighting wherever these men are at work."

The army had by this time passed through the built portion of the city, and the advanced guard had already passed the pontoon over the Schuylkill, and in the course of an hour or two more the whole body had crossed, and were formed on the other side.

The thousands of citizens who had accompanied them to the east bank gave a parting cheer as the army resumed its march, and then returned to their homes.

That evening the army encamped at Chester

CHAPTER IV.

The next morning a messenger came to Ellis Clayton's troop from the general, requiring the captain's presence at head-quarters.

He repaired thither at once, and found Washington alone.

"I have need of your services, Captain Clayton," said he. "You will leave the camp at once, and reconnoiter the country between here and the Chesapeake carefully. I received information last night that the enemy had landed at a place called Turkey Point, at the mouth of Elk River. You will go there, keeping your eyes open on the way, hover around in the neighborhood of the enemy, and send me as good an account as you can procure of their force and probable movements. Also see how the people generally stand affected."

"Does thee wish me to take the whole troop?" asked Clayton.

"By no means. So large a body would only encumber your movements. A dozen or twenty of your best men will be ample. You will have to detach some of them, occasionally, to carry intelligence. Avoid observation as much as possible."

"I think it would be better to have all at work in different directions," said Clayton. "We can go in separate bands of about twenty each, under the command of my officers, each of whom can manage quite as well alone as under my orders. We can co-operate with each other then, if need be, without being suspected; and if an opportunity should offer to strike a blow, we can do it effectually in a body."

"Well, be it so," said the general; "you seem to have a system of tactics of your own. Do the best you can; but be careful not to be taken."

"We'll look out for that," said Clayton; and, leaving the house, he hurried to the quarters of his troop to give the necessary orders.

In two hours the troop had left the camp, and were on the march down the road to Wilmington.

When within about two miles of the town, they halted in a wood off the road, and Clayton called one of his lieutenants aside.

"Levi," said he, "it will be necessary for the troop to separate here, in order to avoid observation. Let them divide into squads of from ten to twenty, and scatter along the roads between here and Elk, and pick up all the information they can. No two squads must be seen together or know each other, unless it becomes necessary for one of them to call in the help of the others. Our business just now is to keep watch, and make report of what we see; but if they should light on any parties of the British where there are not more noses than can be counted, I suppose they had better try to persuade them to retreat or surrender. If they should be foolish or obstinate enough to refuse, thee understands it may be necessary to urge them strongly."

"I understand, sir," said the lieutenant, who, though a Quaker, had dropped his plain language when he put on his sword-belt. "We'll try to convince them."

"The men know the signals; thee will impress upon them not to be out of hearing of each other any more than they can help; and now I am going on alone," said Clayton, divesting himself of his arms, with the exception of a pair of small pistols which he concealed in his breast.

"Why, where are you going, captain?" inquired Levi, in amazement.

"Right into the heart of the British camp: they won't suspect a plain Friend of any evil intention," said he, with a smile, "and there's the place to get information."

So saying, Ellis Clayton rode off in a quiet jog-trot, his horse, with drooping neck and tail, looking like nothing but an ordinary farm-beast, and they passed down the road out of sight.

The lieutenant turned to the troop.

"Boys," said he, "we've got work to do. Wheeler, Wetherill, and Bettle, each of you take twenty men and make for Elk separately; that is, don't be seen *together*; at the same time, keep within hearing of each other's carbines."

"Are we to go through Wilmington?" inquired Wetherill.

"No; go around it. I'm going through there myself, with the rest of the men. Keep off the roads and in the woods as much as possible; scatter the men while under cover, each of you, however, keeping his own squad within hearing of a call."

"Suppose we see any of the British," said Bettle, "what shall we do?"

"At them, if they are not strong enough to eat you," said Levi.

"Very good," answered Bettle; "now we know what to do. Come, boys." And he galloped off, followed helter-skelter by the twenty most reckless daredevils in the troop, put under his command by Clayton, who knew him well, on the good old principle of "like master like man."

"He's going to skirt the road," said Levi. "Wetherill, do you bear off more into the country; Wheeler, you take the other side of the road; and keep a sharp lookout, both of you."

The two detachments moved off in the directions indicated, and when all were fairly out of sight in the woods, which lined the greater part of the road on both sides, Levi Barton, the lieutenant, put himself at the head of the remaining forty men, and moved briskly down the road.

When he arrived at Wilmington, he found the town in commotion. The inhabitants were packing up their valuables for flight, and the streets were crowded with wagons and carts loaded with grain and household goods, barrels of liquor, sacks of salt, worth almost its weight in silver, beds, spinning-wheels, dry goods, and groceries, in fact, almost everything portable, making their way out of the town, to go up the Brandywine toward the forks in Chester county, in order to be out of the track of the enemy, who it was expected would, as a matter of course, march through and plunder Wilmington.

They were accompanied by a guard of the American light-horse, which had been detached to escort them.

From them Barton obtained the latest news from the enemy's army, but heard nothing that he deemed of sufficient importance to send to head-quarters, and passed on his way to New Castle. He halted near the town, it being by this time near evening, and rested for a couple of hours, to give the men time to at supper and feed and groom their horses.

It was night when they resumed their march, but the full moon was shining, and they pushed on rapidly long through New Castle and down the road, the moonlight breaking through the trees, here and there, with uncertain gleams, and the fire-flies or "lightnin'-bugs" sparkling in the air around them.

They had gone about five miles in silence, except for the trample of the horses and the rattling of their equipments, when Barton suddenly heard the shrill, spiteful note of a "katydid" directly behind him. The whole troop stopped instantly.

"What is it, Frank?" he whispered, as one of the men silently moved forward a few steps till he reached his side.

The man pointed, without speaking, to a light at some distance to the left, in the woods.

"It's nothing but a farm-house," said Barton.

"Nothin' but yer granny," said Frank Lightfoot.

This was not exactly respectful from a private to his officer; but the rank and file of such a troop were necessarily rather rough fellows, and, while perfectly obedient in all matters of discipline, were allowed, and always used to its full extent, the liberty of expressing themselves in the most terse and straightforward way.

"My granny's at home, knitting stockings, I expect," said Barton, coolly. " What do you think it is, if not a light in a farm-house window ?"

" Too low down, an' the light's too big," said Frank, laconically.

" I believe you are right," said Barton, taking a second look. "Go in and see what it is; we'll stop here unless we hear an owl-hoot: if we hear one, we'll move on around the turn of the road; if we hear two in succession——"

" What do you mean by 'succession'?" said Frank.

" Two in a row," answered Barton, gravely.

" Why couldn't you say so, then, an' not talk so big ?"

" Very well: when we hear two calls *in a row*, we'll understand that you want help; so now be off."

Frank dismounted, took off his sword, which he tied to the horn of his saddle, and moved off cautiously into the woods, armed only with his knife and carbine.

For about a quarter of an hour his companions sat still, listening intently, but hearing nothing. The light was too far off to allow them to see anything but itself shining among the trees, and Barton, beginning to feel uneasy, was thinking of moving forward himself into the wood to see what had become of Frank, when the tremulous owl-note was heard, apparently some distance in advance. All listened intently, but the cry was not repeated. At a sign from Barton, the men tucked their swords under their left legs, pressing them against the saddles to prevent any rattling of scabbards, unslung their carbines and took them under their right arms, and then, filing off to each side of the road, where the ground was not beaten so hard as in the middle, rode at a slow walk toward the turn in the road which Barton had indicated.

At a short distance below the turn, a narrow cartway led off into the wood, on one side of which was a space comparatively open, the trees having been a good deal thinned out. Halting here, Barton, after listening a moment and hearing nothing, uttered a cry like a whip-poor-will, and listened again. The long, doleful hoot of the owl quavered right over his head, from among the branches of the tree beneath which he was standing. The next moment Frank slid down the trunk and stood before him.

"Well," said Barton, "what do you make of them?"

"A hundred and fifty Tories around a fire," said Frank.

"What are they doing, and how far off are they?"

"Some asleep, some playin' cards, some drinkin' whisky,—half a mile," said Frank, categorically answering both questions at once.

"How do you know they are Tories?" asked Barton.

"New English muskets; officer got a red coat."

"A hundred and fifty men," muttered Barton, musingly; "that's rather heavy odds against forty, unless we can surprise them. Have they posted sentries, Frank?" he added, in a louder tone, though even then his voice would have been inaudible twenty feet off.

"Yes," answered Frank, "'cept where they're wanted."

"How do you mean?" asked Barton.

"Why, look'e here; they're pitched round a spring down there, and their fire's built on the bank of the run that comes from it. The run goes between deep banks, with plenty of bushes on each side. There's where they want a sentry. Got none, o' course. Officer's a greenhorn. Young ensign with bought commission, I reckon."

"That was where you got near them, then?" said Barton.

"To be sure; crep' up within thirty feet. Heard 'em talkin' how they were goin' down to Elk to-morrow mornin'. But that ain't all. Look'e here: Bettle's boys is down there in the hollow a-watchin' em, too!"

"Bettle's boys!" exclaimed Barton. "Do they know we're here?"

"Yes: they're a-waitin'."

"Good!" said Barton; "that makes sixty; we'll have them. Now, how is the ground? fit for horses?"

"No; covered with brush; must be done afoot."

"Very well. Dismount, men; Simpson and Parker, lead the horses farther in among the trees, and wait there."

This conversation occupied but a few moments, and the party were soon on their march under Frank's guidance. The horses, each with his rider's carbine and scabbard tied to the saddle-horn, had been led out of sight among the trees, and the party, taking to the stream, which ran, as Frank had stated, between deep banks overgrown with bushes, moved along in single file through the water, each man with his pistols in his belt, and his sword tied by a thong to his wrist.

In about ten minutes they reached Bettle's men, who were impatiently awaiting them, and could see through the bushes the fire, and the enemy around it occupied very much as Frank had described. They were about a hundred yards distant, but the fire, fed with dry brushwood, which lay plentifully scattered around, burned brightly enough to enable them to see that the arms were stacked in a position to be easily reached by their owners. A sentry was pacing up and down in front of them. Nearly all the men who were not asleep were playing cards, and had been drinking freely. It was getting late, however, and one after another lay down to sleep, until, in the course of half an hour, during which the concealed party had watched them in grim silence, all whom they could see were snoring, except the officer in command—who still sat by the fire, his horse, the only one in the party, tied to a sapling near him—and the sentry who was on guard over the muskets.

The latter was pacing up and down his beat, humming to himself some old tune, evidently acting upon the feeling that the duty he was performing was more a matter of form than of any special necessity.

The bushes immediately around the spring and over the space occupied by the company had been roughly cleared by hacking down the low brush and piling it into couches, on which the sleepers lay in their half-drunken slumber, as they had carelessly thrown themselves down.

They, of course, occupied some considerable space, extending from the spring down the course of the stream. The bushes had been cut away only to the edge of the sloping bank, and the muskets were stacked near the edge in the corner of the cleared ground about twenty yards from this clump of bushes, casually turned to glance at the sentry as he reached this point, when, at the instant the latter turned on his heel to go back, the officer caught a glimpse of something like a cord sweeping through the moonlight clear over the point of the man's bayonet, with a shrill " whish" like a switch cutting rapidly through the air, and the sentry went down backward into the bushes, disappearing as suddenly and utterly as though the ground had opened beneath him. The officer sprang to his feet and shouted an alarm. His men, thus suddenly roused, and stupid from the effect of their previous drinking, scrambled up confusedly, and huddled together for a moment like a flock of sheep.

"To the guns! to the guns!" he shouted, drawing his sword and springing toward the stacked arms, his men, who had recovered from their momentary bewilderment, rushing pell-mell after him.

But, while the cry was on his lips, a crowd of dusky figures poured from the bushes, and, before he had cleared half the distance to the guns, had possessed themselves of them, and were formed in solid column right in his path, holding him and his unarmed rabble covered with their own weapons. The other sentries had run in at the alarm, and he shouted to them to fire They hesitated a moment, for there were only three or four of them; and then the first voice which was heard from the attacking party, spoke.

"Hold! if you fire a shot, if a single hand is raised, you shall die to a man. Ground your arms!"

The four muskets struck the ground with a single "thud."

"You are outgeneraled," said Barton, who was

he speaker, calmly, to the officer; "deliver up your sword."

"I deliver my sword to no leader of banditti, sir," said the officer, scornfully; "I will deliver it to any regular officer, if such a man can be found in your gang."

"You are wasting breath, my friend, in hard words," said Barton, as calmly as ever; "you will deliver it to plain Levi Barton, in command of a detachment of the irregular cavalry of the rebel army, or it will be taken from you; I care not which "

"Take it, then, if you can!" said the Englishman, frantic with rage and mortification; and, springing forward, he made a furious lunge, which would assuredly have left but little more to be said about Barton, had the latter been one whit less wary and prompt than he showed himself.

As it was, he only saved himself by instinctively throwing down his left hand and seizing the blade near the point, turning it aside, while the Englishman, losing his balance as his arm was wrenched aside, came full against the breast of his antagonist.

Half a dozen bullets from the captured muskets, fired aimlessly in the hurry, whizzed past the young officer's head as he sprang forward, and as many men darted from the ranks of the Americans to the assistance of their leader.

"Back!" shouted Barton; "back, I say! leave me to deal with him!" and, twitching the straight cut-and-thrust sword which hung by its thong from his wrist, into his hand, he made a step in advance as the Englishman recovered himself, and the blades crossed.

It was a splendid night for such a passage at arms.

The full moon was shining directly overhead, without a cloud, giving a light almost as bright as day. The fire of brushwood near the spring was still blazing, though partially burnt out, and its flickering light cast a weird, uncanny glare on the flashing swords which were now busy, on the ghostly-looking trees, and the masses of eager faces between which the two combatants were stamping and circling around.

For two or three minutes nothing was audible but the sharp clink of the swords as they struck together, or the low rasp as blade grated along blade, as the combatants stood warily upon guard for a moment. Then from one a gleam would dart across the moonlight straight at the other's breast. A quick turn of the wrist, and it would swerve, slide back, and the blades would play across, around, and past each other so rapidly that the spectators could discern nothing but the flashing gleams as the weapons glanced in the moonbeams or in the light of the fire.

The whole affair was over in five minutes; but in that short time, justice compels me to state, Barton was as many times within a hair's-breadth of losing his life. So far as skill and practice were concerned, his antagonist was fully his match; and he owed his life to the coolness which his Quaker training in self-command had made a second nature, and which, though he fought with energy and in stern earnest, he never lost for an instant, contenting himself at first with standing on the defensive, and parrying as well as he could—and it took all the skill he had—the furious lunges with which his antagonist, half mad with rage, attacked him. He had also the advantage of a more muscular and better-knit frame, and, above all, of what, in fencing, other things being equal, will almost infallibly secure a victory,—a suppler and stronger *wrist*. The Englishman, in his blind fury, had thrown himself open repeatedly, but Barton, though he did not fail to see it, took no advantage of it, as he did not intend to kill him if he could help it.

Warily standing thus on his guard, he watched his adversary keenly, and seeing him, at length, beginning to breathe hard and quickly, he suddenly changed his plan, at the last minute, and attacked in his turn.

There was a sudden thrust, a parry, a locking of hilts, a quick spring of Barton's wrist, and the Englishman's sword flew out of his hand, and he stood unarmed and panting.

"Will you give up your sword?" said Barton, in the calm, unmoved tone he had used all along, to his antagonist.

"You have disarmed me, sir, and I am in your power," said the officer, gloomily. "Do with me as you please: I will thank you if you will pass your sword through me, and end me and my dishonor together."

"You surrender, then, unconditionally?" asked Barton.

The officer bowed. "I can do no better, sir."

"Frank," said Barton, "bring me that sword."

Frank picked it up from where it lay at his feet, and handed it to Barton.

The latter turned toward the officer, who was looking at him in some bewilderment, and placed the hilt in his hand, saying, kindly,—

"Take back your sword: it couldn't be in a braver hand, nor in any that knows better how to use it. It is no disgrace to have been disarmed by a stronger man—I can't say a better fencer."

"I thank you, sir," said the officer, in a low tone, and speaking with much emotion. "You have treated me most generously. I am aware that, by the laws of war, I have forfeited my life in attacking you as I did, and you give it to me without asking."

"We'll let that pass," said Barton; "brave men are not plenty enough to be killed unnecessarily, even if they are enemies."

"Well, sir," said the officer, "you have made one enemy less, and one friend more, if you will allow me to call myself so."

"I had rather have that sword of yours for me than against me," said Barton, smiling, "and had a good deal rather have its master for a friend than for an enemy. I must do an unfriendly act, however. It will be necessary for me to take you and your men with me to the camp as prisoners."

"Of course," said the officer: "it is your duty to do so."

He then turned to his men and ordered them to form in column, and the sentries, who still retained their muskets, to stack them with the rest. When they had done so, and stood looking rather sheepishly at each other, he said to Barton,—

"We wait your pleasure, sir."

"Boys," said Barton to his troop, "each of you take two of those muskets, sling one to your backs with reversed bayonets, and keep the other in hand. I don't distrust you," he said, in a low tone, to the officer, "but I do distrust your men, and, with such a force, must use every precaution."

"You have reason to, sir," said the latter, in the same tone; "for a set of greater scoundrels never went unhanged than half of them are. If it were not for the shame of being surprised through my own carelessness, I would feel inclined to thank you for having released me from the command of them."

As he spoke, he turned suddenly to one of his men, who had stepped forward and whispered something in his ear.

"Take that, you infernal scoundrel!" he exclaimed, dashing his sword-hilt against the fellow's mouth with a force that sent him reeling back into the ranks with his front teeth knocked out and his jaw broken.

"What's the matter?" said Barton, in great surprise, while the sharp click of gunlocks cocking ran along his own ranks.

"Only an illustration of what I just told you," said the officer, bitterly. "That fellow proposed to seize you and hold you, so that your men could not fire on them without killing you, while they made terms for their own safety."

"They wouldn't have gained much by that," said Barton, coolly: "my men are used to hitting nothing but what they aim at, when they have time to aim at all."

"Well, let him go," said the officer. "I believe I have spoiled his talking for awhile."

The Tories were then ordered to march forward into the woods, the Americans guarding them on each side, and so they proceeded along the course of the little stream, leading the horse with them, until they reached the junction of the roads. A whistle from Barton was answered from a little distance in the woods, and soon after the horses of the troop issued forth, following the soldiers who were mounted on the foremost. The whole party reached the American camp, without any further disturbance, about daybreak, and Barton reported himself at head-quarters and delivered his prisoners.

CHAPTER V.

WHEN Ellis Clayton reached Turkey Point, he found the army debarked and encamped about a mile back in the country, with the exception of three brigades of Hessians under Knyphausen, which were posted near the landing. The ships lay off the mouth of the river, with boats passing to and fro between them and the shore, busily engaged in landing what remained of the army stores and equipage.

Approaching an officer who was standing near the landing, superintending the work that was going on, he said to him,—

"Friend, does thee think there would be any objection to my going within the camp? It is a new and strange sight to me, and I feel a curiosity to see it more closely."

The officer stared hard at the meek-looking individual who addressed him so blandly, but at last answered,—

"Well, I don't know that there would, Friend George Fox. But what interest can a man of your cloth take in such worldly matters as soldiers and camps? However, go in; but don't talk to any of the men on duty."

So Clayton quietly walked in,—I forgot to mention

that he had left his horse at a house about half a mile from the landing,—and sauntered quietly and with apparent listlessness through the camp, but with his eyes about him, noting everything,—the bad condition of the horses,—the artillery, which had not yet been removed, carefully fixing in his mind the number and weight of the guns and the supply of ammunition, as well as he could judge of the latter,—but finding his attempts to gain information from the soldiers he met, a little impeded in consequence of not understanding a word of German, and of those he spoke to not understanding a word of English except the one word "reb'l."

The only answers he received, "Nein"—"Ya, meinherr"—and "Wier no sprechen reb'l"—being unsatisfactory in their nature, he gave it up, and contented himself with making the circuit of the camp, marking two or three places on the outskirts where he thought a night attack might be advantageously made, and finally reached the point he had started from, where he found the officer still on duty.

"Well, Friend George," said the latter, "what does thee think of the appearance of things? This is only a detachment of the army; but it's a fair specimen. Do you think we would have any chance if Mr. Washington should catch us?"

"That would depend upon how many troops thee had, and especially how many cannons like those I saw over yonder; if the rest of the army has as many in proportion, my impression is that thee might be able to persuade him not to molest thee."

"Oh, that's all the artillery," said the officer; "but, besides, we have about seventeen thousand men. Did you happen to have heard how many Mr. Washington has?"

"No," said Clayton, who, as it happened, had never heard the number mentioned, though he could have made a shrewd guess; "I have not heard, but I should suppose nearly as many as what thee mentioned."

"Do you think so?" said the officer: "then there'll be so much the more credit in routing them when we meet. But there's the gun," he added, as the heavy report of the evening gun boomed through the camp and rolled over the still water of the bay; "you must get outside the lines."

"Well, farewell, friend," said Clayton. "I am obliged for the privilege thee has given me, and hope to be able to repay thee some day."

So saying, he walked away, while the officer looked after him suspiciously, his attention having been attracted by a slight change in the tone of the last words. "I've half a mind to stop that fellow," he muttered to himself; but Clayton was walking quietly along, so calmly, and with so little appearance of suspecting that he was suspected, that the officer, whose attention was also called to something else at the moment, relinquished his half-formed purpose, and soon forgot, for the time, all about the circumstance.

Clayton went back to where he had left his horse, and, mounting, betook himself with all speed to the point occupied by the small force of Americans which was in the neighborhood. These had been sent down more for the purpose of assisting in the removal of the stores, and protecting those who were employed in this way, than with any idea of their fighting.

6*

The next morning, about daybreak, he was aroused by a great bustle in the camp, accompanied by a cheer or two, which, however, were promptly and sternly silenced by the officer in command.

"What's the matter?" he inquired of a soldier who was hurrying past him to the commander's quarters.

"Don't know, exactly," said the soldier; "some prisoners brought in, I b'lieve."

Clayton hurried forward with the rest, and there, sure enough, in front of the commander's tent, were Barton and Bettle with their sixty men, surrounding, as well as they could, their one hundred and fifty prisoners.

Barton glanced at him as he came near; but a slight knitting of Clayton's brows, for an instant, warned him against any public recognition of him. The men glanced from one to the other and understood the hint at once, and gave no sign of recognition whatever, but sat still on their horses.

A few words from Barton to the commander sufficed to explain matters; the prisoners were placed under guard, with the exception of their officer, who was released upon his parole not to leave the camp; and the troop was dismissed.

"So thee's been at work?" said Clayton, after the crowd had scattered, so that no one was within hearing. "Where did thee pick up this party?"

"About ten miles back in the woods," said Barton, who then gave him a detailed account of the occurrence, though much more concisely than I have done.

"It was well done," said Clayton, "and I am the more pleased that thee managed it without shedding blood. Has thee seen Wetherill and Wheeler?"

"No," said Barton; "I presume they're not far off, but there's been no sign of them as yet."

"After thee and the men have had breakfast and taken some sleep, I want thee to send Bettle and a dozen men to look for them. I shall want them, perhaps, to-night; I want thee, also, to send a trusty messenger to Chester to General Washington. Tell him that the enemy have landed in good condition, with the exception of the horses, which are down in flesh in consequence of their long voyage; they have a full train of field-pieces, with plenty of ammunition; they are preparing to march up into the country, and will probably pass through Wilmington; the people, generally, are discouraged, and inclined to accept the protection which Howe has proclaimed. That is about all, except what relates to thy own affair last night."

About sunset, the remaining forty rangers, under Wetherill and Wheeler, came in, bringing with them a few stragglers whom they had cut off from the main body of the enemy, around which they had been hovering all day; and in half an hour afterward came Bettle with his party, to report that they had not been able to find them; they had been reconnoitering one side of the army, while Wetherill and Wheeler were hovering about the other.

Wetherill informed Clayton that one of his men had been in the camp disguised as a laborer, and had gathered from the talk of the soldiers that they expected to march the next morning.

"To-morrow morning," said Clayton. "Are the horses fresh enough for service to-night?"

"Oh, yes," said Wetherill; "they've had no hard work to-day."

"The moon will go down about nine o'clock," said Clayton, "and it is getting cloudy: it will be a dark night, and I believe I'll give them some exercise."

"What are we to do?" inquired Wetherill.

"Call the other lieutenants," said Clayton.

Barton, Wheeler, and Bettle made their appearance, and Clayton unfolded his plan briefly.

"I'm going to try if we can't reach Knyphausen's tent and carry him off to-night. Each of you take his squad and meet me in the woods on the hill beyond the camp at one o'clock in the morning. Go separately. You will have to depend upon signals to find the meeting-place after you get into the woods."

Clayton had explained the character of his troop to the officer in command, and had shown him an order from Washington, instructing him to allow them to come and go at discretion, so that, at the appointed time, being furnished with the pass-word, they found no difficulty in passing out, though the sentinel on duty where Wheeler's division passed, stared hard at them, and muttered to himself,—

"I wonder what devilment the fightin' Quakers are up to now."

"We're going to a 'meeting for discipline,'" said Wheeler, who overheard him.

After some little time, having walked their horses slowly, to avoid noise, the four divisions reached the wood at different points, and, after entering fairly among the trees, halted in silence, waiting for signals.

Barton, with his forty men, had entered on the side farthest from the camp; he had been there but a few moments when the well-known owl-hoot quavered from a point near the center of the wood.

"There's the captain," said he, as he answered it
with a whistle, "and there's Wetherill," as the cry of
whip-poor-will sounded from the left; "forward,
boys, quietly."

In a few minutes, guided by the first signal, which
was repeated at short intervals, the whole party were
assembled around Clayton.

In his calm, impassive way, he gave them their
orders in a few brief words, and the troop emerged
from the wood, which was about two miles from the
Hessian camp.

The sky was by this time covered with heavy clouds,
the thunder had begun to mutter in the distance, and
there was every appearance of a storm.

As soon as the troop emerged from the wood they
separated, and descended the hill in small parties,
silently and cautiously, the tramp of the horses being
but slightly audible on the soft sward, as they proceeded
at a slow walk. The wind also was rising, and blowing directly from the encampment, decreasing materially the danger of being heard. A ravine lay across
their course at some distance from the camp, with a
space of about a hundred yards of open meadow-ground
between its brink and the nearest sentinel. It was
fringed with trees on both sides, while at the bottom
ran a tumbling brook, which, at one point, pitched over
some obstructing rocks in a series of irregular cascades,
falling, altogether, some seven or eight feet; this, of
itself, made sufficient roaring to drown the noise of
horse-hoofs proceeding so cautiously.

The scattered troop assembled again in the ravine,
and crossed the stream just above the cascade, where
the water was foaming and splashing over the rocky

bottom, the sure-footed horses feeling their way among the slippery stones, with the reins loose upon their necks, until they had all reached the other side, and formed on the slope of the nearer bank, just below the meadow level, and screened by the trees which grew upon the brink. In another minute, three of the men had dismounted, divested themselves of all their arms except a long knife and a light cord of twisted rawhide, such as had been used upon the unlucky sentry at the spring when he disappeared so suddenly in the bushes, crawled over the edge of the bank, and were worming their way, flat upon the ground, through the long grass, toward as many different sentinels. The sky had grown blacker than ever, and the darkness was intense; it was utterly impossible for the sentries to distinguish any object, not above the level of the ground, ten feet off, while the three scouts could distinguish, dimly, though surely enough for their purpose, the forms of the sentries against the sky, which, black as it was, was lighter than the ground, as they paced up and down their respective beats. That of the nearest was terminated by a large chestnut-tree, at which Frank, who was one of the scouts, had observed him turn and retrace his steps. That of the second was terminated by a bend of the ravine, which swept, in that direction, half round the camp. That of the third, and most remote, terminated at an orchard surrounded by a worm fence.

The three men wormed their way stealthily along toward the various points I have mentioned, as the sentinels paced drowsily to and fro, until they had all reached their destinations, Frank lying flat in the, if possible, deeper darkness under the tree, while his companions were crouched, one behind the bank of the ravine, the other in an angle of the fence, beneath the overhanging branches of a large old apple-tree.

As the sentinel whose beat extended to this place reached it, he turned, marched a step or two back, and then, stopping, lowered his musket to the ground, and stood with the bayonet leaning against his shoulder, while he emptied and refilled his exhausted pipe. As he did so, a dark form rose silently and swiftly behind him; there was a quick whirl of its arm, a slight "whish," and the raw-hide cord, armed with a leaden ball at the end, swept against the gaiters of the unlucky Hessian, coiling around his ankles instantly, while a powerful jerk given at the same moment snatched his feet backward from under him with a force that brought his nose and mouth into contact with the earth before he had time to utter an exclamation.

He was scarcely down before his captor was upon him, with one knee between his shoulders, at the base of the neck, effectually preventing him from raising his head enough to raise an alarm, while he coolly, but with wonderful precision and rapidity, tied his hands behind him with the end of the cord. The scout then, by a sudden pull, turned him on his back, clapping his hand over his mouth as he did so, thus preventing any imprudent outcry, and then, without wasting any words, which the other would not have understood, enjoined silence by the low "sh" which is intelligible in all languages, enforced by a slight but expressive pressure of his knife-point upon the side of the neck, between the ear and the edge of the leather stock. He then slightly relaxed his grasp upon the mouth, to see whether his prisoner had discretion enough to take the hint and keep it shut. As may be supposed, the fellow was half stunned, and a good deal more than half confused, by his fall: he was just beginning to recover his faculties as his captor eased his hand from his mouth, and immediately showed that he had very little discretion, by opening it to shout for help, whereupon his captor, who had untwined the cord from his legs, clapped his left hand upon his throat in a way that made him open his mouth to its full extent for breath, and incontinently thrust the leaden ball, about as large as a walnut with the hull on, into his wide-stretched jaws, cleverly filling up the cavity and effectually stopping any noise from issuing thereout. Tying a handkerchief tightly around the mouth, to keep the extempore gag in its place, he led his prisoner cautiously, but rapidly, away in the shadow of the orchard, until he reached the ravine, diving into which, he hurried up to where the troop was stationed.

Frank and the remaining scout came in at the same time. They had been less fortunate, in one respect at least, for both had killed their men. Frank had been compelled to do so; for as he put his hand down to raise himself behind the tree under which the sentinel had at that instant turned, he placed it, and pressed with his whole weight, right upon a cluster of chestnut-burrs, which some urchin in passing had clubbed down. Though he made no exclamation, the sharp, unexpected sting made him start slightly, and the soldier heard him and turned. There was no time to lose; and, leaping upon him, before he had time to lower his musket to fire, he seized it by the barrel, and drove his knife into the luckless Hessian's throat. With a single effort to shout, which only produced a low, choking gurgle, the man fell dead, and Frank sped back across the meadow, crouching low until he came within the shadow of the trees that lined the ravine.

The other had taken the same plan as had been taken with the sentinel at the spring, and had jerked the cord against his throat with such good will that the man actually rolled down the bank with his neck broken.

So far all had been successful; and, long as it has taken to tell it, was accomplished in a few minutes. Clayton immediately put the troop in motion, calculating to pass the lines before the relief guard should come around. The storm was drawing nearer, and the thunder was beginning to roll heavily, and almost continuously, effectually drowning the sound of the horses' feet, and they reached the lines without being discovered; but it happened that the officer whom Clayton had seen the previous evening was in command of the relief guard, and after he had returned from placing the sentinels, the thought of Clayton's last words, and the half suspicion they had roused, recurred to him, and he determined to visit the outposts again before the time was up, to see what the sentries were doing. Reaching the bend of the ravine, where the upper one was stationed, he found the post vacant.

"The scoundrel's deserted!" said he, with an oath; "forward, men, and let's see what's become of the next one."

At this instant, a broad glare of lightning blazed across the sky, showing him the whole of Clayton's troop crossing his track between him and the chestnut-tree, not more than thirty yards off.

"Fire!" he shouted; "fire, you dogs, and then make for the tents!"

He was answered by the instant discharge of all the muskets of the patrol, without effect, however, in the intense darkness, while the troop, paying no attention to his party, now that the alarm was given, put their horses to their speed toward the center of the camp, where stood Knyphausen's marquee.

In a moment after the fire of the guard, they heard the long roll of drums in every direction; there was the tramp of hurrying feet, and voices of officers issuing orders rapidly and sharply, as the men poured, half dressed and "drunk with sleep," from their tents, and formed hastily to repel an attack of they knew not what.

Then came a rattle of musketry, fired in the direction of the roar of hoofs which were sweeping on like a hurricane, but fired so hurriedly and at random that not a shot took effect. The next instant, however, came the heavy bang of a field-piece, which had been hastily unlimbered and loaded, and a twelve-pound shot hummed through the troop, emptying five or six saddles at once.

A leap of Bettle's horse brought him alongside the gunner, who dropped under the gun just in time to save his head from being swept off by a back-handed blow of Bettle's sword.

Another broad glare of lightning, and then another and another flashed over the sky in such rapid succession, that for several seconds the whole expanse of meadow and forest and camp was visible in the glimmering light, showing the rows of tents, with the general's marquee in the midst, not thirty yards off; but

same glare showed the whole camp alive with
soldiers hurrying to their respective posts, and twenty
or thirty men rapidly unlimbering the cannon. The
game was blocked, and nothing was left but to escape
as well as they could. It looked like a forlorn hope;
but Clayton, whose coolness and watchfulness nothing
ever disturbed, fertile in resources, as he now and
many a time afterward had sore need to be, was ready
for the emergency. His keen eye had observed, while
the lightning was flashing, that the only force actually
opposed to him was the small detachment whose ineffectual fire he had just received, and which was only
half formed. He determined to charge their flank, cut
his way through, if possible, and pass across their rear
before the others could join them, and so run the gauntlet of the irregular fire, or turn on them again before
they could form, and scatter them.

He gave his orders instantly, and the column wheeled
and dashed headlong at the enemy, riding down all in
their way, the horses, trained to their work, striking
furiously with their forefeet and seizing with their teeth
every one within reach.

The enemy turned, promptly enough, as they gained
the rear, but their line, such as it was, was hopelessly
disordered, and in another moment there was a confused hurly-burly of horse and foot in deadly hand-to-hand strife, man to man.

They were so mingled that it was impossible for
those coming up to fire without killing their own
friends; but the nearest body, consisting of about
fifty or sixty, having had time to form, came up in
solid column with the bayonet. Another body, rather
stronger, was advancing on the other side, and Clay-

ton saw, in the now almost incessant blaze of the lightning, that he was hemmed in.

"By the piper," said the officer at the head of the smaller company, "if it isn't George Fox, with a carnal weapon in his hand! Thee's done for, Friend George."

"Perhaps thee's mistaken," said Clayton, who had recognized the voice of the officer to whom he had been talking at the landing; "perhaps thee's mistaken. Away!" he shouted, and his men, who had been in a solid square, instantly streamed out into two lines, as if by magic, and darted between the opposing forces at full speed, crouching low behind their horses' necks, and pouring from beneath them, on either hand, a fire from their pistols, which was instantly returned, though without much effect on either side. Another moment, and they were clear, and a hundred yards off in the meadow, but now separated into half a dozen squads, and scattered from one end of it to the other.

Battalion after battalion came up and poured in their volleys, but with little effect, as may be supposed, upon an enemy which showed no two men together to fire at, and of whom every individual was constantly in rapid motion, never standing still for a moment. On the other hand, the carbines were cracking singly from all directions in the meadow, as the riders circled about like hawks, preserving, in all their apparent looseness, a symmetry of evolution which showed plainly that some incomprehensible kind of discipline was at work among them. This irregular fire did a good deal of mischief in the solid ranks, nearly every ball telling. By this time, however, the artillery was brought up, and a storm of grape from half a dozen guns at once whistled across the meadow, knocking three or four more men off their horses. It was now time to leave in earnest; and, Clayton having given the order to retreat, without which his men would have stood their ground all night, they gave a parting volley from their carbines, and rode off toward the ravine, followed by another ineffectual discharge of musketry, and in five minutes more were in the wood from which they had first emerged.

"Well, of all the—isn't a Quaker the very d—l?" said the officer who had recognized Clayton; "to slip through our fingers that way! 'Bout face; march!" and back they marched through the rain, which was now pouring furiously.

CHAPTER VI.

THE attempt had failed; not from want of care or management on the part of Clayton, but from one of those awkward contingencies which cannot be foreseen, and against which there is no guarding. It gave Knyphausen, however, a glimpse of a new feature, to him, in the tactics of the enemy. With regulars he knew very well what to do, but this kind of heretical manœuvring, this way of attacking, like a nest of hornets, a sting and away, leaving nothing for him to attack in return, was as uncomfortable and confusing to him as it became to a good many more of his Majesty's faithful officers before the war was ended.

The next day the British forces moved forward to Gray's Hill, and from that time until the 11th of September they were occupied in working their way to Chad's Ford, harassed by continual skirmishes and desultory attacks, in which our Quaker corps was by no means idle.

It was evening, the 11th of September. The battle had been fought gallantly against odds in numbers, in training, in discipline; and it had been lost. The broken columns of the bulk of the American army were flying down the road from Birmingham Meetinghouse to Dilworthstown. General Greene still stub-

bornly held the narrow defile commanding the road, where he had stationed himself by Washington's orders as soon as the retreat became inevitable. La Fayette, wounded in attempting to rally the flying troops, was lying helpless at the house of William Jones, about half a mile north of the meeting-house. Pulaski, with his cavalry, was covering the retreat. The old meeting-house was turned into a hospital, and the surgeons were busy with knife and saw and tourniquet.

When it had grown dark, and the pursuit had ceased, Greene withdrew from his position in the defile, and marched with what remained of the American forces in good order toward Chester, which had been fixed upon by the commander as a rendezvous.

Clayton, however, who had stationed himself with his troop in the same defile, under General Greene's orders for the time, separated his force from Greene's as soon as they were fairly on the road, it being no part of his purpose to accompany the retreat of the army; and, making a wide circuit to the eastward to outreach the British, struck the Brandywine again on the east branch, at Jefferis' Ford, and thence proceeded along the road described in the first chapter, till he reached the quaint little old brick house which I have already described. His force was sadly reduced, consisting now of not more than thirty-five or forty men, with some twenty extra horses, which had kept in the ranks after their riders had fallen, and now followed in good order in the rear. It was now about eleven o'clock at night, and all was still, except the occasional bark of a watch-dog, breaking sharply and harshly through the monotonous roar of a dam higher up the stream, and the gurgling of the small "run" which crossed the road they were on, just below the house.

The building, or rather the barn* belonging to it, came into view first, from a point in the road some two or three hundred yards below, where it turned the corner of a high bank on the east side. On arriving at this point, Clayton gave the order to halt, in a low voice, and, turning to Barton, who was riding near him, inquired whether he knew the place or anything about the country.

"No," answered Barton, "I don't; but Frank, here, is from somewhere in this neighborhood, and ought to know."

"Does thee know whose place this is, Frank?" said Clayton; "the men and horses are tired and hungry, and I would like to find some place to rest and refresh them."

"Well, I reckon I know it," said Frank; "and we couldn't ha' lit on a better place. Look'e here, this is old Tommy Sanford's place,—as good a Whig as the country can turn up, only he's got so many Tory neighbors he can't show it, for fear o' bein' tuk an' handed over to the Britishers if they git the upper hand."

"Well, I suppose if we take possession of the house and barn without his consent, he won't mind it particularly," said Barton.

"No, I 'xpect not," said Frank. "But jest look'e here; hadn't I better go up by myself an' take a squint round first, to see if there's any bloody Tories about

---

* It no longer exists; the present barn is on the west side of the road, between the house and the Strasburg road.

there? It wouldn't be nice to tumble on to a hundred or two of 'em without bein' ready, would it?"

"Not very," said Clayton. "Go on, then, and see if thee can perceive any signs of them."

"All right," said Frank; "you keep still, this side o' th' bridge, till I come back or call. If you hear an owl, there's danger, and you'd better git into the cornfield, off from the road, an' then I'll know where to find you."

So saying, Frank dismounted and proceeded toward the barn, while one of the other men, by Clayton's order, silently took down the bars that led into the field, where the corn was standing high enough to conceal a man on horseback, in order that they might, if necessary, get out of the road without noise. This done, the troop stood silent, the men with their carbines under their left arms, and their swords tucked in between thigh and saddle, as they always rode in night marches.

In the mean time, Frank proceeded cautiously along the road, keeping well in the shadow of the bank, until he reached the corner of the barn-yard, which was upon the edge of the road. Here he stopped, and, crouching by the wall, peered over. The night was too dark to see anything distinctly, but he thought he could perceive, in the deep shadow beneath the upper part of the barn, which projected some twenty feet over the lower portion and was supported by rude pillars of heavy masonry, something like the figures of five or six animals,—whether horses or cattle he could not tell. He also heard sounds within the stables, apparently among the stalls, which seemed to indicate a larger number of occupants than he knew the old farmer was accustomed to keep.

He kept along the yard, crouching below the top of the wall, until he reached the corner nearest the house, where he could get a clear view of the gangway and of the space between the house and barn. Before reaching the corner, he laid himself at full length, and snaked, or "snigged" his way, as he termed it, along, so close to the ground that there was no possibility of seeing him, had there been a dozen sentries. But none was visible, and Frank cautiously raised himself and moved on tiptoe up the gangway to the barn-doors, where he stood for a minute listening intently. While in this position, he felt his left hand, which was hanging carelessly behind him, touched by something cold. Startled, he turned promptly, hand on knife, but found nothing but a dog, which he had given to the old farmer about six months before, and which had recognized him, and was now rubbing its cold nose against him and whining joyfully.

"'St, Carlo, old boy, 'st," said Frank, in a whisper; "keep that throat o' yourn still." And, giving the dog a light pinch on the ear, the intelligent brute lay down close to the ground, giving no signs of life except a wary turning of the head occasionally.

After listening a minute longer, and hearing no sound, except the occasional movements of the horses below, Frank pulled the latch-string of the small door which opened in one of the large ones, opened it noiselessly, stepped over the bottom board, and entered the threshing-floor of the barn. A few moments satisfied him that there was no one there but himself, and, coming out again, he proceeded toward the house.

If he had found silence in the barn, he did not find it when he reached the kitchen-door; for the kitchen at

ast was evidently full of men, who were as evidently arousing. He could distinguish certainly not less than om forty to fifty different voices amid the confused ubbub which prevailed, and, stealing to the window, small·narrow opening, glazed with lozenge-shaped gbts set in lead, and destitute of shutters, he looked a, standing a foot or so back, however, that his face light be hidden in the gloom outside.

What he saw was this. The kitchen full of men, ome asleep on the floor, some sitting around a table, a company with a demijohn and an uncouth-looking ariety of mugs and cups for drinking, and some athered near a corner of the room where sat, eviently prisoners, Thomas Sanford and his two sons, ohn and Mahlon. The old man's countenance wore a expression of gloomy thought, and he took little otice of the efforts of his wife and Jenny, who sat eside him, to cheer him up. The younger men sat ill, with a look of dogged endurance, but with a drawg together of the eyebrows, and a compressed squareess about the lips, which told of anything but amiable elings at work within.

At this moment one of the men, a lean, shambling llow, with a long, peaked nose, rose from the table, id, crossing the room to where the girl was sitting, ith that excessively precise step which marks the age of intoxication graphically designated as a "brick his hat," squared himself before her with a vacant ok of maudlin sentimentality for a moment, and then, fore she could suspect what he was at, deliberately ooped over her and attempted to take her face been his hands and draw it toward his own. As the rl thrust away his hands indignantly, and made an unsuccessful attempt to rise from her chair, the two young men, who were sitting near, both sprang to their feet at once and seized him by the throat. They were instantly grappled with, however, by half a dozen of those who stood around, and were dragged off, struggling furiously.

"Let me go!" exclaimed John; "the drunken coward has insulted my sister!" and both renewed their struggles so vehemently that it required all the strength of the six men to hold them.

There was a hurly-burly of voices,—"Let 'em at him." "Fair play; one at a time." "He *shall* kiss the gal." "He sha'n't." "It's a shame." "Knock the young rebels on the head,"—some attempting to drag the fellow away, some striving to prevent it. All who had been sitting at the table had sprung up and were joining in the scuffle, those who had been asleep on the floor were "picking themselves up" and staring around in the confusion of their sudden awakening, and there was every prospect of a general mêlée.

Blows were beginning to be exchanged, and several of the combatants, extricating themselves from the crowd, made toward the muskets, which were stacked in the opposite corner of the room. This had been foreseen from the beginning, however, by the cooler heads of the party, and a dozen of them had formed themselves around the pile of arms, and stood quietly and firmly in a quarter-circle, whose arc bristled with bayonets from wall to wall.

This was an unanswerable argument, which the others did not attempt to controvert, but turned back again, to resume the fight "pugnibus et calcibus."

By this time, however, a few of those who were nearest to being sober had interfered, and managed to separate the combatants and restore some kind of order.

The whole affair did not occupy more than a couple of minutes, and the men resumed their places, some at the table and some on the floor. The girl, however, sat with her face buried in her hands, while her mother bent over her, striving to comfort her, and her brothers sat grinding their teeth in powerless rage.

Frank had beheld the whole scene from the window, and at the moment the fellow stooped over the girl he was covered by the cocked horse-pistol in Frank's hand. Another instant, and he would have fired; but, while his forefinger was pressing the trigger, the two brothers had sprung directly into the line of fire; and from that time, until tranquillity was restored, no opportunity occurred for him to fire without imminent danger of hitting the wrong man. It gave him also an opportunity of recovering his coolness, which had at first been somewhat disturbed by his sudden wrath.

"Look'e here!" said he, addressing nobody in particular, and quietly uncocking the pistol; "by the hokey! well it wasn't Bettle, 'stead o' me, saw that rascal try to kiss Jenny Sanford; he'd a' been among 'em slap dash, an' got his throat cut, sure. Blamed if I wasn't nigh doin' a desp'it foolish thing myself, to go to shoot him then. I reckon Bettle wouldn't 'a' thanked me much for takin' that job off his hands, anyhow. Now I'll jest take a squint round the house an' see if there's any sentries out, an' then back an' report."

So saying, Frank moved cautiously around the

building, as noiselessly as a snake, and satisfied himself that the Tories, in their fancied security, had overlooked this very important precaution.

Hurrying back to where the troop were standing, he reported what he had seen to Clayton.

"Can we take them?" asked the latter; "or are they too strong? The men and horses are tired out, and not fit for fighting. I would like to save those people, too, particularly as thee says that Bettle is interested in the young woman. Suppose thee tells him, and sees what he thinks."

"No; reckon we'd best not tell him jest yet," said Frank; "Bettle's skin wouldn't hold him, if he know'd it. He'll fight hard enough, if there's any fightin' to be done, without knowin' anything about it. But there needn't be much fightin', if we go to work right."

"Well, what does thee propose?"

"Why, look'e here: we don't want to take 'em at all; wouldn't know what to do with 'em if we had 'em; but we can rout 'em off, an' save old Tommy an' the rest of 'em, jest as easy as snappin' your fingers."

"How?" inquired Clayton.

"Why, I'll tell you as we go along; leave a dozen o' the men here, with the loose horses in front of 'em; bring a dozen more up to the barn-yard, an' put 'em behind the wall with their carbines—they must leave their horses out o' sight, behind the barn—send half a dozen up the road, between the house an' the Lancaster road, an' let me have the rest, an' we'll fix 'em good."

"Be it so," said Clayton. "What next?"

"Tell you that as we go along," said Frank.

Clayton then ordered Barton to remain where he was with a dozen of his men, telling him to form the loose horses in front as suggested by Frank. The detachment for the barn-yard was sent forward under Wheeler, while Wetherill was sent to occupy the road above, and Bettle, with his men, accompanied Frank, at the latter's request. Clayton also went with this detachment. A few minutes sufficed to place the different parties at their respective posts and put them in possession of their orders.

It was a ticklish thing to get Wetherill's detachment past the house without noise; but, partly by taking to the meadow, and partly owing to the noise in the house, where the Tories were now in high revel, it was accomplished successfully.

The road ran nearly north and south, directly in front of the house. The barn was about fifty yards to the south of the house, with only the width of the barn-yard between it and the road.

The men who occupied the latter were posted behind its northern wall, facing the house.

Frank's and Bettle's men now dismounted, and, leaving their horses also behind the barn, with three men to guard them, stole quietly and noiselessly to the side of the house nearest the great road, which was about four or five hundred yards distant. When all was ready, Frank stole back to the corner of the barn-yard, and, picking up a small stone, flung it across the yard into the field beyond, where the guard was stationed with the horses. A moment or two after, a faint light was seen rising from that side of the barn. Frank waited another moment till the light grew stronger and began to throw something of a glare upon the sky; then, yelling, "Fire! fire!" at the top of his voice, he ran at full speed toward the house and, banging and kicking at the door, he shouted again,—

"Fire! Hello, there! The barn's afire!—Turn out, Tommy Sanford, or your horses 'll be roasted like rats!"

The door was thrown open instantly, and out poured the disorderly crowd from the kitchen, intent upon saving their horses. Taking no notice of Frank, who sprang a little on one side to avoid being carried away by the rush, the whole party went helter-skelter toward the barn, receiving, when within twenty yards of the wall, the fire of a dozen carbines, right in their faces. They stopped short, completely bewildered; and, before they had recovered from their surprise, a dozen heads, magnified by the sudden fright into a hundred, were raised above the wall, and another volley from a dozen pistols came, sending them to the right about, in full stampede for the house. As they came near, they were met by another volley from door and window, when they dashed down the bank on which the house stood, and up the road, only to be turned again by the carbines of Wetherill's men, who immediately moved down to the house and stationed themselves in front of it.

The terrified fugitives ran in a confused crowd down the road past the barn, taking another discharge from the carbines of Wheeler's men as they passed, and had the consolation, first, of seeing the dying flame of a pile of burnt brushwood which Frank's quick eye had noted as he came up at first, and which he had made use of to raise all the hubbub, and then, as they slackened their pace for a moment, of hearing the cracking of a new dozen of carbines, and the whistling of the balls about their ears, from Barton's division at the bridge.

The next moment came the order "Forward," and then the tramp of galloping hoofs, and then the wild vision of a roadful of riderless horses coming upon them. They broke at once; and, scrambling, leaping, tumbling over anyhow, across the fence and into the meadow, they ran for life, while the spare horses of the troop swept by like a small hurricane, trampling into a jelly one unlucky fellow, who had stumbled in his hurry and was unable to recover himself before they were upon him.

As the fugitives cleared the fence, a quick, sharp order came from the rear. "Over, and head them off!" The pursuers wheeled promptly; but, to Barton's chagrin, the tired horses absolutely refused to take the leap, and, after two or three ineffectual attempts to spur them over, they were obliged to give it up, contenting themselves with sending a random discharge from their pistols after the now invisible enemy. They then rode to the house, where they found the rest of the troop collected, together with those horses which had been stopped by Wetherill's men.

As soon as the Tories had left the house, at the first alarm, Frank, Bettle, and Clayton, with the men under their command, had entered it, greatly to the alarm of the old farmer and his family, who supposed them, at first, to be another party of the enemy.

The next instant, however, just as the first volley

8*

from the barn-yard wall rattled on the air, Thomas Sanford recognized Frank, and at the same moment Jenny sprang from her seat, exclaiming, joyfully,—

"Oh, father, it's William! it's William! Now we're safe!" and straightway gave vent to her joy in the most inconsistent manner, by clinging to Bettle's neck and sobbing pitifully. Bettle sustained her,—it was necessary to put his arm around her waist to do it,—and whispered a great many consoling things, but in so low a voice that I really can't tell what they were.

Indeed, he was so pleasantly engaged that, for a wonder, he paid no attention to the fighting that was going on for the five minutes or so that succeeded their first entry into the house, hardly deigning to look around even at the discharge from the door and windows as the Tories rushed back from the barn.

By the time the fray was over and the whole troop was assembled, Jenny had become sufficiently composed to be able to sit on her chair without the assistance of Bettle's arm, and the farmer, turning to Frank, inquired,—

"How did thee manage to be here just at the right time? I thought thee was in Philadelphy."

"Don't you know me well enough yet, Uncle Tommy," said Frank, "to know that I'm always where people don't expect to find me? Look'e here; if we hadn't been whipped down at Brummadgem, an' had to run for it, I reckon you'd ha' been in an ugly fix——"

"Whipped!" interrupted one of the brothers; "we heard the firin', and knew there must be somethin' goin' on. But where's the rest of the army?"

"Gone to Chester or Hook; don' know which," said Frank.

"Then the country will be too hot to hold you," said Thomas, "and us too, after this night's work."

"I reckon *we'll* make it hot enough to burn anybody's fingers that meddles with us," said Frank. "But look'e here, Uncle Tommy; there's forty men of us here, and sixty hosses, that hain't tasted bit or sup since noon, an' done a good deal o' hard fightin, besides. Got anything in the house to eat, an' some cider or whisky, an' some fodder for the beasts? We're all mortal hungry an' dry."

"We have plenty in house and barn," said the old man; "only we haven't room to put up the horses."

"Never mind that," said Frank; "toss it out on the ground, an' the hosses 'll take care o' themselves."

The two sons then went out with Frank to procure food and water for the horses, while Jenny and her mother busied themselves in preparing supper for their unexpected guests.

This Frank Lightfoot, who has figured rather prominently in the events I have detailed so far, is worth a more particular description than I have as yet given him.

He was an old Indian-fighter, having been a wagon-boy in Braddock's army at the defeat of the latter near Fort Duquesne, in the month of July, 1755. He had seen his elder brother, a teamster, shot down by his side at the first volley from the bushes, and, seizing the musket of a fallen soldier, had at once thrown himself into the ranks of the Virginians under Washington,— the only corps in the whole army that had the slightest idea of how to manage such an affair, and who were already scattering among the trees,—and had done a man's full share in the work of saving the besotted regulars, and such of their officers as survived the murderous storm of rifle-balls which were pouring into their solid ranks.

From the day of that disastrous blunder of old-fogyism, to the commencement of the Revolution, he had employed himself as a scout and Indian-fighter, attaching himself as a volunteer to every expedition that was sent against the savages, and always rendering valuable service by his skill and daring, and his intimate knowledge of all the stratagems used by those most perplexing of all enemies.

He was, at the time he joined Clayton's troop, about thirty-five years of age; thin, wiry, with one of those prematurely seamed, old-looking faces which you sometimes see upon young men, sallow in complexion, with strong black hair, and burning black eyes gleaming from under it; with iron muscles, and no nerves at all; he would ride, if necessary, for forty hours at a stretch, without sleep or food, except a biscuit now and then, and a draught of water. No fatigue seemed to exhaust him, and no danger deterred him in carrying out orders. He was attached to Barton's division of the troop, and was his right-hand man, the one to whom he always looked whenever anything of difficulty or danger was to be undertaken.

He was also a great favorite with Bettle, to whom he was strongly attached; the two, though of such unequal age and education, being drawn together by some occult sympathy of their dare-devil temperaments, and having now the Sanford family, with whom Frank had lived previously to his enlistment, as a further bond of union.

Bettle had by no means made him a confidant as to his feelings toward Jenny, but from some expressions he had let drop, at different times, after his return from his expedition in July, Frank, with his natural acuteness, had no difficulty in seeing how matters stood.

To resume. After supper, the tired men and horses passed the rest of the night in the sound sleep they so much needed after their stormy day; the former on the barn-floor, which John and Mahlon Sanford had covered thickly with hay thrown from the mow, and the latter on the ground outside.

Jenny had left the room as soon as possible after supper was ready, feeling decidedly embarrassed at the demonstration she had almost unconsciously made when she first saw Bettle.

The officers were accommodated with rooms so far as could be done in a house that had only two unoccupied, one of which belonged to the farmer's two sons, who had volunteered to stand guard for the rest of the night; and in a few minutes nothing was heard but the long, heavy respirations of the tired sleepers, through which rasped harshly, audible all through the house, the prodigious snore of Mike away up in the garret under the roof.

The brothers stood on guard until after sunrise, but no further disturbance took place. The eventful scenes of the next twenty-four hours, however, we must leave for another chapter.

CHAPTER VII.

By the time the sky began to redden over old Deborah's rock, with the reflected light from the east, Frank was up, and out in the open air. He was a restless fellow, that Frank; getting awake at all manner of unseasonable times, and sleeping, when he did sleep, only by short naps, and as lightly as a weasel. He had acquired, perforce, in his exposed and adventurous life, two other faculties in this connection, which had more than once been of signal value to him,—the power of going to sleep at a minute's notice, anywhere, and the power of waking at any moment he chose, and of staying awake for almost any indefinite length of time.

He had slept longer than was usual with him on this occasion, for even his cast-steel frame had felt the effects of the tremendous labor of the day and evening. He was the first one out, however, leaving all the rest, officers and men, in profound slumber.

He found John and Mahlon Sanford still on guard, patrolling up and down, each with one of the Tories' muskets on his shoulder. It was light enough by this time to see distinctly, and the first things that caught Frank's eye were the dead bodies of five of the Tories lying a short distance from the barn-yard wall, as they had fallen before the two volleys fired from behind it. Two more were lying in front of the house, and in the middle of the road lay the unfortunate fellow who had been run down and trampled to death by the horses.

"Look'e here, boys," said he to the two brothers, "s'posin' we git these here corpusses out o' the way afore your mother an' Jenny comes out. No use in them a-seein' 'em. Let's drag 'em round behind the barn, an' after breakfast we'll have 'em buried."

This was done, the propriety of the suggestion being manifest; though the young men, less accustomed than Frank to the sight of dead bodies, went about the ghastly business with undisguised repugnance.

As they came back to remove the last one, they found Mike standing over it, looking first at it and then at Frank, in a state of utter bewilderment.

"Arrah, now, Misther Frank, an' is it yerself that's here! an' what's the matther, anyhow?"

"Matter, you dunderhead!" said Frank; "where were you last night, that you don't know what's the matter?"

"Where was I, is it? Sure, an' wasn't I aslape in me own paceful bed, all the blessed night?"

"Well, if you could sleep through all the firin' that was goin' on, you've got more lead in your brains than I thought," said Mahlon.

"Firin', is it?" said Mike, slowly; "well, now, I thought I heard some noise wanst, an' I was goin' to git up an' see what it was; an' thin jist as I got up, d'ye see, I didn't git up at all, be rason that the slape was heavy on me; an' thin, afore I know'd it, I was down agin, an' divil a haporth did I know till I got awake a little while ago, an' seen John an' Mally here a-walkin' up an' down wid guns on their showlthers, an' all the horses lyin' about; an' thin I got drissed an' hurried down, an' bedad they were gone whin I kem ; an' I saw this poor fellow a-lyin' in the road, an' I was lookin' at 'im an' thryin' to make it all out, when yees kem up."

"Look'e here, Mike," said Frank, "you must 'list in the reg'lar line for a sentry. Here's the house tuk by Tories, a battle fit in an' round it, the Tories druv off, an' you slep' through it all. Just the fellow for a reg'lar sentry. Here, bear a hand, an' let's git this carron out o' the way afore anybody sees it."

"But how did you git here yerself, Misther Frank?" inquired Mike, as they returned toward the house; "an' who was it druv off the Tories?"

"Come last night, with what was left o' the troop, from Brummadgem."

"The throop!" said Mike, in amazement. "Is it the throop that's here? Sure, I wonthered where all the horses kem frum. Is Misther Bettle among 'em?"

"Yes," said Frank.

"An' that rampin' divil of a horse of his! Be the powers, Misther Frank, but ye ought to have seen the fright he gev me whin he was here in harvest."

"Yes, I heard somethin' about that," said Frank. "You tried the wise trick of lashin' him 'cause he flung you. If it hadn't been for Bettle, you'd ha' been a dead man. He's got the same hoss here now; you'd better keep clear of him."

"Bedad, I'll do that same," said Mike, as they walked toward the house.

Clayton and his officers were seated within, engaged in close consultation about something which did not appear to be of a very pleasant nature, judging from the knit brows and grave, earnest tones of the speakers.

As Frank appeared at the door, Clayton called him within.

"Does thee know this country well?" he inquired; "I am informed that there is a large force of Tories in the neighborhood, of which those we routed last night were only a detachment. I had rather avoid a fight at present, particularly against odds, if it can be done."

"How many are they, Uncle Tommy?" asked Frank, addressing Thomas Sanford.

"About two hundred, Riah Wood'r't told me. They're stationed at his mill just up the creek; thee knows where it is."

"Reckon I do; 'bout quarter of a mile above the cold spring. If there's that many, we'd better git away from this without losin' time. They're too strong for us."

"If they know *our* strength, they are," said Wetherill; "but I rather think they were too much frightened last night to have much idea of our number: headed off in so many directions, I think it more likely they will suppose us to be four or five times as strong as we are."

"They may do that," said Clayton, "but the truth will soon be discovered. Besides, our ammunition must be short; how much did thee say there was, Levi?" he added, addressing Barton.

"Six rounds apiece for the carbines, and about twice as many for the pistols."

"Not quite so bad as I feared," said Clayton.

"We have the cartridge-boxes of the Tories, too."

"Plenty of powder, but no balls that will go in our pieces. We might use their muskets, it is true, but with our numbers we could only make a fight behind shelter, and when the ammunition was exhausted we would be at their mercy. Nevertheless, we'll take the cartridges with us."

"Why, there's Mary Woodward!" exclaimed Jenny, suddenly, pointing to the figure of a girl on horseback, who was approaching at a rapid gallop along the road; "she must have something to tell, or she wouldn't be coming over so early in the morning."

The girl came up at a sharp gallop, and, checking her horse, without dismounting, exclaimed, "Father sent me over to tell you to leave at once! They know how weak you are, and as soon as the men have had their breakfast they'll be over and attack you, with Black Rawdon at their head. They'll be here in an hour."

"A good deal can be done in an hour," said Clayton; "but there's no time to lose. Have the horses got ready, Frank; we must eat *our* breakfast in the saddle. The loose horses had better be left behind: they will only encumber us."

In a few minutes the troop was in the saddle.

"Now," said Clayton, addressing Thomas Sanford, "one thing more; it won't do for thee and thy people to remain here if the Tories are coming back. They will revenge last night's work on anybody they may find. Has thee any plan in view?"

"No," said Thomas, "there's nothing that I can do; there are plenty of neighbors where we would be welcome, but we would be no safer than here, and would draw them into danger besides. No, we must take what comes."

"You'll take what comes to us," said Clayton: "if

we escape, you escape; if we are cut off or taken, it may be that you will have to share the lot with us; not if we can help it, though, even then. Whatever may befall us, you shall be saved, if possible."

It was then arranged that the old farmer, his wife, and Jenny should go forward at once under the escort of Bettle and what remained of his division,—some fourteen or fifteen, including 'Riah Woodward's three sons and four of the other men he had obtained on his former visit,—under Frank's guidance. Two of the farmer's horses were already equipped with side-saddles, and Bettle felt a pleasant glow of pride as he saw how lightly and gracefully Jenny sprang to her seat from Frank's hand and gathered up the reins, and how easily but steadily she sat in the saddle. Her mother mounted in a more staid and sober manner, as became a matron of advancing years and comfortable ponderosity; but, once in the saddle, she was evidently nearly as much at home there as her daughter.

All being now ready, Frank started with his party, and, proceeding down the road as far as the bars near the little bridge, turned at once into the cornfield, carefully putting up the bars after all had passed, and made for the woods, intending to keep as much as possible under cover until they reached the place he had indicated as a rendezvous. This was a spring, a little more than a quarter of a mile south of the old Lancaster road, which I have already mentioned, but which is now better known as the Strasburg road, and just at the western edge of West Chester.

The spring lay in a little hollow, between the present State road and Market Street, and was at that time surrounded by woods, which covered a considerable portion of the country, particularly to the south and west.

Heading well southward until they struck the run which flows from the spring and empties into the Bradywine at Jefferis' Ford, they followed the course of the stream, only deviating from it where it passed through open meadows, and carefully avoiding the traveled roads.

All this care was owing partly to Frank's habitual caution, and partly to the fact that he had a strong suspicion that the route of the British would lie somewhere in this direction. Even should the main body not cross in the neighborhood, he felt very sure there would be enough foraging parties prowling about to make it advisable to keep out of sight as much as possible.

They were proceeding in this cautious manner, with Frank about fifty yards in advance, on foot, when they saw him stop suddenly near the side of a narrow cart-road which ran across the course they were pursuing, throw himself down with his ear to the ground for a moment, and then, springing up, wave them back with his hand, and swarm like a squirrel up the trunk of a tall hickory-tree that almost overhung the path.

The party stopped instantly, and the three farm-horses, with their riders, were led behind a clump of saplings which stood near, and which screened them effectually from view at any distance. In the mean time, the trained horses of the troop, at the word of command, had crouched flat on the ground, each with his rider lying behind him, with carbine unslung and sword hanging at his wrist. In this position, a slight rise in the ground prevented them from seeing the

ad, and they lay there in grim silence, awaiting such
gnal as Frank might give.

A few moments of anxious suspense followed, and
ettle was about to move forward to a position whence
e could command the road, when suddenly a light
ep was heard among the trees to one side, and the
ext moment Frank appeared.

"What is it, Frank?" said Bettle. "British or
ories?"

"Red coats," said Frank. "A hundred reg'lars
comin' double file down the road yonder. Git the
omen furder back among the trees. We're all too
ear."

"Is there time?" asked Bettle, anxiously.

"Time enough if we don't stand blatherin' about
, but git to work. They're quarter of a mile off
et."

Orders were at once given accordingly, and the troop-
s retreated rapidly and silently until they reached a
ot about a hundred yards back, where the trees
ere thicker and the ground overgrown with bushes.
As soon as Frank had given his information, Bettle
ad gone to where Jenny and her parents were wait-
g anxiously.

"We must go deeper into the woods," he said,
lmly, "as there is a party of British near us that I
d rather avoid just now."

"Is there danger, does thee think?" inquired Martha
anford.

"No, not if we are prudent; but we had better
ove." So saying, he took the bridle of Jenny's
rse, and the whole party moved forward, the men
companying them in close order on either side and

9*

in the rear, until they reached the spot already mentioned, where the troop-horses again crouched down like cats among the bushes, with their riders behind them.

The farm-horses, not having been trained to this, remained standing, and Bettle wasted no time in vain attempts to make them lie down, but, turning to the nearest man, said, with a slight gesture toward Jenny and her parents,—

"Woodward, lead their horses down into the hollow there around the bend of the run, and stay there until you hear a whistle. If there is but one, come back; if there are two, make ready for a start, but keep close; if you hear three, wait for nothing more, but *run!* their safety will depend on you then."

Woodward took his post at once, and was about to lead them off, when Jenny beckoned to Bettle, who immediately stepped to her side.

"Is thee going with us?" she whispered, bending down toward him.

"No, Jenny," said he; "my place is here among my men."

"So is mine, then," said she: "if there is danger, why shouldn't I share it?"

"It would do no good, Jenny; it would only unnerve me and the men to have you exposed to danger. I hope they will pass by without seeing us; but they may see our tracks and follow them, and then a tree-fight will be inevitable, and you would lose your life without accomplishing any good whatever—or, what is a great deal worse, you may fall alive into hands that know neither honor nor pity. No, no, Jenny, you must be as safe as I can make you, or I can do nothing.

You may pray for us all, if you will, for if it comes to a fight we'll need it."

"Thee is right, William; I'll go," said Jenny, pressing his hand, "and I'll pray that their eyes may be held, so that we may escape without bloodshed."

Several precious moments were lost in this conversation, and Bettle watched the receding figures with a great deal more anxiety than he had manifested while talking, until they turned the bend of the stream and passed out of sight.

As he crouched down by his horse, he could hear the regular heavy tramp of what was evidently a considerable body of men passing along the road below, though, owing to the nature of the ground, he could see nothing.

Frank, however, had already climbed the tree behind which Bettle lay, and, completely hidden from view by the leaves and branches, was watching the enemy closely.

Suddenly came from the road the command, "Halt!"

Bettle gave a light tap on the tree with his sword-hilt, which was immediately answered from above.

"What are they doing?" he inquired, in a low voice, laying his mouth close to the trunk, that the sound might be better transmitted.

"'Xaminin' the tracks," said Frank, in the same tone; and then continued, "Lay low: they're looking this way; now they're tryin' to count 'em; there's four or five of 'em working up on the trail; now they've lost it again."

"Well?" said Bettle, as Frank paused.

"Now they've gone back to talk to the officer; they're pointin' this way; the officer's a-comin' this way himself, now; no, he's stopped, an's shakin' his head; now he's gone back, an' the men are formin' agin."

"Fall in, men, fall in," came the order, in an impatient tone, from below; "we've no time to get into an ambuscade hunting rebels in the woods, if there are any there at all. Fall in; forward, march!"

To Bettle's intense relief, the steady tramp became audible again, and in a few minutes passed out of hearing.

Frank slid down from the tree.

"That was a mighty close graze," said he, coolly; "reckon they'd ha' treed us, sure, if old Eli Flint had been with 'em an' got holt o' one end of a trail like they did, an' he'd ha' told how many there was of us, too."

"Who's Eli Flint?" said Bettle.

"An old fellow-scout o' mine, an' the best hand on a blind trail I ever seen. He could find sign where an Injin himself couldn't, and he'd follow it like a hound. But I reckon we'd better git on."

"Yes," said Bettle, "we've lost time enough; I want to reach the spring by noon."

While all this was going on, the party in the thicket were waiting the result, straining their ears to hear any sound that might indicate the course events were taking.

The first sound they heard was a low whistle.

"What's that?" inquired Thomas Sanford, hastily.

"Leftenant Bettle's call," said Woodward, shortly. "'St! Listen if another comes."

No other came, however, and Woodward, exclaiming, "All's right, then," prepared to return with his charge, when there was a rustling in the bushes behind him, and a large dog sprang from them to the side of Jenny's horse, and with a joyful whine rose upon his hind legs, and, placing his fore-paws upon the skirt of her riding-dress, rubbed his black muzzle fondly against the hand which was now patting his head.

"Why, Carlo, what brought thee here?" said Jenny.

"Sure enough," muttered Woodward, compressing his lips, "what did bring him here? Well, we'll see directly."

They now left their concealment and joined the others, Carlo frisking about his old friends the farm-horses.

"Frank," said Woodward, "just search about the dog: he ain't here for nothing."

"Here, Carlo," said Frank; and, as the dog came close to him and stood by his side, he noticed a slight bulge in one part of the leathern collar, around which a bit of twine was tied. Slipping his finger beneath, he discovered a folded scrap of paper. Detaching and opening it, he handed it to Bettle, who read, roughly traced with a pencil:—

"The Tories are on us, two hundred strong. We have gained the rock, and can hold it for a little while. If there is any place where Thomas and his family can be placed in safety, leave them and come back; if not, push on to Philadelphia with all speed, and bring such help as thee can, as soon as they are safe.

"CLAYTON."

The dog had evidently swum the Brandywine, for the paper was wet, and so discolored by the wet leather of the collar that Bettle had at first some difficulty in making it out.

CHAPTER VIII.

HERE was a complication of the business, with a vengeance! What was to be done? With his already weakened force reduced by one-third, and that third composed of the best fighters in the troop, Clayton, though his position on the rock was a strong one, was in by no means an enviable situation.

He had left the house with his force, soon after the departure of Frank and his party, but had not proceeded a hundred yards down the road, before the Tories emerged from the wood near the house and instantly gave chase. At least they thought they were giving chase.

But the small body of men in advance of them did not seem to have reached the same conclusion; for, as the Tories came within some sixty or seventy yards of them, they halted, faced about, and delivered their fire in a volley which cut sharply among their ranks.

The whole body halted for an instant, staggered, not so much by the fire itself as by the cool hardihood and effrontery of the handful of men from whom it came. The halt was but momentary, however, and the next moment saw Clayton and his men in the meadow which lay between the road and the Brandywine, making at full speed for the creek. Some fifty of the Tories, who were mounted, leaped into the meadow at the same moment, and there was a desperate race across it, one

arty making for the creek, the other trying to head
them off and turn them back upon the footmen, who
had by this time formed along the road and were
keeping up a brisk but ineffectual fire upon the flying
troop.

Disregarding the fire both from the road and from
the horsemen, which their rapid motion rendered harmless, Clayton and his men spurred toward the stream,
and reached the bank about thirty yards ahead of their
pursuers, who, not so well mounted, had lost ground
in the endeavor to bear down upon their flank and turn
them.

The foremost rider,—Clayton was in the rear, the
commander's place in a retreat,—as he reached the
bank, spurred his horse at it, without a moment's
check or hesitation, and went into the water with a
flying leap that carried him at once twenty feet from
the bank. He knew the stream, however, and had
selected a spot where the water was shallower than
it was higher up and nearer the rock. Even there,
however, it reached nearly to the horse's girths. The
whole troop followed him, spreading out, however,
both to avoid striking each other as they leaped, and
to present a less compact mark for the fire of the
Tories' pistols as they were crossing.

The next minute the horses were leaping and scrambling up the opposite bank like cats. As the last one
gained his footing on the firm ground, Clayton, who
was still in the stream, halted for a moment to look
round at his pursuers.

Their horses, the ordinary farm-cattle of the neighborhood, which they had seized and pressed into their
service, were swerving from the leap, and rearing and

plunging as their riders strove to spur them over the bank. Clayton's men also halted, standing in the open order in which they had reached the land.

The leader of the Tories, an old campaigner,—none of your militia captains,—reined up his horse upon the other bank, and, leveling his pistol at Clayton, fired; the ball grazed his ear, but did no harm beyond drawing a drop or two of blood.

"Thee ought to do better than that, so near," said Clayton, in his cool, grave way. "I'll give thee a lesson." And, leveling his own pistol in turn, he fired.

He was not in the habit of missing his aim, and the Tory leader would have reached the end of his fighting on the spot, had he not, with a readiness that showed practice, at the instant he saw Clayton raising his hand, forced his horse to rear. The ball struck the poor brute just in front of the girth, and he rolled over with his rider upon the grass.

While the latter was recovering himself, Clayton reached the bank, and put his troop in motion.

By this time two or three of the enemy had forced their horses into the water, when the rest followed without hesitation, and the whole body were crossing the stream; the footmen also had reached it farther down, and were crossing.

Clayton might possibly have escaped, but his plan from the first had been to gain the rock, not being willing to risk a long chase or running fight, in the tired condition of his horses; for, though the few hours they had slept on the preceding night had refreshed them a little, they still needed rest. He knew the rock and its capabilities for defense pretty well, from descriptions Bettle had given him; and, with the promptness which was one of his characteristics, he had taken the bold resolution, the moment he saw the enemy, to reach it if possible, and hold it until his horses were rested or help came. Twenty-four hours would do for the former; less might bring the latter.

Turning to Mahlon Sanford, who was riding beside him, he inquired if he knew any path by which they could reach the top with horses, without going around by the ridge.

"Yes," answered the boy, promptly: "when Bettle was here in the summer, I told him there was none; but since then me an' John's been tryin' the place to see if there was, an' we found one where I think we can get up. It's pretty rough, though. Are the beasts sure-footed?"

"As squirrels," said Clayton.

"Then we can do it," said the boy. "Can't we, John?"

John nodded, and they rode rapidly on to the foot of the rock.

There was no time to lose, for the enemy's horsemen had already reached the bank, and were in motion toward them, a little more cautiously, however, now that they were near the shelter of the trees with which the back and sides of the rock were at that time covered, while the footmen, who had also crossed, were pushing forward from below.

Placing the two Sanfords in front, and taking the rear himself, he gave the word, and they moved forward on their break-neck expedition.

Up they toiled, now scrambling over moss-grown boulders, now leaping over fallen tree-trunks, the horses in advance, following the one which Mahlon was leading, the men on foot covering the rear, and holding the enemy in check with their carbines, until they reached the top, breathless.

Here, for the time, they were safe; for, as Bettle had said, they could have held it, with plenty of ammunition and provisions, against an army.

"Now," said Clayton to Wheeler, dryly, "I want to send a message to Bettle. If thee can tell me how to do it, I'll be obliged to thee."

"I can tell thee how to do it," said Mahlon; "jest thee write it down, and I'll send it."

Clayton looked at him, but he was evidently in earnest; and accordingly he tore a leaf out of a small memorandum-book, and hastily scribbled down the note which ended the last chapter, and handed it to Mahlon. The latter immediately fastened it in the way I have described to the collar of the dog Carlo, who had accompanied them throughout the whole scene.

"There, now, Carlo," said he, when he had secured the paper, "sik Jenny; sik 'em out, old boy; hi on!"

The dog looked up with his bright, intelligent eyes into the boy's face as he spoke, and then started down the hill, running the gauntlet of the enemy's fire, but escaping without a scratch, crossed the stream, and made directly for the house, where, after smelling around for a few moments, he gave a short, quick bark or two, started off at a gallop with his nose to the ground, and came up with the fugitives just late enough to avoid betraying them to the regulars who had passed along the road below.

When Bettle had read the note to himself, he read it to Frank.

"By the hokey!" said the latter, "look'e here! we're in what old Eli used to call a 'corn-twisted diffikilty;' we can't leave the folks here; if we take em on to Philadelfy, it's a chance if they don't chaw up the whole troop afore we can git back—Stay! I know a place off here, right in the woods, out o' the way o' stragglers, where they'll be safe enough till we can come for 'em."

"Whose place is it?" said Bettle.

"Why, long Johnny Mac Allan's," said Frank; "ef I hadn't had my skull so full of other things, I'd ha' thunk o' him at first."

"Will he be willing to run any risk?"

"Well, I reckon he won't trouble himself much about that; he'll take 'em if I ask him; an' I'd like to see the man that 'd meddle with anybody he promised to take keer of."

"We must try him," said Bettle; and then, approaching Jenny, he read the note to her, saying, "I'm afraid we must go back at once, Jenny; Frank knows a place here in the woods where you can all stay in safety until we return, or until the coast is clear, so that you can get home again. It is at the house of an acquaintance of his, named Mac Allan."

"I've heard of him," said Jenny, "and if Frank says so, and thee thinks best, we ought to go. I'll tell father about it."

She communicated the state of affairs briefly to her father, to whom, also, Bettle read the note.

"I know Mac Allan well," said the old man; "it's the best thing we can do; thee must go back at once to the rock, and help the captain."

Nothing more was said, and the party struck off into

the woods toward Mac Allan's house, which was about a quarter of a mile off.

It was a tolerably large, but rudely-built, log house, with perhaps half an acre of cleared ground around it. As they emerged from the wood upon this open space, they were greeted by the open-mouthed rush of half a dozen savage bull-dogs at them, while Frank's eye, which never missed anything, detected the muzzles of two or three rifles poking out from loop-holes in the wall.

First speaking to the dogs, who recognized his voice and stopped, though they eyed his companions suspiciously, he called, "Hello, Johnny, take down them shootin'-irons an' come out; I want to speak to you. Ha' you forgot Frank Lightfoot a'ready?"

The door opened, and a tall man stepped out; one of those long, double-jointed, broad-shouldered, big-footed, big-fisted, slab-sided fellows, in whom all grace and symmetry have been sacrificed to make room for a double quantity of simple sledge-hammer strength.

"Why, Frank," said he, in a voice a good deal milder and smoother than his appearance indicated, " why, Frank, is that you? And Tommy Sanford, I swan! What's the matter? What's brung you all into the woods this mornin'?"

"'Cause we wanted to get the wimmen-folks out o' Black Rawdon's clutches, an' we wa'n't strong enough to fight him."

"Black Rawdon! Is he up in the neighborhood? That's a bad lookout, sure. How many men has he?"

"Why, about two hundred; an' that ain't the worst; look'e here, Johnny; he's got the captain, with only

out twenty-five men, treed on Deborah's Rock; we
st got word by old Carlo here."

"How?"

"By old Carlo; note fastened to his collar."

"My sakes alive!" said the old man, "that's wus
' more of it. What are ye goin' to do? Who's these
th you? Part of the troop?"

"Yes," said Frank, in a low voice; "the officer's
e o' the leftenants,—Bettle. We want you to take
arge o' the wimmen-folks an' the old man, an' keep
n safe while we go back to the rock; for the captain
want all the help we can give him. Will you do it?"

"Certain," said Mac Allan; "light down, folks, an'
me into the house."

They did so, and, after seeing them safely within,
ttle went to the old man, and, taking his hand, said,
rnestly,—

"Now, John, will you take care of them truly and
thfully? Will you defend them as you would your
n family, while you can fire a shot or strike a
ow? I'm not a man to forget those who show kind-
ss to me or those I care for."

Mac Allan looked hard at Bettle for a moment, and
en glanced with a look of interrogation at Frank,
o answered it with a wink and a slight screw of his
ad.

"We'll take care of 'em, leftenant; never fear: if we
n't do it by fightin', I've got a place to hide 'em in
at all the Tories in the country couldn't find."

"Well," said Bettle, who had already bidden Jenny
od-by, "then we'll go back as fast as we can, and——"

"Wait a bit," said Mac Allan; "I reckon you won't
any wus off for a little extra help." And, taking

10*

down a tin horn that hung by the door, he blew a long blast on it; it was answered in a minute or two by the appearance of ten stalwart young men, all of the same powerful, double-jointed frame as the speaker.

"There," said he, "there's ten boys that can bark a squirrel off a tree an' never raise the fur. Boys, git your rifles an' powder-horns; we're goin' to Brandywine to have a lick at Black Rawdon an' his gang."

"All right, dad; hurray!" shouted the boys, as they hurried into the house, and reappeared directly, each armed with a long, heavy rifle and accouterments, and with a tomahawk in his belt.

"But," said Bettle, "won't this leave the place without protection in case of attack?"

"What! with the old woman an' the three gals, that can all handle a rifle as well as I can, or the boys? I'd like to see the rapscallions git in while they're there! Never fear, leftenant; the gal an' the old folks 'll be as safe as if they were in the middle of Washington's camp."

"All right," whispered Frank, answering a look from Bettle; "I know 'em all; the old woman an' the gals 'll fight like she-painters, an' they're as cunnin' as Injuns. We'll find em all safe, *if we ever git back.*"

The old man then went into the house to give final directions to his wife and daughters. When he came out again, the party, strengthened by this valuable addition to their force, moved rapidly back through the woods toward the Brandywine, heading, however, for Jefferis' Ford, which they crossed, and proceeded up the west bank of the river, keeping in the woods with which the country at that day was pretty much covered.

On the way, Frank gave Mac Allan a description of the events of the preceding day and night, which occupied the time until they reached the neighborhood of the rock. The old man listened attentively, giving a slight grunt now and then, until Bettle ordered a halt.

"You know the country, Woodward," said he to one of 'Riah's boys, who was riding near him. "How near can we get to the rock without being seen?"

"Within a hundred yards; but not now. We must wait till night."

"I want to let the captain know we're in the neighborhood," said Bettle. "Can you get around so as to let him hear you whistle from above, near the ford?"

"Yes," said the young man, "I can do that; an' if you'll let me have Jim and Harry——"

"Your brother and Dandy Harry?"

"Yes; let us all go, and we can raise the whistle in three different places; I want to puzzle Black Rawdon's men, and lead 'em off on a wild-goose chase, if I can. After we've whistled, I'll go up to the mill and let Mary know we're about. She's a quick-witted girl, and may be able to help us a good deal."

Permission having been given, the three young men started together, on foot, and before many minutes a long, clear whistle, more like the shriek of a small locomotive than any sound coming from human lungs and lips, was heard from the direction of the ford; another came from the old Lancaster road; and a third from the woods at some distance west of the rock. Almost simultaneously with the last they heard an answering whistle from the top of the rock, showing that the party there had heard and understood the signal.

CHAPTER IX.

On reaching the top of the rock, Clayton had seen all its capabilities at a glance. He saw that there was hardly a possibility of reaching it, in the face of an enemy of anything like ordinary vigilance, from any point except the back of the narrow ridge I have already described. This could be barricaded, and *must* be barricaded, or the Tories could come up in full strength and drive them bodily over the face of the precipice. It was a miserably confined place, however, for so many horses to stand, much less manœuvre. Indeed, the latter was impossible, as a single false step of one of the upper horses on the dry, slippery grass might have sent himself and half the others with him rolling down the steep bluff

They were arranged, therefore, in as compact order as possible, on the small plateau on the south side of the ridge, and made to lie down, while all hands went to work to pry up such of the smaller boulders as appeared at all manageable, and roll them to a point indicated by Clayton, at about one hundred and fifty feet back from the brow of the rock. He had selected this because he had observed that several large trees stood in a line across it, close enough together to afford a reasonable hope of being able to fill up the spaces between them with stones and logs for a sufficient distance to block up the only avenue of approach.

They had no axes, of course, but several of the men were armed with hatchets and tomahawks; and they set to work to cut down such saplings as were not too large, and laid them along the barricade, interlacing them between the trees; they contrived, finally, to erect a breastwork, which, flimsy as it would have been on open ground or against artillery, looked as though it would answer its present purpose very well.

The enemy had stationed themselves on the ridge and along the northern bluff, satisfied that no attempt at escape would be made in any other direction, and intending to wait until night before they ventured an attack. They had heard the signal whistles, and the answer from the rock, and knew that help was at hand for the besieged, but had no idea to what extent; they were not aware, of course, of the detachment having been sent off with Jenny and her parents, and supposed that they had the whole force in their clutches; they were greatly puzzled, therefore, by the signals, coming from so many different directions, and the evident understanding between those who made them and the besieged party.

On the other hand, Clayton, satisfied that his message had been received, and that Bettle, with his force, was in the neighborhood, gave himself no further trouble, but quietly waited, keeping a vigilant watch, however, through the rest of the day, prepared to second any plan that Bettle and Frank might adopt.

Night came on without any more signals having been given; but still the handful of men waited patiently around a fire they had built near the breastwork, so as to throw a strong glare of light among the trees on the ridge beyond.

About an hour after sunset, Barton's ear caught a low whistle proceeding from somewhere about the front of the rock. He answered it softly, and it was repeated in the same tone, followed instantly by the sharp chirp of a katydid.

"That must be Frank," said Barton, rising to go toward the sound. A hand was laid upon his arm.

"Better let me go," said Mahlon Sanford, in a whisper. "Does thee see the sky?" pointing overhead to the dense black clouds with which it was covered. "Once out o' the firelight, an' thee couldn't see a step before thee; thee'd roll over the edge before thee thought o' bein' near it."

"But why should you go into danger to save me?" said Barton.

"'Cause the troop 'ud git no good by thy goin', and 'ud git some loss if thee tumbled over the rocks in the dark, as thee'd be most sure to do, not knowin' the ground; *I* know every step of it, an' so does Frank, if it's him. Besides, if anybody's to be lost, I can be best spared; boys ain't much 'count, anyhow."

The boy gave this concluding estimate of the value of his branch of the species, not in a whining or sentimental or didactic or misanthropic manner, but in the simplest and most natural way possible, as if it were merely an abstract proposition that had no particular interest for anybody.

Barton was touched by it; but he saw its force, and allowed the boy to pass him, while he followed as well as he could in the darkness, which, among the trees in the shadows of the rocks, and under the cloud-covered sky, was intense.

Keeping well to the right, Mahlon felt his way among

he stones to where the ground became much broken, ut with a general, rapid slope toward the edge. Here e stopped, and waited till Barton, who was a few feet ehind, came up.

"He's right under that big piece," said the boy, ointing to a large oval mass of stone which stands alanced, as it were, on the very edge of the precipice, ut which then looked only like a spot of somewhat nore intense black in the surrounding darkness. " I now he's right there; but it's so dark there's no telling vho's who, an' if we come too near him without lettin' im know who we are, he might shoot, thinkin' we was Cories. Thee knows the signals, I don't; s'pose thee ries 'em."

"I will," said Barton; "I'm not afraid of his shootng at us, if it is Frank; but it may be one of the wolves that are lying in wait for us out yonder."

"What will thee do, if it is?" inquired the boy, in he same noiseless whisper in which the whole conver-ation had been carried on.

"Over!" was the laconic answer, followed by a whistle, clear and distinct, but which would have been naudible a hundred feet off. An answer came in-tantly from the very spot Mahlon had indicated.

"So far, good," muttered Barton to himself; "let's ee if he'll answer the katydid."

The note was sounded, and was immediately an-wered by another from the same spot, followed by the hrill twitter of a tree-frog.

"Frank," said Barton, in a low tone, "is that you? t's all right; come out."

"Keep where you are; I'm comin'," said a voice; nd then Barton heard footsteps making their way slowly and carefully along the dangerous route, and in half a minute more Frank was by his side.

"By the hokey!" said the latter, "but that *was* a climb! It's bad enough in daylight; but such a night as this!—Look'e here! all safe?"

"Yes; not a man lost"

"Anybody hurt?"

"Captain's ear grazed; that's all."

"Hosses up?"

"Yes, just above. Where are the boys?"

"Off in the woods yonder, jest across the meadow, an' long Johnny Mac Allan, with his ten double-fisted sons, with their rifles."

"Johnny an' his boys!" said Mahlon, joyfully; "are they here? Gosh! but we'll have somethin' like fightin', now!"

The two men and the boy had been making their way back to the fire during this conversation.

"Why, Frank!" said Clayton, as they approached, "how did thee contrive to get up here?"

"Scrambled, somehow," said Frank; "there's a sort o' path up around the big rock that sticks out over the water, but it wouldn't do for anybody to try it at night unless he knew the ground. But look'e here! that ain't what I come for." He then told Clayton pretty much the same in substance as he had already told Barton, adding, "Some of us went to Sanford's house, an' found everything just as we left it; so we carried off the muskets an' cartridge-boxes the rascals had left there, over to Wood'r't's Mill; took all the provisions too; Jim an' Harry's been at the mill all day, runnin' bullets an' makin' cartridges for the carbines an' pistols. Mary an' the old woman's been busy bakin' an' cookin', an' at midnight the scow 'll be down here under the big stone with a load o' provisions an' ammunition, an' feed for the hosses, enough to last a week."

"Then we are safe enough," said Clayton; "they *can't* drive us from here, if we have food and ammunition; and I think it likely, with our force in front, and Bettle with his men to worry them in flank and rear, we may contrive to hold them a little uneasy. I see thee has thy cord with thee."

"Certain!" said Frank; "don't ketch me travelin' without it, nohow."

"Does thee think," said Clayton, dropping his voice so as to be barely audible to Frank, who was sitting close beside him, "does thee think—don't look around yet—thee could find the body that belongs to that head—don't move thine, look out of the corner of thy eye—that is peering above the bank close to that big hickory? The third one from the end of the breastwork."

"Wait," said Frank, in the same tone; "may-be he's heard too much." And, changing his position slightly, as if to rest himself, he managed to sink lazily into a recumbent position, with his elbow on the ground and his head resting on his hand, with his face turned sufficiently toward the point indicated to allow him to see without the appearance of scrutinizing it particularly. Sure enough, there, right at the base of the tree, and partly hidden by it, was a clump of green leaves, which Frank was certain had not been there when he first came up. A close scrutiny through his half-closed lids showed him a pair of eyes gleaming from under the leaves, in the light of the fire.

Satisfied as to this, Frank then said, in a louder voice,—

"I'm goin' to lay down where the fire won't shine in my face, an' try to get a nap."

So saying, he sauntered off a few feet toward the farther side of the ridge, and lay down behind one of the large fragments of rock near its edge, so as to bring it between himself and the spy, who still maintained his position. The moment he was out of sight, however, he worked his way along close to the ground to the outside of the breastwork, crept along in front of it, and around through the trees so stealthily, that he approached within seven or eight feet of the owner of the head, without being perceived. The latter was lying flat on his face, still absorbed in watching those around the fire.

Stepping lightly from behind the tree which he had last reached, Frank, with about a foot of the cord stretched tightly between his hands, the ends coiled around his wrists and fore-arms, steadied himself, braced his feet firmly, and then, with a spring as fierce and as noiseless as that of a panther, leaped right on his victim, alighting on all fours with a knee on each side of the unlucky Tory's loins, and the tight cord across the nape of his neck, pinning him down firmly, with his nose flattened against the root over which he had been peeping.

There was not much chance for outcry at best; but Frank put an end to all attempt at it by stooping over his man, still holding the cord firmly down, and hissing in his ear,—

"Look'e here! if you make a whisper, if you breathe a loud breath, I'll hang you without a gallows! Raise

your head a little. What, you won't! By the hokey! f you make me tell you again, I'll shave it off and pitch it down the bank for your men to play foot-ball with. Think I don't know you, Black Rawdon?"

The start the prisoner gave at this question brought he back of his neck into sharp contact with the point of the knife Frank had drawn, and showed him that his captor was in stern and unmistakable earnest.

Rawdon—for it was the dreaded leader himself—raised his head from the root, and in an instant Frank had encircled his neck with two or three folds of the cord, just tight enough to keep him reminded of the danger of loud talking, and then, bidding him get up, secured his arms with the remainder of the cord as he did so, and led him, grinding his teeth in impotent rage, to where Clayton sat by the fire in that everlasting Quaker calmness of his.

"I've got him, captain," said Frank. "Do you know who he is?"

"No; does thee?"

"*I* reckon," said Frank, laconically; "Black Rawdon."

"Black Rawdon!" exclaimed those who were nearest, pressing around the two men in great curiosity; for the prisoner's name was known and dreaded throughout the whole country-side. "Frank's caught Black Rawdon," was buzzed through the whole party, and a half-circle of eager faces was formed around the prisoner and Clayton, who were regarding each other in silence. At last Clayton spoke:—

"Thy fate has overtaken thee at last, friend Rawdon. I have been on the lookout for thee for some time, and thee has put thy neck in my hands with a halter already twisted around it."

"How have I put my neck in your hands?" growled Rawdon.

"By playing the spy," was the answer, in the same grave, impassive tone which always marked Clayton's conversation; "by playing the spy; thee has been taken in the act; and should I have thee thrown headlong from this rock, thee may be very confident that no account will be required at my hands of the manner of thy death."

Rawdon looked at him with an ugly scowl on his swarthy face, mingled with a puzzled expression of countenance at the plain Quaker language in which he was addressed, and growled, again,—

"Who the devil are you, that talk of taking a British officer's life?"

"At present," said Clayton, quietly, "I am thy master; and it will depend a good deal upon thy own behavior whether thee finds me a hard one or not. Will thee promise me to sit still and give no trouble if I have thee loosed?"

Rawdon nodded.

"Loose him, Frank," said Clayton, and then added, in a lower voice, "As thee has been thrown into my hands a prisoner, let me advise thee to keep as near to me or Frank—the man that took thee—or Lieutenant Barton, here, as possible. There are men in the troop who have sworn to skin thee alive if thee should ever fall into their hands. Thee will see the prudence, therefore, of always keeping us in sight."

Rawdon, who had been glancing uneasily around during these remarks, and had seen more than one pair of eyes watching him with savage eagerness, again nodded sullenly.

Clayton had seen it too, and added, "Thee sees: any attempt at escape, by force or stratagem, and I turn thee over to those who will show thee as much mercy as hungry wolves."

Rawdon seated himself on the ground near Clayton, with his elbows resting on his knees, and his chin buried between his clinched hands, the personification of despair. And well he might; for, at the hands of at least five of those on the rock, he had earned his death three or four times over. I have neither time nor space nor inclination for any detailed account of this man. Suffice it to say, two of the five I have mentioned were in his debt, one for a father, and the other for a brother, murdered on their own door-steps, and of the other three, two for sisters carried off by him, and the other for a bride torn away on her wedding-night, and—well, there is no use in details; there is but one fate for women in the hands of such men as Black Rawdon and his gang.

Matters remained thus till midnight, when a slight tapping as of a hammer on stone was heard from the water's edge.

"There they are," said Frank; and, taking two of the men with him, they proceeded to the edge of the rock. A tap from the haft of Frank's knife was answered from below, and he immediately proceeded to make a line by splicing the cords carried by himself and his companions: this done, he crept forward cautiously until his head was over the edge of the precipice, when he lowered the line. It was caught from below, and in a moment more was shaken as a signal to raise it.

The next half-hour was spent in bringing up baskets containing quantities of bread and other provisions, cartridges, a huge demijohn of whisky, with bundles of hay and sacks of oats for the horses, and then the scow was silently poled across the stream, made fast to the large tree which stood close to the bank, and its occupants returned home.

The garrison, if it may be called so, was now provisioned for a week at least.

"Where are thy men?" said Clayton, turning suddenly to his prisoner.

The latter remained in sullen silence.

"Where are thy men?" asked Clayton, again, after giving him ample time to answer.

Still silent.

"Frank," said Clayton, "call up four or five of the men, and hang him up to that limb above the breastwork."

"All right, captain," said Frank; "I know five of 'em 'ud want no better fun."

Rawdon looked rather aghast at this exceedingly prompt way of doing things, and by the time Frank was on his way back with the men, had come to the sensible conclusion that he would not sacrifice his life for the sake of men who would be far enough from doing anything of the kind for him.

"They are out yonder, among the trees, not fifty yards from your breastwork."

"When will they attack?"

"At three o'clock."

"Without thee to head them?"

"They have orders to wait for me till then; if I don't come, then to attack without me, under my first lieutenant."

"How many are there?"

Rawdon hesitated.

Clayton repeated his question, calmly, with a glance first at the men who were standing around him in grim silence, and then at the tree.

Rawdon then stated his force to be about two hundred; but admitted, in answer to Clayton's questioning, that there were less than a hundred who could be relied upon after the first or second volley. He was evidently pretty well satisfied that if the enemy didn't run by that time, *they* would.

This information was given sullenly and reluctantly enough, and not without more than one allusion to the alternative suggested at the beginning of the conference.

"Three o'clock," said Clayton; "it's now one: we'll anticipate them. Levi," he added, addressing Barton, "put him under strict guard in the rear."

This being done, Barton was at his commander's side again, awaiting orders.

The latter, who had been in the mean time consulting with Frank, told him to give the signal to Bettle's party.

At once, the tu-hu hu-u-u-u of a screech-owl quavered dolorously from the rock, and was answered immediately from the woods to the eastward.

An anxious ten minutes of suspense followed; then the same boding cry arose directly on the line of the ridge, and nearer than before.

The party on the rock were by this time all at the breastwork, with carbines, knives, and pistols ready.

Frank gave another signal, which was answered from the same direction as the last, but nearer still.

At the same moment his ear, which had been all alive, caught the click of a gunlock just over the bank to the left. He nodded to Clayton, who ordered the prisoner again to be brought before him.

"Thee will give the signal for thy men to attack; and thee will please to understand that if thee gives a false one, or if thee has told me one atom of anything but truth——" and he pointed to the tree.

"Oh, yes, I'll give the signal," said Rawdon, who had been looking stealthily around him while Clayton was speaking; he snatched a pistol from the belt of one of the men near him as he spoke, cocked and fired it in an instant, almost in Clayton's face, and then, hurling it at him, went, with a furious bound and scramble, right over the breastwork!

The ball, fired hurriedly, missed Clayton; but his face was burnt and blackened by the powder, and he was staggered for a moment. As Rawdon disappeared in front of the breastwork, a shower of balls whistled over his head, all fired, in the surprise, one instant too late.

"After him!" shouted Clayton, as he recovered from the shock, springing forward in time to see Rawdon, about thirty yards off, running down the slope of the ridge, like a deer.

There was a momentary glimpse of this figure bounding along—of a cloud of dusky forms springing into the light to meet him—then the whip-like crack of a single rifle from the left, behind the bank, followed by the reports of seven or eight others in rapid succession; a convulsive spring upward of the solitary figure, which then fell forward upon its face—and a number of figures armed with clubbed rifles leaping up the bank and hurl-

g themselves with wild whoops pell-mell among those
ho had advanced to meet Rawdon. There was no
straining his own men now, even had Clayton wished
: they poured tumultuously over the barricade, and
a moment were all engaged in the hurly-burly of a
nd-to-hand fight, where no man could see his adver-
ry ten feet off.

The Tories, dispirited by the loss of their leader, and
ken by surprise by the sudden rush of the Mac Allans
or the rifle-shots had come from long Johnny's tribe),
ere falling back to cover, followed hotly by the latter
d by Clayton's men, who were by this time pressing
em hard, in spite of their superior numbers. At this
oment shots were heard in the rear, and then Bettle's
ice, in stern, rapid orders, as the slender force under
s command pressed forward silently up the ridge.

This new attack upon the rear of the Tories, which
as backing down the slope in tolerably good order
der the irresistible pressure of the front ranks, which
d given way under the sudden furious rush of the
hole body of the Rangers upon them, checked it, and
ove it forward again upon the front.

Bettle pursued his advantage, throwing himself with
handful of men, like wild-cats, upon the confused
owd which was now jammed together upon the nar-
w strip of fighting ground which the rock afforded;
ayton, from above, did the same thing; while the
ac Allans, on the flank, slashed away promiscuously
th their tomahawks and clubbed rifles.

The Tories, however, though hemmed in on all sides,
overing a little from their surprise, now began to
ke their numbers tell. Forming three fronts, so as
face all their assailants at once, they were now stub-

bornly holding their ground and keeping them at bay. Fortunately for the reinforcement, the darkness prevented the Tories from seeing how scanty it was, while the fury of its attack gave them the impression of a much larger number than it consisted of.

Matters were now becoming serious for the Rangers, when Frank, after a hasty whisper to Clayton, who nodded assent, disappeared, in company with Parker, in the direction of the horses. A moment afterward there was a stir among the latter as they scrambled up to the top of the ridge; then a voice shouting,—

"Stand clear, there! Away, now!"

The Rangers knew what was coming, and separated instantly; while down the slope, in solid column, swept the riderless horses, like an avalanche, headlong upon the surging mass of the enemy, kicking, striking, and biting at everything in their way, and scattering the compact mass of men as if a mine had exploded beneath them; while, as soon as the storm of thundering hoofs had passed between them, the two divisions of the Rangers closed upon their track, and threw themselves upon the disordered crowd more furiously than ever.

Flesh and blood could not stand this; all command was lost, all discipline at an end, and the panic-stricken Tories, hemmed in in front and rear, and utterly bewildered by this incomprehensible attack of wild beasts, turned sharp off to the left and dashed headlong down the south slope; with what result in the dark, I leave any one to judge who has tried to work his way down it by daylight, with his head cool and plenty of time to look where he was stepping.

A loud whistle from Clayton recalled his men from

the pursuit they were recklessly making at the imminent risk of their necks.

Some of Bettle's men had caught the foremost of the horses as they reached them ; the rest had stopped at the word of command, and were now quietly returning. This "fighting on their own hook" was one of the out-of-the-way things in Clayton's system of tactics, which had now stood him in good stead.

As they moved back toward the breastwork, Clayton stumbled, in the darkness, over something soft that lay on the ground. A brand was brought from the fire that was still burning, and by its flickering light they turned over the body of a man who was lying face downwards, and saw the coarse black hair and swarthy features of Rawdon, who lay there with his black eyes wide open, glaring upward at the cloudy sky.

"He was a bold, bad man," said Clayton, turning away, "and has gone to his account with a heavy load of sins to answer for."

"He was near going in good company," said Barton, to whom he spoke, dryly: "it isn't often a man gets the smoke of a pistol in his face, without getting its ball too."

CHAPTER X.

I'M tired of all this fighting. Here for six successive chapters we have never had our nostrils free from the smell of gunpowder. But what could I do? I have undertaken to chronicle the doings of as uneasy and reckless a set of men as ever turned a quiet neighborhood upside down; and I must tell what they *did*, when I had a great deal rather tell what they *ought to have done.*

When morning came, Clayton, having previously made up his mind what to do, called a council of his officers.

This was a "way he had;" it saved a vast deal of trouble in balancing between conflicting opinions and weighing diverse propositions. His practice was to hear all that was to be said upon the subject, and then to announce his decision.

In the present instance, the majority were decidedly in favor of retreating immediately toward Philadelphia, before the Tories could assemble in force again.

Bettle, anxious about the safety of Jenny Sanford and her parents, urged this course strongly.

Barton, however, argued that, being deprived of their leader, it was not likely that they would come to a head again in the neighborhood, particularly as they were necessarily ignorant of the strength, or rather the weakness, of the reinforcements which had come up so opportunely, and, it was most probable, had greatly overrated them: his plan, therefore, was to remain in the strong position they held for a few days, until the men and horses were rested and refreshed.

This happened to be precisely the conclusion to which Clayton had arrived; and he therefore broke up the council by announcing this determination.

This settled, his first movement was to order a detachment to Thomas Sanford's house, to see if the bare horses had been driven off; for, it will be recollected, they had been compelled to leave them in the hurry of the retreat on the previous morning.

They found everything as they had left it, even to the horses of the Tories they had routed on the evening of the 11th. Leaving these, and taking their own horses, they returned to the Rock, where, after feeding them, they addressed themselves to making a breakfast of the provisions which had been sent from the mill.

When the meal was finished, all hands were set to work throwing up a breastwork of earth and stones, about fifty yards farther back, across the ridge, in order to allow more room. A number of saplings were also cut down with axes which had been brought from the house, cut into lengths, sharpened, and planted firmly along the top of the breastwork, forming a very complete chevaux-de-frise.

The post thus fortified, the men spent the balance of the day in absolute rest, no work of any kind being done but the necessary grooming of the horses, preparing the meals, and standing guard; the last Clayton *never* omitted, anywhere or under any circumstances, by day or by night.

With these exceptions, however, the men did as

best pleased them; and that which best pleased the most of them was to go to sleep in the shadows of the rocks and trees, regardless of considerable firing, which appeared to come from the direction of the "Turk."

So the day passed. The demijohn was emptied, and a fearful inroad was made upon the provisions; for, having nothing else to do, the men were nibbling nearly all the time they were awake.

Toward evening, or rather as it began to grow dark, old Mac Allan came to take his leave, saying he "reckoned he must sort o' think o' travelin' home and seein' how the women-folks was a-gettin' on, an' what all that firin' had been about."

"But," said Clayton, "thee don't mean to go to-night, does thee? Better wait till morning. There may be some of the Tories prowling about in the neighborhood yet."

"Well, s'posin' there is," said the old man; "I reckon I can see 'em as fur as they can see me, any how."

"Perhaps so," said Clayton; "but that won't do much good if a dozen or twenty of them should see thee at once."

"Sakes alive, capt'n," said the old man, "I'd be a mighty poor shoat if I couldn't dodge a dozen Tories in the dark. No fear o' me, at all."

"I suppose, however," continued Clayton, "that thy sons will return with thee, and will make a guard strong enough to protect thee against any party thee's likely to meet."

"I s'pose they won't do any such thing, if you'll let 'em stay," said Mac Allan, very promptly; "I've jest been talkin' to 'em, an' they're all high up for a turn with the troop. I reckon the old woman an' me, with the gals, can take keer o' the cabin."

"I shall certainly be very glad to have ten such men in the troop as thy sons," said Clayton; "but, in the present state of affairs, I think it would hardly be right to leave thee with so little defense."

"Hut tut! don't trouble yourself about that, capt'n," said the old man: "if we're once inside, with the door barred, there's nothin' 'll git through short of a canon-ball. No, no! the boys is wanted more where they are than at home; so good-night."

And, without waiting for an answer, he strode down the ridge, with his rifle on his shoulder, and in a few moments was lost to sight in the woods.

The men had built two or three fires, which, with their fitful glare upon the trees and rocks around, gave a wild, weird look to the scene, that would have delighted old Salvator Rosa, could he have seen it. They were gathered around them in groups; and Clayton, rising from his seat, made his way to that which contained the ten sons of long Johnny Mac Allan.

Sitting down upon the grass among them, he said to the nearest,—

"Thy father tells me you all wish to remain with the troop. You can all ride, of course?"

"Oh, yes," said the other: "we can all ride well enough a-straddle on a horse's back; but we can't ride on his flank, and under his belly, and out on his tail, or between his ears, like these chaps here. We ain't never larnt to do them things. I reckon we can do the best kind o' fightin' afoot. But if you want fellows that can put a man's eye out as fur as they can see it, or hit a squir'l on the jump with a single ball, we're the ones to do it."

"You know the country well?"

"Every tree an' fence an' path, every hill an' hollow an' spring an' run, for five miles round."

"That will do; I want just such men as you, for outlyers. You can follow a trail?"

"Like fox-hounds; anything like Injin-fightin' we're up to."

"Very good. Now, as you are the freshest of the party, I want you to scatter to-night and try to strike the trail of the Tories we fought last night; bring me word of where they are and what they are doing; also, take your father's house in your round, and see how they are getting along there. This is Seventh day; at this time on Third day evening I shall expect to see you back; earlier, if you have anything important to tell."

"Come, boys," said the one to whom Clayton had been talking, addressing his brothers, "come along; we're got some trail-work to do."

The other nine young giants—the youngest was a lad of not more than perhaps sixteen, but nearly as big as his brothers—arose from their seats around the fire, and, giving themselves a hearty shake, "to settle their supper," as one of them remarked in an explanatory way, and filing out one by one through a narrow opening which had been left on one side of the breastwork, descended the slope in the direction their father had taken, and disappeared in the darkness.

Those on the rock, in the mean time, were occupying themselves according to their respective humors and tastes. Some were cleaning their arms, some lying on the ground asleep, some sitting around a boulder, watching two of their number who were engaged in a quiet game of cards by the light of the fire; for though Clayton and his officers, with their Quaker principles, which, with the exception of fighting, they firmly adhered to, disapproved of such amusements, they had too much sense to attempt enforcing them on their wild followers, beyond a strict and stern prohibition of gambling. Any attempt at this was punished summarily and pitilessly; so much so, that he had never had occasion to administer it but once.

The game to-night had been going on for an hour or so, when one of the players threw down his cards with a look of disgust, exclaiming,—

"There! I'm tired of this; you've got all the luck to-night, Harry, and I won't play any more. S'pose you sing us that song you made up t'other day, when we were down at Turkey Point."

"How will the captain take it?" inquired Harry, a young fellow of about twenty-two or three, apparently; rather more refined in his appearance than most of those around him, and the same who had accompanied young Woodward to give the signal of the approach of Bettle; "how will the captain take it? May-be he won't fancy such vanities."

"Oh, bother!" said the other; "if he's not too much of a Quaker to split a red-coat's head open, as I saw him do with a dragoon at Brandywine, I reckon he ain't too much of one to stand a good song."

"The song, Harry! the song!" echoed those around who had been watching the game; "let's have the song."

"Here goes, then," said Harry; "only you mustn't

laugh at it, if it don't turn out as good as Jem seems to think it."

So saying, he broke forth, in a clear, ringing tenor voice:—

> "Hark! from a roused nation breaking,
> Like the roar of a hurricane awaking,
> The cry all the broad land shaking,
>   Columbia shall be free!
> Up! you that lie there dreaming,
> The first rays of morn are streaming,
> Back from our foes' arms gleaming,
>   The foes of Liberty!
>   Arouse!
> For the cry all the land is shaking,
>   Columbia shall be free!
>
> "March on them, shoulder to shoulder;
> The Britons in slavery would hold her,
> But never chain shall enfold her,
>   Her sons shall make her free!
> No Lion-flag long shall hover
> The beautiful green land over,
> But toil-harden'd freemen, who love her,
>   Her masters soon shall be.
>   Arouse!
> For the cry all the land is shaking,
>   Columbia shall be free!
>
> "Loudly the bugles are pealing,
> And morn's faint light, o'er us stealing,
> The stars on our flag is revealing,
>   The stars of Liberty!
> Strike while that flag floats o'er us,
> Strike till the foe flies before us,
> Shout till the sky rings in chorus,
>   Our country shall be free!
>   Hurrah!
> Shout till the sky rings in chorus,
>   Our country shall be free!"

The song was sung to a wild, stirring air, to which, perhaps, more than to any merit in the words themselves, was owing the enthusiastic applause with which it was greeted.

"Dandy Harry sings like a lark; don't he, Frank?" said one of those who were seated by another fire a few feet off.

"H-m-m-p!" grunted Frank; "never heard a lark sing such booktionary words as them. Look'e here! what's the use o' squawkin' up here like a crow on top of a hick'ry-tree, to tell everybody where we are?"

"Oh, you be durned, you cussed old growler! what hurt could his singin' do, that our fires hain't done long ago? I don't b'lieve you keer about hearin' any music but an owl's or an Injin whoop. Harry's got a voice like a meadow-lark, or a nightingale."

"Well, may-be he has," said Frank, stretching his arms above his head and yawning fearfully, "may-be he has; I never heered a night-what-ye-call-'em; I've heered a night-*hawk* many a time, an' it ain't like *that*."

To tell the truth, Frank was woefully deficient in what is called musical "ear," and had in a high degree of perfection that so-called "practical" turn of mind that could see little use or beauty in anything that couldn't be made to pay in some fashion or other.

Harry Darlington, who had got his nickname of "Dandy" from a little more fastidiousness about his dress and equipments than was altogether fashionable in the troop, and from a certain indefinable picturesqueness in his dress and manner which were natural to him, and betrayed a poetic and artistic character of mind, which would have been of more use to him in some other situation than the present, was, nevertheless, entirely wanting in the most distinguishing characteristics of the animal whose name he bore: he had not a particle of its affectation, he had none of its dawdling indolence and indifference, but was as quick as a steel-trap, always ready for action, and was one of the bravest, and, where recklessness was of any use, one of the most reckless, fighters in the troop. In person, though tall, he was slender almost to delicacy, with small hands and feet; his hair was light and wavy, and his skin, in spite of the exposed life he was leading, was almost as fair, and his blue eyes, when in repose, as mild, as a girl's. He was the only one of the whole troop whose appearance could be called effeminate; and yet he was one that none who knew him cared to anger; for within that slender frame were muscles like catgut, and beneath that mild, gentle exterior were hidden the fire and resistless energy of a steam-engine.

He was good-humored, however, and merely laughed at Frank's grumbling depreciation of his musical powers, which he had overheard.

"Well," said he, "I'm about sleepy enough to turn in. Pull the curtains, will you, Jemmy, and tuck in the sheets," he added, as he threw himself down upon the dew-laden grass, with his blanket rolled up for a pillow. "Oh, dear! I wonder what my fidgety old aunty would say if she could see me? The last thing she said to me was, 'Now, Harry, whatever thee does, be sure and always have plenty of bedclothes, and, mind, don't let the night-air blow on thee.' I'm afraid this mattress is a little damp. Draw the curtains, Jemmy, and tuck me in."

The rest of the men soon followed Harry's example, and in a few minutes more all were asleep, in a silence which was broken only by the trumpeting of one or two inveterate snorers, the measured tramp of the sentinels, and the occasional restless movements of some of the horses.

Just before dawn, Bettle was startled from his sleep by a voice crying, "William! William! save me." The voice was Jenny Sanford's! He heard it and recognized it as plainly and distinctly as he had ever heard it when talking to her face to face, though now it was full of the sharpness of agonized fear.

Springing to his feet with a bound, he listened with painful intensity for a repetition of the cry. But he heard it no more; and all around was still, except the slight sounds mentioned before. Gradually, as he looked around him, recovering his faculties, which, except the single one of listening, had been for the moment set utterly adrift and wool-gathering by his startling awakening, Bettle stood with his heart beating violently from the sudden reaction of his excitement.

"I wonder if that *was* a dream," he muttered to himself; "it was fearfully like reality; I could have sworn that I heard her call me. Sam Diller," he added, stepping over to the sentry who was nearest him, "has anything been stirring?"

"Nothin' at all, sir; hardly a leaf turned, it's been so still."

"You haven't heard anything, then?"

"No, sir; leastways, nothin' but Jemmy Wood'r't

an' Sanford's Mike, over there, tryin' which can snore the loudest. Did you hear anything, sir?"

"No, I suppose not; it must have been a dream. I thought I heard a voice in the woods below."

"Them dreams is queer things," said the sentry, pacing up and down his short beat, with Bettle, who was too thoroughly excited to sleep again, pacing beside him, "queer things they are, an' no mistake. I've had 'em of all kinds; knocks at my door and my name called, and never a mortal hand or voice to give knock or call; I've been chased by Injins, an' could run like a rabbit till I come to one big buttonball-tree—always the same one—an' then it appeared like I couldn't lift my feet off the ground, an' jist as they was a-goin' to skelp me I'd git awake; an' offen an' offen I've found myself at a huskin' or quiltin' frolic or an' apple-parin' bee, in a room full o' gals, with nothin' on but my shirt, savin' your presence, an' my breeches a mile off at hum, an' sich a time as I——Hark!"

Sure enough! High and clear, piercing the calm morning air, this time, with unmistakable and terrible distinctness, rang a woman's voice from the woods at the foot of the ridge, shrieking for "Help! Help! Help!"

"By the Lord Harry!" exclaimed Diller, throwing down his carbine and springing like a cat to the top of the breastwork, "that's old Sanford's daughter! I know the voice."

Bettle was beside him in an instant, and again the cry came up.

"Stand fast here, Sam, while I rouse some of the men," said Bettle, hurriedly; and, springing down again, he darted to where Frank had been lying, but found him already on his feet, awakened by the voice. Frank's faculties were always on the alert, and, no matter how sudden or startling might be his arousing, he always knew exactly where he was and what he was doing. He had already roused the men nearest him, and was just saying to Clayton, who was also on his feet, "By the hokey, capt'n, that was Jenny Sanford, as sure as death!" when Bettle rushed to the group, exclaiming, " Follow, quick! All the boys you can gather, Frank!" and, turning about, sprang toward the opening in the breastwork, with Frank and some half-dozen of the men close behind him, and darted at full run down the ridge in the direction whence the alarm had come. The bustle had awakened the rest of the men, who, comprehending that there had been an alarm of some kind, but ignorant of what it was, were hurriedly attempting to get their horses saddled, when the calm voice of Clayton, whose coolness all the excitement had not disturbed, was heard.

"Let the horses be; there's no time to get them ready. John," turning to the elder Sanford, "we heard thy sister's voice in the woods, calling for help. Levi, take thy division; Wheeler, thine, and follow; the rest stand fast."

John Sanford ground something very much like an oath between his teeth, Quaker though he was, as Clayton spoke to him, and was out through the opening with Barton and his division before the whole order had passed Clayton's lips. Harry the minstrel and Mahlon Sanford had gone before, without waiting for any orders, clearing the breastwork, stakes and all, side by side, at a flying leap, like two panthers.

"Sentries, to your posts!" exclaimed Clayton, sharply,

observing that they had forsaken them to crowd forward to the breastwork. "Who ordered you to leave them? Diller, stay up where thee is, and keep eyes and ears open. Some of you go now and saddle the horses and have them ready."

These orders having been promptly obeyed, Clayton sat calmly down upon a stone to await the result.

CHAPTER XI.

When the pursuers reached the bottom of the slope, there was no appearance of those they were pursuing, and, to ordinary eyes, no trace of their passage. Here Frank's early training in running by scent, as it were, came into play. The dawn had broken, and, as the gray light stole over the sky, the group stood around Frank, who was crouched on one knee, carefully examining the ground in the still imperfect light.

"I've got it, by the hokey!" said he, raising his head and looking a little in advance. "Stand away, you in front there, till I see how it leads out."

The group separated, and Frank, rising to his feet, ran his eye for a moment along the ground, and exclaimed,—

"Yes, there it goes, as plain as a wagon-road;" and then, taking the lead of the party, fell at once into a long, loping trot, dodging in and out among trees, round clumps of bushes, his eyes mostly fixed upon the ground a short distance in advance, but losing no unusual appearance among the bushes which grew thickly along the course they were pursuing, never halting or hesitating for a moment, except, occasionally, at a remark from some one, louder than he thought prudent, when he would turn half around, put his finger on his lip, shake his fist at the offender, and then resume his trot, with a speed which kept them busy to avoid falling behind.

"How many of them are there, Frank?" said Bettle, who was pressing on beside him.

"Ten hosses; one of 'em's lame."

"How do you know the number?" said Bettle.

"Tracks; plenty o' sign," said Frank, laconically; for he never wasted words or vouchsafed minute information when on a trail.

"Any footmen?"

Frank shook his head impatiently, and the party moved on in silence for half an hour more, when he suddenly stooped, picked up something which lay on the ground, and stopped short with his finger on his lip.

"What is it?" inquired Barton, who happened now to be nearest him.

Frank handed him a woman's slipper, simply saying,—

"Jenny's. 'St; not a hundred yards off!"

"How do you know that?" exclaimed Bettle, who had seized the slipper unceremoniously.

"Warm," said Frank; "put your hand inside; not been off two minutes. She's dropped it o' purpose."

Bettle thrust his hand into the slipper, and found that the keen guide was right, for the warmth of the foot from which it had dropped or been plucked still lingered about it.

"Well, push on, then," said Bettle, impatiently; "push on, and don't give them time to get out of reach."

"Easy, leftenant, easy," said Frank, quietly; "if you want to git the gal agin alive, they mustn't see or hear us till we strike."

"What do you mean?" inquired Bettle, anxiously.

"Why, look'e here! if it's any o' Rawdon's gang,—n' I'm afeard it is,—they're jest the fellows to cut her throat or shoot her, sooner 'an let us git her, or be bothered with her in a race, if we go at 'em bull-headed and let 'em see us in time."

Bettle bit his lip till the blood came, for he was in a fever of excitement; but he saw the wisdom of Frank's advice, and acquiesced at once. He explained it rapidly to Barton, and the whole party stood silent, awaiting the development of Frank's plan.

The latter continued:—

"There's a farm-house about half a mile furder on, an old Tory's, where I reckon they'll halt an' git breakfast, if they don't hear us after 'em; that 'll be the time to light on 'em. I'll go on now, an' the rest o' you keep about fifty yards behind, but don't git out o' sight; when I want you, I'll beckon."

So saying, Frank resumed his march, but much more slowly and cautiously than before, the others following at the same pace at about the distance he had named.

Bettle, who had retained possession of the shoe, which he would have considered it sacrilege to throw away, was a little embarrassed to know what to do with it, but finally thrust it into his belt for temporary safekeeping.

As yet none of the party had caught a glimpse of those they were pursuing, but simply followed on in a blind reliance on Frank's judgment. In the course of ten or fifteen minutes after their last start, however, they saw him stop and beckon to them.

When they reached the spot where he was standing, they found themselves near the edge of the wood, with a meadow in front of them, beyond which, at about a hundred yards' distance, stood the farm-house of which Frank had spoken. In the yard stood ten horses, all of whose riders, except three, had dismounted; and in these three Bettle, Frank, and the two brothers at once recognized Jenny Sanford and her father and mother.

Some of the men about them appeared to be urging them to dismount, and one raised his hand and attempted to take Jenny's for the purpose of assisting her. She shook her head, and withdrew her hand out of his reach.

Finally the party went into the house, leaving Jenny and her parents with two men to guard them, having first taken the precaution of hobbling their horses so that they could not run.

Our party saw all these manœuvres, and prepared for work. Adjoining the meadow and the woods, stretching past the back of the house, and then sweeping around it on the farther side close to the fences, was a large cornfield. Into this Frank at once plunged, and led his party rapidly toward the house.

"If we only had a couple of Johnny Mac Allan's boys with their long rifles here," muttered Frank, "we could fix this off beautiful."

"How?" said Barton.

"Pick off the guards while we got into the house; but our carbines can't be trusted for such nice work."

"We *must* secure the guards first," said Barton.

"Or the gal's dead, an' most likely the old folks too," said Frank: "I know the two scoundrels that's standin' guard."

On the side of the house next the woods was a kind of out-house, used as a shelter for the pump, and as a summer kitchen; next to this was the corn-crib, not exactly adjoining, but with a space of perhaps three feet between it and the out-house.

When they reached the part of the cornfield immediately behind this, Frank ordered a halt; the command of the expedition had been tacitly allowed to him, or rather he had assumed it as a matter of course, as being the only man there who could conduct it; and his orders were obeyed implicitly.

"Fust an' foremost," said he, "them two guards is got to be got out o' the way afore we can do anything else. Some two of us must sneak on 'em, as soon as the rest's ready to surround the house."

"I'll be one of the two," said Bettle.

"And I'll be t'other," said Mahlon Sanford.

"No, no, Melly," said Frank; "'twon't do for you; you're as spry an' lissom as a young painter, but you hain't got the gristle yet to handle a grown man, an' I want these two settled with the knife or tom-axe. Leftenant," he added, turning to Bettle, "unless you're detarmined, you'd better let *me* take your place; you see, these men have got to be *killed* out o' hand; it won't do to try any half-an'-half doin's; an' you wouldn't want to cut a fellow's throat or split his skull right alongside o' *her*, would you?"

"No, I would not," said Bettle; "but why kill them at all?"

"'Cause two of us couldn't take 'em both at once; an', if either of 'em gits time to shoot or strike, it'll be right at the gal or the old folks."

"Why not shoot them from the cornfield on the other side?"

"Too much risk; might miss; might hit the wrong person; might only wound 'em, an' that 'ud spile all. Better let Dandy Harry an' me manage it," said Frank, who, if he did not appreciate Harry's music, did fully appreciate his uncommon strength and activity, as well as his reckless bravery.

Bettle reluctantly acquiesced in this plan, and the party proceeded to put their design into execution.

Frank and Harry stole cautiously around through the corn, while the rest divided; some guarding the back of the house, while the others passed quietly through the opening between the corn-crib and the out-house, and remained just out of sight around the corner of the latter.

Jenny and her parents were seated on their horses, looking eagerly across the meadow towards the woods from which they had recently emerged, and the two guards kept their eyes in the same direction. The Tories were at breakfast in the best parlor, which was on the opposite side of the house, opening upon a space, not more than a rod in width, between it and the edge of the cornfield where Wheeler and his men were concealed.

"Tommy," said one of the guards, whining his words with a sarcastic drawl through his nose, "Tommy, does thee expect anybody to come aout the woods yonder to help thee aout the hands o' the Philistians, Tommy?"

The old man made no answer, nor did Jenny, to whom the other was addressing some ironical pleasantries of the same kind. Neither of them was aware of light steps stealing through the grass behind them, and they continued their brutal taunting; and the one who was speaking to Jenny, growing bolder, and irritated by her silence, had on his lips a vile and obscene jest, when a blow from a tomahawk, cleaving through cap and skull to the eyebrow, spoiled its point by interrupting its utterance at once and forever. At the same instant the other received a downward stab from Harry's knife, which struck him at the base of the neck, just within the collar-bone. Both men fell in their tracks as if struck by lightning. Before the prisoners had recovered from their astonishment, three rapid strokes of Frank's knife had cut the hobbles, the gate was opened, and he exclaimed, "Ride, now, ride for your lives! Back across the meadow into the woods, an' wait there."

Prompt, quick-witted, and possessed of the invaluable faculty of obeying an order instantly and without question or explanation, Jenny gave rein to her horse and flew through the gate in the direction indicated.

Martha was less wise, and began to ask what they were to do in the woods, when Frank unceremoniously cut short her queries by seizing her horse by the head, running him through the gate, and starting him, by a furious kick in the ribs, at full speed after Jenny, who was flying across the meadow, with her father followng close behind.

The Tories, as I have said, were at breakfast in the best room, on the opposite side of the house from where these things occurred. The leader, who was in fact Rawdon's lieutenant, and a worthy successor of that estimable individual, while doing ample justice to the good things that were bountifully supplied, kept his ears wide open; for, suspecting strongly that Clayton's force was still on the Rock, he was far from feeling a comfortable degree of assurance that Jenny's call for help as they passed it would not be answered yet.

He was on the point of rising to order the prisoners to be brought into the house, where they might be under his own eye, when his quick ear caught the faint crash of Frank's tomahawk as he struck down the guard. The next instant he heard his voice, and the quick patter of hoofs as the horses galloped from the yard.

"What the d—l!" he exclaimed, springing to his feet, and sending his chair spinning through the paper screen that closed the fireplace; "the prisoners are off! Follow!"

He darted into the next room toward the yard, but stopped when half-way across it, for in the door stood Bettle and Barton, right in his path, sword in hand, and each of the two windows was darkened by the figures of men with leveled carbines. Behind the two officers, in the out-house, he saw other armed men also.

"Drop your sword," said Barton; "your game is played out; you are prisoners."

The other Tories had gathered into the room by this time, however, and their leader, recovering from his first surprise, shouted to them, "Fire, men, fire! and sweep the windows!" and, drawing a pistol from his belt, fired at the two who were standing in the doorway.

Bettle had sprung in front of his companion toward the Tory as the latter spoke, but staggered back a step or two, at the report of the pistol.

"Are you hit, Bettle?" said Barton, throwing his

rm out to catch him, as the room filled with smoke
om a dozen carbines fired through the windows.

"Not hurt," said Bettle, recovering his balance, and
ouching the shoe at his waist, in the heel of which the
ball was half buried. "At them, boys!" And, springing
orward again, his sword crossed with that of the Tory
eader.

The men poured in through the door and windows,
eceiving a hurried random fire from the enemy's pis-
ols, and then the small room was for a few moments
a confused hurly-burly of clinking sword-blows and
cracking pistols, and clouds of smoke, thick with the
oaths and curses of the Tories, for the Rangers fought,
as they always did, with clinched teeth and in silence.

It was getting too hot for the Tories, and they at-
empted to retreat through the room they had just left,
out found their retreat cut off by the reserve of the
Rangers, who had forced their way into the house
rom the back, and now held them covered with their
carbines.

"Don't thee think it's about time to stop?" said
Wheeler, mildly, as he seized the foremost man by the
collar, and held the point of his sword to his throat.
"If thee makes any resistance, I'm afraid I shall have
to constrain thee." And, as he spoke, the Tory felt a
light pricking pressure upon his throat, just upon the
"Adam's apple," that admonished him strongly of the
olly of further resistance.

"I surrender, on quarters and fair treatment," said
e, sullenly.

"I reckon thee'll just *surrender*," said Wheeler, in
he same placid tone; "thee and all thy men can do
, alive or dead, just as you choose; but you'll *do it*."

All the combatants were by this time in the breakfast-room, and Wheeler, who still kept his hold on his prisoner, spying Barton, said,—

"This friend wants to make terms, Levi; thee's captain here; shall he have them?"

"Yes; such terms as Captain Clayton chooses to give. Are you the commander of this gang of banditti?" said Barton, addressing the Tory.

The fellow glared at him savagely for a moment, and nodded.

"Do you surrender?"

"Yes," said the other, grinding his teeth: "what's the use of trying to fight with only three men against twenty?"

"Not much," said Barton: "you might have discovered that before. Order your men to lay down their arms."

This ended the fight; the victory was won, it remained to see at what cost.

Ah! that cost! that cost! It always comes in at a victory, like the skeleton in the old Egyptian feasts.

There, in the front room, beneath the window through which he had sprung, lay Mahlon Sanford, dead.

Beside him lay a gigantic trooper, with the upper part of his face crushed out of all semblance to humanity, by a blow from a carbine-butt; and standing there, with one foot pressing heavily upon the broad chest, his arms folded, his brows drawn together, and his lips compressed to a ghastly whiteness with the intense agony of his grief, was John Sanford. His carbine, with its blood-splashed butt, lay where it had fallen across the trooper's thighs, unnoticed. The body of the Tory leader (the one who had surrendered to Barton had assumed command on the death of his superior) lay in the middle of the room, where Bettle had struck him down. The men were standing around in mute sympathy, for Mahlon was a favorite with them all; but the brother saw nothing but the slight, boyish form which lay motionless before him. At last Bettle, wishing to rouse him from his stupor, touched his arm and spoke to him, "John"—but his voice faltered.

The single word broke the spell, however, and John, turning suddenly, seized Bettle's hand with both his own, and, wringing it, exclaimed, passionately,—

"Oh, Bettle, Bettle! *how* shall I tell this to mother? The youngest, her pet, her darling! How *can* I go and tell her he's dead?" And the strong man broke down utterly, and, burying his face in his hands, shook all over with the convulsive sobs that burst forth uncontrollably.

Tears were trickling down the bronzed faces of the wild Rangers who were gathered around, over cheeks which had not been wet by tears for many a day.

At last Harry went to John, and, passing his arm across his shoulders, walked into the yard with him, saying, in a low voice, "Come, John; you'd better not stay here any longer. Leave Melly to us; we'll do all that remains to be done for him."

"He must be brought with us," said John.

"Of course; we'd better take him to the Rock for the present, and then we can decide what shall be done," said Harry, adding,—

"We must get back as soon as possible, for there's no telling how many of the scoundrels in the neighborhood have heard the firing, and——Halt, there!"

The sudden exclamation was drawn from Harry by a glimpse of a shadow flitting across the space between the corn-crib and the out-house. Darting through the passage, he leaped into the cornfield, and disappeared for a moment; there was a sound of scuffling among the corn, and then Harry reappeared, dragging after him a stout boy, who was hanging back, whimpering and protesting that he "wan't goin' to do nothin'; he wan't on'y jest goin' to the spring-house."

"That's right in the middle of the meadow here," interrupted Harry. "Sonny, when you undertake to tell a lie to an old bird like me, you ought to tell a straighter one; this one's as crooked as the route you were taking to the spring. Now, where are the soldiers you were going to see?"

The boy remained in sullen silence.

"Oh, very well," said Harry, perceiving that the other Rangers were all in the yard ready to move, four of them in the rear, bearing the body of Mahlon, which lay on a shutter they had lifted from the old-fashioned strap hinges which sustained it, a pillow under his head, and a clean white sheet laid carefully over him. "Now, my son, you're going with us; you're going to have the post of honor in front, between me and this gentleman," pointing to Frank; "and at the first sound you make above a whisper, the first sign you make with head or foot or hand, or the first appearance of an attack on us, sign or no sign, *you'll die in your tracks*, whoever else escapes."

The boy, though not particularly sharp-witted, was brilliant enough to understand these practical remarks, and took his place submissively between Harry and Frank, and they moved silently and sadly across the meadow toward the woods, where they joined the Sanfords, thence toward the Rock, without further alarm or disturbance, Jenny and her father riding on one side of the rude bier, and Martha, with her other son at her bridle, on the other.

About half a mile from the Rock, the men in advance stopped, and Frank, leaving his charge, on whose arm Harry instantly fastened a grip like a vice, whispered a moment to Barton, who nodded.

"Is the way clear from here to the Rock?" inquired Frank, returning to their involuntary guide. "Listen afore you answer. The rest are goin' on; you're goin' to stay here with me an' Harry till we're ready to move. Now, if anything goes wrong, by the hokey! you know what you're got to look for."

The boy asseverated strongly that he "be derned if there was a Tory nearer 'n five miles off, as he know'd on."

Frank nodded to Barton, who moved on with his party, while he and Harry coolly seated themselves on a log, with their prisoner between them.

In the course of fifteen or twenty minutes more a long, shrill whistle came from the direction of the Rock.

"There's Sam Diller," said Harry: "he has a pipe like ten thousand plovers."

"They're there, all safe, then," said Frank. "Now you may go home; and if you see any of the Tories, tell 'em we've got fifty men on the Rock ready for 'em."

After the boy had gone, Harry said to Frank,—

"I supposed we stopped here to keep that young scoundrel from seeing what force we had. What the deuce made you tell him?"

"Why, look'e here!" said Frank, "'cause he's jest about sharp enough to make certain I was a-lyin', or, if he ain't, so much the better; 'cause if he tells any of the Tories they'll make sure I was, an' be afeard o' gittin' into a trap."

The two men now went on to the Rock, where they found, in addition to those who had gone on in advance, long Johnny Mac Allan, his wife, and their three daughters.

The women were sitting apart with the Sanfords, beside the body of Mahlon, while Mac Allan was talking earnestly to Clayton.

Martha Sanford gave way to no noisy demonstrations of grief, but sat motionless, her hands crossed in her lap, her eyes fastened on her boy.

Her husband sat near her, his features clothed with that rigid, stony, almost fearful calmness which belongs to feelings forcibly and sternly kept down.

Jenny sat between, weeping silently but plentifully, the only one to whom the relief of tears had come.

"Oh, William, William," said the mother, at last, as Bettle drew near with John Sanford, "didn't thee promise me my boy should not go to battle? How could thee let him?"

"It wasn't William's fault, mother," said her son, gently; "if he or any of us could have stopped him, we would; but he and one of the men were out ahead of all the rest, as soon as we heard Jenny call; and when we surrounded the house he got into another division, and William and I both lost sight of him till it was too late."

"I don't understand it at all, John: I only know my boy is dead."

At this moment, Clayton, having finished his conversation with Mac Allan, approached Martha, and, taking her hand, said, earnestly,—

"We all share thy grief, Martha; we all mourn for him, for he had endeared himself even to the wildest and roughest of the men; not one of them but would have saved him at the cost of his own life, if it could have been; but it was ordered otherwise, and we can only bow to the will of Him who holds all our lives in His hand."

"I know we must, Ellis; but, oh, it's hard, it's hard, to lose him so suddenly, without any warning, and in such a way! But I will not grieve wickedly for him. The Lord gave him, and He hath taken him in His own good time and in His own way. I will not question His providence."

Clayton led her gently away, followed by Jenny, who clung with both hands to Bettle's arm, sobbing convulsively, while Mrs. Mac Allan and her daughters prepared the body for burial, which it was necessary should take place as soon as possible, it being uncertain at what moment they might be attacked or be obliged to forsake the Rock; though Clayton intended to hold it, if possible, until all his scouts had come in.

He had explained the necessity for this apparently hurried burial to the family; and they made no objection.

In the course of an hour, Mac Allan stepped quietly up to Clayton and informed him that they were ready.

They stood around the shallow grave beside which the boy lay, still upon the shutter, with the sheet wrapped around him, the troopers with heads uncovered and arms reversed, and the stricken family looking sadly at the last they would see on earth of him they all loved so well.

He was lowered on the shutter as he lay, his face covered with a fold of the sheet, some thick branches were laid carefully above him to prevent the earth from touching him when the grave should be filled, and they turned away again, in a silence broken only by the voice of Mike, which rose and fell in the Irish "keen" for the dead, with a cadence inexpressibly wild and mournful.

CHAPTER XII.

On the previous Friday night, when the Tories had retreated, beaten from the Rock, they scattered at first, in a panic at the loss of their leader. Gradually, however, dropping in, sometimes one at a time, sometimes two or three together, about a hundred of them were assembled in a wild, secluded spot beside the creek, which had been previously used as a place of rendezvous after their forays.

They brought no plunder with them this time, however; only chafed tempers, which found vent in a good deal of crimination and recrimination as to their defeat. This brought on a hot discussion as to the strength of the reinforcement which had come up so opportunely. Some averred that they had counted a hundred, some fifty, some twenty; some said they were regulars, some that they were riflemen, some that they were both, and one fellow, besides, swore a huge oath that he had seen two six-pounders grinning over the breastwork.

"Yeou be blamed," drawled a sharp, nasal voice from the foot of a tree a few feet off, where its owner, who had until now taken no part in the conversation, sat leaning against the trunk, engaged in whittling a stick which he had cut from a bush near him for that especial purpose; "there wan't nao six-paounders, nor nao other kind o' paounders, 'cept them on two legs, an' the cussed, rampin' hosses 'at paounded us daown the bank."

"Wall, naow, I reckon not," said the other, mimicking him: "you hadn't much chance o' seein' what there was, the way them long legs o' yourn carried your ugly mug out o' the way when them big teeth an' thrashin' hoofs come tearin' in among us."

"Yaas," said the other, coolly, "I beat ye, didn't I? I heern them little pins o' yourn a' pittipattin' consider'ble quick arter I passed you, but they were too short to keep up. Naow, I'll tell you what; there wan't no regulars, but there *was* riflemen, an' mighty good shots too; an', what's more, I know who they were."

"Who were they?" inquired the leader.

"Long Johnny Mac Allan an' his ten double-fisted sons; an' naow I've got a plan: there ain't nobody but the women-folks about the old fellow's haouse; let's go an' burn it to pay him for meddlin' with our business."

This proposition was agreed to unanimously; and just before daybreak, under the guidance of the Yankee, they reached the place.

The inmates of the house were aroused by the furious barking of the dogs in the yard, and Keziah, peeping out through one of the loop-holes, saw it full of the Tories.

"Up, gals, up, an' take to the loop-holes, with the rifles," said she. "Here's a purty kittle o' fish; if there's one Tory, there's a hundred in the yard. Hannah, you take t'other loop-hole in front, here; Jemima an' 'Rushy, you take the back ones; an' I reckon we'll give 'em some trouble yit, afore they git in."

The girls each seized a rifle, four of which, with

powder-horn and bullet-pouch for each, all well filled, hung upon their several hooks around the lower room, to which all had descended.

Briefly telling Jenny and her parents to place themselves in the corner of the room, out of the line of fire from without, the stout-hearted woman thrust the muzzle of her rifle through the opening at which she had stationed herself, and coolly awaited the summons.

"Open the door, in the King's name," said a voice from without.

The only answer was the click of her rifle, as she cocked it.

"Aha," said the leader, whose quick ear had caught the sound, "that's the answer, is it? Surround the house."

It will be remembered that there was a considerable body of footmen attached to the party. These immediately divided, about half of them going around to the rear of the house; while those who were on horseback dismounted, and, leading their horses a little back, tied them among the trees, and then returned.

The leader again ordered the door to be opened; but, no answer being received, they proceeded to force it. Their plan for doing this was extremely simple: they procured axes from an out-house, where some had been carelessly left in the hurried departure of the men, cut down a stout sapling, and, raising it in their hands, prepared to make a rush with it at the door.

Keziah had been watching their manœuvres, and, as the men poised the sapling in their hands, exclaimed to her daughter, who was guarding the front with her,—

"Now, Hannah, as soon's they git in a run with that pole, I'll give the word, an' do you pick off the foremost on your side."

Hannah nodded.

After "hefting" the sapling once or twice, the twenty men who held it started for the door at a run. If they had reached it, the door must have gone down, strong as it was. But in the midst of their rush came, almost as one, the sharp crack of two rifles, one from each side the door, and the two foremost men fell. The sudden loss of support for the forward end of the battering-ram, as it might be called, thus unexpectedly throwing the additional weight and leverage upon those who were next in the rear, caused it to sway downwards, striking the ground, jerking it out of their hands by the sudden check, and bringing it to the earth with a crash, and the whole party down with it, each man tripping up the one behind him.

"Pick yourselves up and try it agin, ye villains," said Keziah, priming her rifle, which she had reloaded; "try it agin, if ye want to lose more o' your men; if you don't, clear out and leave us alone! We've shed blood enough for one day."

She was answered by a volley from the muskets in front, the balls from which pattered into the logs around the loop-hole, and one, better aimed than the rest, passed through it, carrying away her cap and comb, and burying itself in the opposite side, about a foot above 'Rushy's head. Keziah only shook her gray locks and laughed.

Hannah's rifle cracked again, but missed; the Tories [be]ing so enveloped in the smoke from the muskets [fired] at it was impossible to see any form distinctly. The fallen men, excepting the two who had been [sh]ot and were lying beneath the pole, had by this [ti]me regained their feet, and the whole party, in obe[di]ence to their leader's command, retreated from the [ya]rd to the trees beyond, among which they sheltered [th]emselves from the murderous rifles.

Keziah heard, at this moment, a heavy creaking and [ra]ttling of wheels at the back of the house, and, at [th]e same instant both of her daughters, who were [sta]tioned at that side, called to her, in a low voice, "Mother, mother, come here, quick!"

"What's the matter?" said she, hurrying over, [lea]ving her rifle, however, poking its muzzle out [th]rough its loop-hole. "What is it, 'Rushy?"

"Why, they've got the big wagon across the fence, [an]' they're loadin' it with dry brush. Shall I shoot?" [sai]d 'Rushy, eagerly.

"My soulds!" said Keziah, in dismay; "if they [a]in't a-goin' to try and burn us up! Keep a sharp look[ou]t, gals, an' pop over every one you kin draw a bead [on]; we must never let 'em git that wagon up to the [ho]use, or we're gone! Oh, if the old man an' the [bo]ys was only here!"

"There's one, mother, with a big bundle afore him, [rig]ht in range," said Jemima. "Shall I shoot? I can't [see] his head."

"Fire at his waistband," said the old woman, [ste]rnly. "Don't miss him."

"Miss him!" said the girl, cocking her rifle and [set]ting the hair trigger. The report followed her words, and the man fell. Another sprang forward to seize the bundle, but Keziah, snatching the rifle from 'Rushy's hands, darted to the other loop-hole, thrust Jemima away, and called through it, "Drop that, or you're a dead man."

The fellow looked up.

"Drop it, I say, and go back, or I'll send you after the dog that brought it."

The old woman's temper was now fairly up, and she spoke sharply and sternly, without any more saving clauses about her unwillingness to shed blood.

A momentary pause of irresolution on the part of the Tory was brought to an end speedily by the crack of Jemima's rifle, which 'Rushy had seized and reloaded, and the sight of another of his comrades who was advancing with an armful of brushwood, reeling back, with a ball through his shoulder. Suddenly snatching up the fallen armful which lay at his feet, he made an ineffectual attempt to fling it on the wagon, and then, dropping on the ground, rolled rapidly over and over till he got behind the latter, his sudden motion just saving him from the ball which the exasperated Keziah sent after him.

While this was going on in the rear of the house, those in front had not been idle. Screened by the trees, they had wasted an immense deal of powder and lead in firing with muskets at slits in the wall, which it would have required rifles, and hands that knew how to use them, to hit with any certainty at the distance at which they were firing. A constant fire was also kept up by the muskets in the rear from behind the wagon, but with no effect, either from front or rear, beyond pitting with bullet-holes the solid logs of which the house was built, and gradually filling the air around with a thick cloud of smoke.

It was a still, sultry morning, the precursor of one of those relaxing, sweltering September days when not a breath of air stirs, and everything in nature seems asleep but the heat and the flies; and even the latter are too lazy to let go where they begin to bite, merely sidling off at each brush of the hand, and immediately dropping back to their place and renewing their stinging attentions.

In consequence of the dead stillness, the smoke, as I have said, hung thick and low around the house; and Keziah perceived, with an uneasiness she did not express, that if it became much more dense it would not be difficult for some of the Tories to approach the house unperceived. They could only tell where they were now by the flash of their guns and pistols; for the leader, perceiving the advantage the smoke was giving him, quite as promptly as Keziah had done, ordered his horsemen to keep up a fire with their pistols, in order to increase it.

There was little fear of the Tories getting into the house by any means at their command, if they could be prevented from firing the brush in the wagon and running it up against the house. Should they succeed in that, its destruction was inevitable; for, built entirely of wood as it was, and very old, it would burn like tinder.

It had not been erected by Mac Allan, who had found it deserted and falling to decay when he took possession of it. From its strength, and arrangements for defense, it had apparently been built by some earlier settler, who had less faith in the pacific disposition of the Indians around than they deserved; for, in addition to the solid thickness of the walls, the small windows, and the loop-holes for firing through, Mac Allan found in the cellar, the sides of which were rudely lined with rough slabs, one slab which appeared to be loose. Trying it, he found it was movable, and, pushing it aside, discovered a small opening cut in the earth, wide enough to admit his broad shoulders with tolerable ease. Following this, he found that it led, by a series of roughly-cut steps, to the well, descending to a point not far from the water's edge. Leading off to the left was a natural opening, formed by a rift in the stratum of rock which lay beneath the surface of the ground. Making his way through this, though it was much encumbered with rubbish, he proceeded by a very crooked route until he reached a point where it enlarged into a rugged cave, with a floor which had evidently been cleared and leveled to some extent by human hands. It was about eight feet high in the highest part, and was large enough to allow some fifteen or twenty people to be seated comfortably.

It had evidently been used, for the sides and roof were black with smoke and soot, and at one side were a few stones, piled up so as to form a rude fireplace, in which was lying an old iron pot. Satisfied that the fireplace could not have been used without some way for the smoke to escape, he searched around the walls more narrowly by the aid of the candle with which he had provided himself, and discovered a pile of decaying logs and brushwood, which had apparently been thrown carelessly against the wall to get them out of the way. Removing these, he found that they covered another opening beneath a shelving rock, high enough to allow him to pass through on his hands and knees.

Following this for about a rod, he emerged beneath a mass of overhanging bushes, which entirely concealed the opening from without, upon the side of the hill upon which the house was built, and about a quarter of a mile distant from it.

The war had begun at the time Mac Allan took possession of the house, and it struck him very forcibly that it would do no harm to have such a place of retreat ready in case of emergency, though he certainly had not much apprehension of ever being compelled to use it; so he cleared away the rubbish, to the great improvement of the passage leading to the cave, and Keziah and her daughters gave two or three days' hard labor to clearing off the soot and smoke from the walls of the cave itself, and then whitewashed it all over, thus transforming a gloomy dungeon into quite a cheerful-looking cell, considering. It had remained in this state, undergoing an occasional renovation with the whitewash-brush, ever since.

The well, from which the passage led, was about a rod from the house, directly between it and the wagon, behind which a number of the enemy were lying, effectually concealed from view by it and the thick smoke in which it was enveloped.

Keziah's thoughts were now occupied with the means of procuring water in case the wagon should be fired and brought up to the house.

There was manifestly no possibility of doing it above ground, for the well was directly in the line of fire from the wagon. It must be brought, if at all, from below.

"Thomas," said Keziah, approaching the Sanfords, "will you take my rifle and watch at the loop-hole while me an' 'Rushy goes down to the well after water? We must have some, an' that soon."

Thomas Sanford was placed in a cruel strait. On the one side were his life-long Quaker principles, forbidding him to fight or resist. On the other was the consciousness that a family of women, on whom his own had no claim whatever, except that which every human being has upon every other for assistance in time of need, had been fighting for him and his, and were now exposed to imminent danger arising solely from attempting to protect him. The very service he was now asked to render had grown legitimately out of the danger to which they were exposed. Besides, Quaker though he was, he had, all along, an uneasy feeling that he was allowing Keziah to do work which, if it must be done at all, belonged properly to him, and not to a woman.

He looked inquiringly at his wife as these thoughts struck him.

"I can't advise, Thomas," said she. "Thee must act as thee feels free to do."

"Surely it don't seem right," said he, "that these friends—women, too—should bear all the burden of the danger we have brought on them, and I, the only man here, refuse to help when asked. It don't seem right. I won't."

So saying, Thomas took the rifle from the hands of Keziah, and stationed himself at the loop-hole she had quitted.

The latter then turned to Jenny, and asked her if she thought she could take 'Rushy's place for a little while.

Jenny shook her head with a melancholy smile.

"I'd be of no use there," said she; "I never fired a gun in my life, and don't know how either to aim or load it. But I can do better than that. Do thee take Rushy's place, and let her and me bring the water. I've had some practice in that," she added, smiling again, faintly.

"To be sure," exclaimed Keziah. "What an old goose I am, to think nobody can work but me! Now, down cellar with ye, an' pass up water as fast as ye can, an' I'll get the tubs ready."

The two girls descended to the well by the passage before spoken of, and for the next half-hour were busily engaged in passing up water, until four tubs, all the house could boast, were filled. Only one of these was in the lower room, the other three having been taken up-stairs and filled there, to be ready when the roof should take fire, there being no doubt that it would be the first thing to go.

The firing from the outside was kept up moderately, the smoke still hanging low and thick, while for some time no shot had been fired from within. Just as Rushy came up, however, with the last bucket of water, an exclamation of surprise was heard from Jemima, followed instantly by the crack of her rifle, and the exclamation, "Missed him, consarn it all!"

"Missed who, Jemima?" said her mother. "Who did you shoot at?"

"Yankee Nat, that used to live here," said the girl, speaking low between her clinched teeth, and busily reloading her rifle; "if he shows that long nose of his'n in range agin, I reckon he won't git away with it."

The girl's face, which had more pretensions to good

looks than that of either of her sisters, was as pale as death, but not with fear, as was very evident from the dilating eyes, which were fairly blazing, and the rigid lips, which were drawn tightly across the clinched teeth. Indeed, Nat—for it was the fellow who had suggested the plan of attacking the house—owed his life to the trembling of Jemima's hand, caused by the sudden overpowering rush of anger which the sight of him had produced.

"Yankee Nat!" said Keziah; "is that sneakin', treacherous varmint among 'em? Keep a sharp lookout for him, gals, and don't let him git away, if you kin see him. We've got an account to settle with him."

"What has he done?" inquired Martha, who, as well as her husband and Jenny, had observed the sudden emotion of Jemima, and did not understand it. "What's the matter?"

"Matter enough," said Keziah, bitterly. "He said things to Jemima when he was here, ay, an'——Well, no matter! if he had been about the place when the old man an' the boys come home that afternoon, he'd ha' behaved himself forever afterward."

CHAPTER XIII.

It had not been necessary for Thomas Sanford to discharge his rifle at all; and he very willingly returned it to 'Rushy, who took her place at the loop-hole, eagerly but unsuccessfully looking out for Nat.

The enemy, having now piled a large quantity of brushwood upon the wagon, succeeded in running it up to the house under cover of the smoke, and placing it sideways against the wall. In this position, and reaching up to the second-story windows, it obstructed the loop-holes effectually, and of course put an end to the danger from the rifles on that side.

It was not many minutes before those within heard the crackling of fire in the wagon, and perceived the smell of burning wood, which stole, with the pungent smoke, through the openings.

Leaving the girls to defend the front against attack on that side, Keziah and Thomas Sanford went upstairs to be ready to fight the fire. They did not have to wait long; for the dry, light brushwood burned almost like straw, and in a few moments light-blue jets of flame came shooting up through the mass, darting forth and back like the forked tongues of serpents. Here and there a bunch of dead leaves would kindle, as one of these sharp tongues shot through it, blaze up into a yellow flame, and then die out.

Faster and faster came the jets, turning from blue to

yellow, and then deepening to red, shooting higher and higher, curling and swaying back and forth with an angry crackle and roar, lapping the sides of the house and the dry eaves greedily. Keziah and her companion had not been idle, but from the first appearance of the flames had been dashing buckets of water upon them, assisted by Martha and Jenny, who had been called up by Thomas.

The occasional crack of a rifle from the room below showed that the girls were on the alert to prevent the door from being forced, some demonstrations of which had been made, at the expense of the lives of two or three more of the besiegers.

Still the fearless woman above, with her companions, battled stubbornly with the increasing fire, till the flakes from the kindling roof began to fall within, and the room was so full of smoke that they could hardly breathe.

They then retreated to the room below, and Keziah, briefly telling Thomas and his companions to follow, descended rapidly to the cellar, and, leading the way to the passage which turned off to the left, directed them to follow it to the cave, and there wait till she and her daughters should join them.

There was no time for parley, and they set out at once.

Keziah hastened back to the room where her daughters were still watching at the loop-holes, and, bidding them collect what food and clothes they could, not forgetting a bag of Spanish dollars which her husband kept stored for emergencies, prepared to follow the Sanfords, leaving the house to its fate.

The whole roof was by this time on fire, and the

sparks were beginning to fall thickly into the room through the stairway. The firing from the outside had ceased, while the besiegers watched the progress of the flames, and the inmates of the house were about to descend to the cellar, when they heard the heavy tramp of a column of soldiers, and the sharp, stern orders,—
"Run that wagon from the house! seize the tongue and away with it to the fence! Quick, you ruffians! By my life, if it stands there one moment longer, I'll have the ringleader tossed into it, to try how he likes his handiwork! Away with it!"

There was no doubt that the speaker meant to be obeyed, and half a dozen of the Tories sprang to the tongue, and ran the wagon, with its burning load, as far from the house as possible.

"Now, who's in the house?" said the voice, sharply.

"Don't know," was the answer; "'cept one old woman an' some blasted good rifles that's knocked over six or eight of us."

"Women!" exclaimed the other, darting around to the front of the house.

As he reached the door, it was opened from within, and Keziah stood before him, her gray locks hanging in disorder, as they had fallen when her comb was shot away, about her smoke-grimed face, and her three daughters, each with her rifle in her hand, standing immediately behind her.

"If you are an English officer, and a man, we claim your protection agin that gang of cowardly wolves," said she.

"You shall have it, madam; you shall have it," said he. "I'm sorry I wasn't able to afford it earlier; I'm afraid there's no hope of saving the house."

"None," said Keziah; "let it burn."

"Are there no men in the house?" inquired the officer, in surprise, as he looked from the grim figure of Keziah to her daughters and back again. "Are you all the force here?"

"Yes," said Keziah, "one old woman an' three gals, with a rifle apiece, is what's kep' a hundred Tories off sin' sun-up, an' would ha' kep' 'em off till sun-down, if they hadn't ha' managed to git the old wagon up to the house an' set it afire."

"Four women holding a log house for hours against a hundred men! If all your countrymen had your courage and determination, we should have been driven from the country long ago," said the officer. "As for you, you cowardly hounds, that attack women twenty-five to one," he added, turning to the Tories, "you have been doing brigands' work, and you shall have brigands' pay. Lay down your arms."

"D——d if we do," said one, who appeared to have some command. "Who the d——l are you, that undertakes to order his Majesty's soldiers to lay down their arms?"

"Your superior officer, sir," said the young captain, "and one who means to be obeyed. 'Soldiers'!" he added, with his lip curling; "a gang of lawless ruffians, rather, that disgrace any cause they fight for. We'll see what General Howe thinks of such soldiers. Deliver your sword to the sergeant; you and your men are under arrest."

The whole house was now on fire, burning furiously; and all present had moved some distance away, to avoid the heat, which was intense.

The temporary leader of the Tories sullenly offered

is sword to the captain, for he saw that his force was greatly outnumbered; the latter, however, turned his back upon him, motioning the sergeant to take it.

"And now, madam," said he, turning to Keziah, "you have been deprived of a home by these scoundrels: is there any place where you can stay, with our family, for the present? We will escort you safely to any place you wish."

"Thank'e," said she; "but there's a neighbor's house not far off, where we can stay till such time as my old man an' the boys can knock up a shanty."

"You have a husband, then?"

"Yes, an' ten boys;" the captain involuntarily raised his eyebrows slightly, but Keziah went on without noticing it: "if they'd been at home, we'd ha' druv' off all these scum long ago."

"Where are your sons?" inquired the officer. "In the American army?"

Keziah hesitated.

"Don't tell me, if you had rather not," said he; "I only wish, however, to befriend them, should it ever be in my power."

"Well," said Keziah, "they're not exactly in the army; they're with Clayton's Rangers now."

"Clayton's Rangers!" said the officer; "I ought to know them. Isn't the first lieutenant a gentleman named Barton?"

"I don't know," said Keziah; "I never seen any of 'em till yesterday. I think the officer's name was Little."

"The same: he was another lieutenant. I don't want to know where they are," he added, in a low voice; "but, if you know, I think, in the unsettled state of the country, you had better get yourself and your daughters under the protection of the troop as soon as possible. Should you see Lieutenant Barton, tell him that Captain Gardner desired to be remembered to him and the other officers."

The soldiers now prepared for departure with their prisoners, Keziah declining any escort, saying "they could git along without any trouble, if he would only drive them wolves away."

Captain Gardner, after repeating his offer of an escort, which Keziah again declined, bade them good-by kindly, and his men, with the disarmed Tories in front of them, filed away through the woods, and were soon out of sight.

As soon as the coast was clear, Keziah and her daughters hurried to where the cave opened on the hill-side.

"Somebody's been through these bushes," said Hannah, pointing to some twigs which were broken off, and at the leaves which were turned in some disorder and stripped off.

"I hope they hain't been so foolish as to come out by themselves," said Keziah.

Stooping down to the mouth of the cave, she called; but no answer was returned.

A sudden exclamation from Jemima brought Keziah away from the cave to the foot of the hill.

"See here, mother," said the girl; "here's horse-tracks. What's that mean?'

"Horse-tracks!" said Keziah; "then there's been treachery somewhere, and they're carried off, sure. Nobody'd be likely to bring horses here for anything else."

"I'll soon see," said Jemima, coolly, "whether they're in the cave or not."

And the fearless girl, armed with her rifle, from which she had never parted, walked to the entrance, crouched upon her hands and knees, and disappeared beneath the bushes and the shelving rock.

The others followed her at once, with their rifles, partly from curiosity, and partly to assist her in case there should be any danger.

They soon reached the interior of the cave; but it was empty. They proceeded along the passage to the well, found the opening into the cellar blocked up with fallen timbers from the house, which was now a heap of smouldering ruins, still finding no trace of the object of their search.

Turning on their steps, they retraced their way toward the cave. When about fifty yards distant, Keziah, who was in advance, suddenly stopped, saying,—

"Hark! what's that?"

All stopped, listened, and heard unmistakably the sound of an axe, falling slowly in heavy blows, apparently proceeding from the cave.

Beckoning her daughters closer to her, Keziah now moved along more slowly and cautiously than before, the girls following close in her rear.

Arrived at a jutting point of rock which projected partially across the passage, just before it opened into the cave itself, Keziah stopped again, and all four concealed themselves behind it and listened again.

The blows of the axe still continued, and, after a moment's listening, 'Rushy, who was next her mother, saw her face, haggard enough before, suddenly grow pale as death.

"What's the matter, mother?" she whispered, anxiously.

"That axe is *outside* the cave, gal, right at the mouth," said Keziah.

"So it is," said she, listening, but unable to imagine why her mother was so agitated. "I wonder who it can be choppin' there, just now."

"Choppin'!" said Keziah; "don't you know the sound of an axe-edge better 'n that? That's the butt of an axe, drivin' a stake in the ground. We're shut in!"

A look of dismay glanced from face to face, and then, as by one impulse, they all hurried past the projection into the cave, seizing their rifles, which had been leaning against the rock, and then to its mouth.

But there they stopped; for, jammed partly under the shelving rock which formed the mouth, was a large stone, closing up the aperture entirely, except one spot at the upper right-hand corner, where the light came, broken by the bushes outside, through a small opening not larger than Keziah's hand.

Placing her shoulder against the stone, and beckoning her daughters to assist her, they all exerted their utmost strength to move it, but in vain. Twenty times their strength, exerted at the disadvantage of their constrained position in the low passage, would have succeeded no better.

They moved back to the higher part of the cave, a few feet from the stone, and crouched on the floor, Keziah groaning aloud in bitterness of spirit.

At this moment the small aperture I have mentioned was darkened, and a voice with a villainously exaggerated nasal twang whined through it,—

"Wal, naow, daon't you feel comf'ble, Keziah? Whar's Jemimy? I reckon——"

What was reckoned did not appear; for the speech was cut short by the report of Jemima's rifle, she having recognized the voice and caught a glimpse, as it peered through the opening into the darkness, of the face of Yankee Nat, and instantly fired at it.

Half stunned by the report, and blinded by the smoke, they were uncertain at first whether he had been hit or not; but the next moment, though they could see nothing, they heard the voice again, exclaiming,—

"Cre-a-tion! what a she-painter! Good-by, Keziar; 'member me to Jemimy." And then they heard a mocking laugh growing fainter and fainter in the distance as the villain rode deliberately off and left his entrapped victims to their fate.

The prospect before them was not encouraging. At the mouth of the cave was the stone, jammed tightly in, and then secured further by two stout stakes driven deeply into the ground close to it, rendering it impossible to move it except from the outside. At the other end of the long passage all egress was barred by the timbers which had fallen into the cellar, so that there was absolutely no way to get out except by climbing straight up the perpendicular sides of the well; a feat to the performance of which neither of the prisoners felt herself competent.

CHAPTER XIV.

WHEN Thomas Sanford and his family, after some difficulty, reached the cave, they found themselves in the clutches of Yankee Nat and six of the other Tories, who were there waiting, not for them, but for the Mac Allans.

" Jee-rew-sl'm !" exclaimed Nat: "this is better still. Haow's thee do, Thomas?" he added, in that devilish, mocking, nasal drawl of his, and snuffling; " didn't expect the pleasure o' thy company to-day. Friends, this is Thomas Sanford, whar we got licked from his house last Thursday night by the bloody Rangers 't licked us yesterday mornin', an' lost five of our best men."

There was something in the voice that uttered this remarkable bit of involved grammar, which Jenny was sure she had heard before ; and, taking a better look at its owner, she recognized in him the fellow who had insulted hèr on the Thursday evening he had now referred to.

Carefully avoiding any sign of recognition, however, but with spirits by no means lightened by this discovery, she stood silent, with her eyes cast down to avoid those of Nat, which she felt were bent upon her.

"Naow, boys," resumed Nat, "I reckon we're got 'baout th' best luck we could ha' had. These here folks is wuth suthin' to captivate. Th' old woman an' er gals wan't no 'caount at all, in comparison o' hese."

"What's that?" interrupted one of the others; "the rin's stopped."

"Wal," said Nat, "'sposin' you squirm out an' see; ou're nearder th' hole 'n anybody else." The man accordingly crawled out to reconnoitre; in a few minutes he was back at the entrance, calling agerly, but in a suppressed voice,—

"Nat! I say, Nat, come here quick!"

Nat dived into the low passage, and made his way s rapidly as possible to its mouth.

"Fetch all hands out," said the fellow: "the house s blazin' like a haystack, but there's the d——l knows ow many Reg'lars around it, an' all our fellows is lisarmed."

"Then we must run for it," said Nat, in a sharp, uick tone, strongly in contrast with his ordinary rawl; "get the horses ready;" and then, backing into he cave again, hurried the other men, with the prisonrs, into the open air, giving the latter, as they emerged, a stern and hurried warning to be silent. The Tories hen mounted their horses, from which, however, three f them, from very shame, soon dismounted, to allow heir prisoners to ride, and all except Nat immediately isappeared in the woods, taking a roundabout course o the rendezvous they had left in the morning.

Nat, instead of going with them, led his horse off out f sight into the woods, and then concealed himself mong the bushes, with which the ground was overun, to await the coming of Keziah and her daughters, ho he felt sure would not be long in looking after heir guests, if they were left at liberty.

He had, as Keziah had said, lived with the Mac Allans for a short time. He had not been there a week before, with his prying Yankee curiosity, he had ferreted out the whole secret of the cave and the subterranean passage to it, in spite of all the care that was taken to keep him in ignorance of it. He was a close-mouthed fellow about his own affairs, however, and always kept his knowledge to himself until he should find an opportunity to bring it into use.

He was satisfied that if the women were not already in the passage, the entrance to it in the cellar was so blocked up by the ruins of the house that the cave could not be reached from that direction.

Accordingly, he had waited patiently in his concealment until Keziah and her daughters had entered the cave. As soon as they disappeared, he crept stealthily up to the mouth, and, having heard their voices die in the distance as they moved toward the well, had rolled up the large stone and secured it as already described.

When he had got through his laugh, he put spurs to his horse, and galloped after his party.

Arrived at the rendezvous, they remained there through the day and the greater part of the night, and about an hour before daybreak started with their prisoners for the farm-house.

It was impossible to avoid passing Deborah's Rock without making a wide detour, which would have consumed too much time, and Nat, who acted as guide, determined to run the risk of skirting it, trusting partly to Jenny's fears to keep her from giving any alarm, and partly to the hope of getting past the dangerous point without her knowledge. He miscalculated both her timidity and her acquaintance with the country, as the event showed.

He had sprung to her side when she screamed for help, and leveled his pistol at her head, but recovered his coolness instantly, and lowered it again; for her death was not consistent with his ultimate designs. It was no lingering gentleness, no touch of pity for the young, helpless girl who had thus been thrown so unexpectedly into his power, that held his hand: Nat, son of Belial as he was, would have snuffled contemptuously at being charged with any such weakness.

Well was it for Jenny Sanford that Dandy Harry's knife so effectually unsettled his plans and sent him home to his master that morning; for the guard whom Harry had dispatched so promptly just before the attack on the house was no other than Yankee Nat. He has gone to his own place, and will appear no more.

All through the day, in the mean time, Keziah Mac Allan and her daughters had remained prisoners in the cave, not sitting with their hands in their laps, but wearying themselves out in vain attempts, now to pry away the stone with their rifle-barrels, now to force their way into the cellar.

At last, as evening came on, completely overcome with fatigue, they sank down on the floor of the cave, and went to sleep.

They slept soundly, whether long or not they could not tell. Keziah was awakened at last by a touch on her shoulder.

Opening her eyes with a start, and catching an indistinct glimpse, in the gloom, of a man's figure, she sprang to her feet, making a grasp at her rifle, which lay beside her, as she rose.

16*

"My sakes alive, K'ziah," said a well-known voice, "but I'm glad to find you an' the gals alive! But what's been up? Here's the house burnt down, an' you fastened here in the cave. Where's Tommy Sanford an' his folks?"

Conquering an instinctive feminine tendency to hysterics, Keziah briefly detailed the events I have described, stating that they had held out till the house was beginning to tumble over their heads, that they had sent on the Sanfords in advance, not suspecting that Nat knew the secret of the cave; their missing and searching for them, and their imprisonment.

"That's what the firin' meant, this mornin', then," said Mac Allan, after she had finished; "we heerd it, an' seen the smoke, but thought it was furder off. Well, we can't do anything to-night; we must go over to the neighbor's now, an' start by sun-up for the Rock, to let Captain Clayton know the Sanfords are missin'."

Accordingly, having spent the night at the neighbor's, they made an early start in the morning, and, as we have seen, reached the Rock just before the Sanfords and the party who had rescued them returned with the dead body of Mahlon.

The account which Keziah had been giving Clayton of the cause of their presence there, had been interrupted by the arrival of the party, and had not been resumed until after the burial; the Sanfords had withdrawn a little apart, and were sitting by themselves; and Keziah, at Clayton's request, stepping out of earshot, resumed her narrative in a low voice.

When she mentioned Captain Gardner's name, he interrupted her to ask about his personal appearance.

Keziah described him as well as she could, and with sufficient accuracy to enable Clayton to recognize him.

"He named one o' your leftenants in partic'lar."

"Was it Wheeler or Wetherill?" said Clayton.

"No, that wan't the name," said she, considering a moment. "I think it was Barnet, or Burton, or somethin'——"

"Barton?" said he.

"Yes,—Barton: that was it."

Barton, who had heard his name spoken by the captain, came over to where they were talking, supposing he had been called.

"Thee remembers the young Englishman thee took the other night, at the spring below New Castle, Levi?" said Clayton.

"Yes," said Barton. "Have you seen him?"

"Friend Keziah, here, saw him yesterday, at a very fortunate time for her. He was the means of saving her and her daughters from burning to death in their own house, or falling into the hands of the remnant of the gang we drove from here on Sixth day night."

"Had he any force with him?" inquired Barton. "He must have got to work without much delay after he was exchanged."

"Yes, he had considerable force," said Clayton. "I'll tell thee all about it after awhile. I would like to hear the rest of thy story, now, Keziah."

"There hain't much more to tell," said she; and then went on to describe the disarming of the Tories, and their own adventure in the cave, their discovery and release by her husband, and their journey to the Rock.

"Then the gang is completely broken up, I suspect," said Clayton; "all their fighting-men, who survive, are prisoners. Our work with them is done. We will stay here, however, till thy sons come in, and then try for a few days whether we can pick up some recruits; for our ranks have been terribly thinned in the last three weeks; only what thee sees—about forty men—left out of a hundred." And Clayton and his lieutenant looked sadly around upon their scanty force.

CHAPTER XV.

On Tuesday morning all the scouts came in together. They had tracked the Regulars, with their prisoners, from the burned house, to the outpost of the British army, supposing that all who had been left in the house were prisoners, and then came back to report.

They were, of course, a good deal surprised to find those they had been seeking, all safe among friends.

The Rangers now abandoned the Rock, and, at Thomas Sanford's earnest solicitation, quartered themselves at his house until they should be ready to leave the neighborhood. Mac Allan and his family also went there, and made it their home for some time after the departure of the troop, Martha absolutely refusing to let them go away until the cabin, which the old man and his sons (whom Clayton had directed to remain for the purpose, and join him as soon as possible afterward) had at once set about building, was completed.

It was on the afternoon of Tuesday, the 16th of September, that the Rangers returned to the old house, from the Rock.

In the five days which had elapsed since their retreat from Brandywine, including the night of that sad day, they had gone through fighting enough to satisfy the most reckless fire-eater among them all; and Clayton and his officers were not sorry to have the opportunity of a few days' exemption from it. Bettle certainly had no objection to the prospect of a little quiet enjoyment of Jenny's society, now that the recent events had brought about a tacit understanding between them, which needed no formal declarations on either side.

The relation between them was by this time as well understood by all the troop as it was by themselves; and by common consent, not expressed, but universally acted upon, Jenny was left to her lover, with no more particular attentions from the other officers than civility and a strong liking for her called for.

Moreover, Clayton—who, though as brave as any man in his troop, and as unsparing in battle when his spirit was fairly up, was no fire-eater—had observed, with some uneasiness, that the constant fighting and excitement of the last two or three weeks had developed symptoms of a taste for blood-letting among the wilder and rougher men of the troop, which was not at all in accordance with his views. He was anxious, therefore, on this account also, to have a little time for them to cool down.

There was but little "soldiering" done, therefore, during the few days they remained at Sanford's, with the exception of training the new recruits, of whom some twenty in all—about enough to mount the riderless horses which had followed the troop from Birmingham—were obtained from the neighborhood.

This was less difficult than might have been supposed, considering the consternation which the defeat at Brandywine had spread over all this section of the country. The knowledge, which spread like wild-fire, that the Rangers, with only forty men, had succeeded in beating off and scattering two hundred Tories with Black Rawdon at their head, besides killing the dreaded chief himself, had produced a strong persuasion of the invincibility of the troop.

With the exception of drilling morning and evening, for the benefit of the new recruits, the men did pretty much as they pleased through the day, though Clayton always had two or three of his hard-riding scouts out scouring the country for information of the enemy's movements.

Those who remained at home employed themselves principally in fishing in the creek or gunning in the woods around, turning their carbines into fowling-pieces for the time, and bringing home many a palatable mess of birds and fish, and, on one occasion, a deer; for deer were still occasionally found in that part of Chester county.

Besides this, they did what they could on the farm, to requite Thomas Sanford for his hospitality. His corn was ready to cut, and on the morning after their return to the house the whole troop turned in, with their swords for "cutters," and had the whole of it cut and shocked by dinner time.

They gathered in the apples from the orchard and stored them away, and finished his fall ploughing, which had been interrupted by the raid of the Tories upon him.

Of course, with so many mouths to provide for, the female portion of the household, strengthened though they were by the addition of Keziah and her daughters, were kept pretty actively employed. It was better, perhaps, that it was so, as it kept Jenny and her mother from dwelling too much upon the loss of Mahlon, at least during the day. But their pillows were wet with tears at night, and for many a night afterward, during that fall and winter.

Mike devoted himself mainly to the horses, carefully avoiding Bettle's Roland, however, having a very distinct recollection of his former experience with him, and seeing very plainly that Roland had not forgotten it either. Whenever he came near the horse, the ears laid back, the suddenly dilated nostrils, the breath hissed forcibly through them, and the glare of his broad black eye as it followed all his motions vigilantly, gave him warnings which he could not mistake, to keep out of reach.

On one occasion, when Roland had inadvertently been placed in a different stall from the one he usually occupied, he suddenly lashed out his heels at the poor fellow, who was unconsciously passing him, and came within an ace of dashing his brains out.

The stable-door, which was opposite the stall, received the blow, and was driven open from its fastenings as if by the shock of a battering-ram.

Mike sprang head-foremost through the door, and, when at a safe distance, stopped and shook his fist wrathfully at the savage beast, exclaiming,—

"Tunder an' turf! ye spalpeen, if ye wasn't Mr. Bettle's baste I'd hamstring ye for that, an' spile them pavin'-stones o' hales for iver an' a day."

Bettle, who was on the gangway of the barn at the moment, heard the crash, followed by Mike's voice, and, suspecting what was the matter, hastened down.

"Mike," said he, "I'm sorry the horse seems to have such an enmity to you, and I really don't know how to cure it."

"Inmity, is it!" ejaculated Mike. "Tare an' ouns! he's a divil entirely for bearin' malice. But, faix, it's me that didn't go near 'im o' purpose; some omadhaun or other put 'im in the wrong stall; if ye'd plase tell 'im to put the brute where he belongs, an' kape puttin' 'im there, I'll know how to kape out o' his way."

Bettle called the trooper who had charge of Roland, and had him removed to his proper stall, after administering a severe reprimand for his carelessness, for the man acknowledged, in answer to his question, that he knew the horse's antipathy to Mike perfectly well, but had changed his place in the stable without thinking.

Bettle and Jenny were not so busy but that they found time in the evenings, after supper, to take a few long, quiet strolls together; and very pleasant strolls they were, through the meadows, and along the banks of the beautiful, quiet stream, which flowed on as calmly and peacefully as if no sound but the murmur of lovers' voices had ever mingled with the sough of the autumn wind through the corn that waved and rustled on its banks, and among the trees that drooped over them.

The lovers had many things to talk about; the trials and troubles that had crowded upon them in the last few days, the uncertain prospect for the future, their reliance on each other,—for these same troubles had swept away all reserve, and they talked freely and unrestrainedly,—and the hope that better times would come, when all these alarms would be at an end.

It would have sounded curiously to those who only knew Bettle as the reckless dare-devil partisan officer, to hear him talk of the delights of a quiet, farmer's life, and of his longing for the time when he could forsake the wild, restless life he was now leading for what he saw, in the light of the new feeling that had come over him, was a far higher and better one; not that he had any thought of leaving it now, however, for the conviction of duty which first led him to adopt it was as powerful as ever.

Neither did Jenny urge it, for she had come to see the question in the same light as he himself did, and would not have persuaded him to abandon his duty, if she could.

With all her quiet happiness at these times, however, the poor girl was sad enough, for she had loved the boy who had fallen in the attempt to save her, with all the fondness of an affectionate nature, and his death weighed constantly and heavily upon her spirits. Perhaps she clung the more tenderly to Bettle for this loss: transferring to him the affection whose tendrils had been so rudely torn away from the object to which they had previously attached themselves.

As they walked along the bank of the creek, on one of these evenings, they had been talking of Mahlon, and Jenny at last said,—

"But, indeed, William, it does seem hard that the youngest should be taken thus, and in the only battle he was ever in."

"It is a sad loss, the more so as he was so young and had attached us all to him so much. Jenny, as we stood around him and John after the fight on that sad morning, I saw the lips working and big tears running, unnoticed by themselves, down the faces of some of my own men, who I suspect had never shed them since they were as young as the poor boy they were grieving for."

"Those wild, stern, reckless-looking men! They look as if nothing could ever move them," said Jenny. "But it is strange that my brother was the only one killed in such a fight as John described to me. How did thee escape, so reckless and daring as he says thee is?"

"I have to thank you, Jenny, for my life in that affair," said Bettle.

"Me!" she exclaimed, gazing at him with that earnest look I have before spoken of. "How could I have anything to do with saving thee?"

"You had all to do with it, humanly speaking, Jenny," said he. "Do you remember the shoe you dropped as you were going along?"

"Yes," said she; "I watched my chance and let it fall from my foot, in hopes that they might have heard me on the Rock when I called for help, and would follow and find it, so as to know we were not far off."

"Just what Frank did. Well, I took the shoe," he said, with a smile, "because it was yours and I thought I had the best right to it, and slipped it into my belt for safe-keeping. When Barton first ordered the Tories to surrender, I was standing beside him, and their leader fired his pistol at us; I had just stepped in front of Barton, and felt myself driven back a step or two as the fellow fired; I had been hit, sure enough, but the shoe stopped the ball, which struck fair in the heel, and buried itself there, leaving me to thank your foresight in dropping it for my life."

"Does thee know," she asked, changing the subject, "whether the captain intends to stay here long? I don't know whether it's right to feel so, but I can't help hoping that it will be a long time before thee is called off to do any more of this dreadful fighting. I can't bear to think of thy being in such constant danger. What would I do if thee should be killed, as my brother was?"

Bettle made no answer to this; nor, indeed, did Jenny expect any, and they returned in silence to the house, where they found the men gathered around Frank, who had apparently been telling them some news, for they were all alive with excitement.

Frank had been absent since the afternoon before, scouting in the direction of Philadelphia, and had just returned with information that the British were posted near Tredyffrin Church, and that "Mad Anthony," with fifteen hundred men, had been detached to annoy his rear and divert his attention while Washington crossed the Schuylkill at Parker's Ferry with what was left of the main army.

There was but little probability that any more difficulty with the Tories would be experienced by the Sanfords, or any other family in that neighborhood; and Clayton at once determined to join Wayne, the service in which the latter was employed being of a character peculiarly in his own line, and the men being eager to be at work again.

Everything, therefore, was prepared for an early march the next morning. A messenger was sent to Mac Allan's to see if his cabin was sufficiently advanced to enable him to do without his boys. The latter came back with the messenger, all ready for service, having just finished putting the roof on the cabin so as to afford some shelter, though the openings between the logs of which the walls were formed had not yet been filled up.

The evening was spent in moulding balls, preparing

cartridges, sharpening knives and swords, and cleaning fire-arms.

The next morning, by half an hour after sunrise, the Rangers had dispatched a substantial breakfast, and were in the saddle in marching order.

In a few minutes more they had passed out of sight, carrying with them the fervent blessings of those they had saved; while Jenny looked after them, with dimmed eyes, through the tears she, this time, took no pains to hide.

CHAPTER XVI.

The Rangers moved rapidly on, not along the main road, but south of it, over the same route that had been taken eight days before by Frank when guiding the Sanfords' escort, till they reached the spot where Mac Allan was at work "chinkin' an' daubin'," as he phrased it, at his cabin; that is, in English, filling up the gaps between the logs with stones and mud.

As the troop halted for a moment, the old man suspended his work, and came forward.

"How do? how do?" he exclaimed, cordially; "you see, we're a'most got into the house agin. They don't build their grand houses in Philadelphy this fast, do they, capt'n?" he added, addressing Clayton.

"No, not quite," said he, dryly; "they generally take a good many times four days to get a house under roof, and then take a month or two after they've done, to finish it."

"But where are ye bound now?" said the old man. "For the city?"

"Not directly," said Clayton, and, approaching Mac Allan, leaned down from his horse and whispered in his ear.

The latter shook his head doubtfully.

"I don't like that much," he muttered; "there's too many Tories about there, that knows the country enough sight better'n Mad Anthony or any of his men.

He'll find himself in a trap afore he knows it, if he don't look out."

"Well, I'm afraid thee's right," said Clayton; "but, if there's any danger of that kind, we ought to be there to do what we can to help him through it, and the sooner and more quietly we get there, the better. Farewell."

"Good-by," said Mac Allan, shaking hands with him and then with his sons, one after the other. "Now, boys," said he, addressing the latter, "you've all done well, so far; I want to hear a good report of you from the capt'n, wherever you're at work. Don't let the old man hear anything about his boys that'll make him feel ashamed of 'em."

The troop now resumed its march, halting again at the spring near West Chester, which I described some chapters back, to water their horses; thence passing along a few hundred yards to the southward of the Turk's Head tavern, where they did *not* stop, and crossing the Lancaster road about a mile east of it at the point now known as Gallows Hill, and then straight across the country, crossing Chester and Ridley Creeks, and threading their way through the thickly-wooded country, until they reached the outposts of Wayne's division. The place where the force lay had been well chosen for concealment. It was deep in the woods, about two miles southwest of where the Paoli Tavern now stands, and was surrounded by hills. There was one narrow defile, the site of a disused road, which Clayton had marked, as he approached, as the point from which danger was to be looked for. Still, the place was so secluded that it would have been perfectly secure from discovery, had it not been for one or more treacherous hounds living near, who knew every defile and ravine in the neighborhood.

Halting his force near the outposts, Clayton rode forward alone until challenged by a sentinel; waiting here until the latter was relieved, he went in with the guard to the tent of the general, to whom he announced his errand and offered his services.

The latter, who had seen the conduct of the troop at Brandywine, and had heard of their daring foray into Knyphausen's camp,—an exploit which, harebrained though it was, chimed exactly with his own adventurous spirit,—received him gladly, as a most valuable assistant.

By the time their quarters had been assigned them and taken up, the sun was set, and the cool autumn twilight was coming on. The red flush had faded from the sky, and then the pale green shone through the broken cloud-masses like the distant meadows of the land of Beulah. Beautiful, with a most exquisite and tender beauty, is this pale, delicate green which spreads over the western sky after the sun has fairly sunk from view, and before the dull gray through which the stars first come out, has crept over it. Few writers seem to have noticed it, and I have rarely seen a landscape, except some of Paul Weber's, in which the artist appears to have observed it at all.

It faded rapidly out, and soon the camp was in darkness, except for the light of their fires, and by ten o'clock all was silent.

Clayton had his own scouts on the lookout, in the defile he had marked, in addition to the regular sentries; and a little after midnight, as he lay asleep with his head resting on the saddle, he was aroused by a touch on his shoulder. Springing to his feet, broad awake in an instant, he saw Bettle standing before him.

"What's the matter?" he inquired.

"I've heard Sam Diller's whistle twice from the ravine yonder," said Bettle. "There it is again!" said he, as a long, clear, powerful whistle came from the ravine, followed by the quick, angry bark of a watch-dog, as if the animal had been roused by some one passing. The latter noise was cut short suddenly, but the whistle sounded again, and then another from the same direction, a little to the right, and another and another from the left, somewhat nearer, and then all at once, as though a detachment of small locomotives had broken loose. "Off to Wayne's quarters at once and rouse him," said Clayton; "there's mischief afoot. Leave me to rouse our men."

While Clayton was doing this, and before Bettle had passed half the distance to the general's tent, a shot was heard from the ravine, followed by three or four more in rapid succession, and the picket guards came running in at full speed, shouting, "The British! The British!" followed closely by a column of infantry with fixed bayonets.

"Tell Wheeler to set his men and Bettle's with the new hands, to saddle the horses; take to the trees with carbines, thee and Wetherill, with your men," said Clayton, speaking to Barton, who had joined him, in the sharp, rapid voice which men use when thoroughly in earnest, "and pick the officers out wherever you can see them."

The order was instantly obeyed, Wheeler's and Bettle's men working rapidly but coolly among the horses, while the rest of the force scattered among the trees and opened a sharp but irregular fire upon the advancing column with their carbines and the rifles of the Mac Allans.

"Forward! forward!" shouted the leader, as the head of the column wavered for an instant; "are you going to be stopped by a dozen bush-fighters? Put them up with the bayonet."

Twenty carbines cracked from as many different trees in answer, dropping some three or four of the men nearest him, but leaving him untouched. The column moved steadily forward with fixed bayonets, dislodging the Americans, who flitted from tree to tree, sometimes in front, sometimes on either flank of the attacking party, keeping up a brisk pattering fire, which, however, in the dim light, did but little execution.

In the mean time the silent bayonets were doing their work upon the surprised and half-armed soldiers, who, in their panic, rushed, undressed, from their tents, in many instances right upon them; many others were slain within the tents, pinned to the ground before they could rise.

The camp was full of half-naked men rushing distractedly hither and thither, seeking only to escape.

So far, the affair had been little but a massacre; but by this time Wayne had succeeded in rallying a few companies, and his voice was heard, "Ready—aim low—fire!" and a storm of balls flew over the Rangers, who, being between Wayne's men and the enemy, had thrown themselves flat upon the ground at the sound of the first order. Volley followed volley, telling with some effect upon the close columns of the British, though most of the balls were either lost by striking into the trees or diverted by grazing them.

The Rangers, while holding their successive trees as long as possible, had been gradually working their way toward their horses, which were by this time ready. Taking advantage of a brief lull in the firing, they sprang to their feet, and, darting from tree to tree, passed out of the line of fire, still using their carbines as they had opportunity, till they reached the horses and sprang into the saddles. At this moment the scene was lit up by the glare of a dozen burning tents, which had been fired by order of Colonel Gray, the commander of the assailants; and then came the cries of wounded men, who were perishing in them. This dastardly piece of ferocity had the good effect of giving light enough for Clayton's troop to act on horseback to much better advantage. Putting his men in motion instantly, he charged on the enemy's flank in solid column; he succeeded in partially disordering them, but they rallied immediately, and he was forced to give back from a mass of bayonets which it would have been utter madness to attempt to ride down.

The Rangers broke at once, but not in retreat nor confusion; and in a moment they were hovering singly or in groups of two or three around the advancing column; in front, in rear, on either flank, these wild riders wheeled and circled like hawks, in and out among the trees, firing with deadly aim into the solid mass of the assailants, while volley after volley whistled harmlessly by them in their rapid and ceaseless evolutions.

The new recruits, who had been employed at first in helping to saddle the horses, behaved quite well as Clayton had dared to hope; he had not been able as yet to procure carbines for them, and several of them had not even swords; they all had pistols, however, and several had brought their fowling-pieces and rifles with them, when they enlisted. With such arms as they had, however, they were at work as busily as the rest, every man "on his own hook;" for there had been no time to drill them in Clayton's peculiar system of tactics, beyond teaching them a few of the more common signals.

In the mean time, Wayne, with the small body he had succeeded in rallying, was stubbornly holding his ground, and covering the flight of the other panic-stricken soldiers, whose officers—vainly, for the most part—strove to check and form them in the rear.

The light of the burning tents, however, showed him how utterly hopeless was the attempt to beat off an enemy evidently stronger than his whole division had been at the beginning; and he reluctantly ordered a retreat.

It was conducted in good order at first, but soon became a flight, with part of the enemy following in hot pursuit, while the remainder amused themselves by bayoneting such of the Americans, scattered about and unarmed, as they could overtake.

Cries for quarter were heard all around, from naked or wounded men, answered by, "No quarter to the bloody rebels!" accompanied by savage oaths and the thrust of bayonets, or the heavy "thud" and the crash as the musket-butt came down upon some naked skull.

The fight was over; but, while the Americans under Wayne retreated, Clayton accompanied them, his troop still harassing the enemy with the irregular but galling fire from their carbines, until they desisted from the pursuit.

The British returned toward the camp, meeting on the way General Smallwood coming to the assistance of Wayne with a detachment of raw militia, who, at sight of the enemy, instantly turned with alacrity and ran for their lives right gallantly, and with a speed which would have defied pursuit, had Colonel Gray made any; a thing he had not the slightest intention of doing. Passing back through what was left of the camp, he collected his forces, gathered up his wounded, and before dawn the place was left in its desolation; and when the sun rose, its light shone upon the bodies of one hundred and fifty dead and wounded Americans lying there, while above the groans of the wounded rose the mournful voice of a soldier's dog, which sat howling over the corpse of its master.

Thus ended the "Paoli massacre," for which General Wayne has been not only severely censured, but most bitterly slandered. He has been charged with having been asleep at a farm-house a mile away from the camp —with having never come near the field—with having been surprised in his tent, and with having escaped from the back of it and fled with his red-lined cloak turned inside out, around his body, passing for a British soldier in the darkness and amid the confusion of the attack! Such lies as these passed current from mouth to mouth, among those who knew nothing of the affair but by rumor. The court-martial convened by Washington about a month afterward, at Wayne's request, came to a different conclusion, after hearing the testimony of those who knew what they were talking about, and decided that "he did everything that could be expected from an active, brave, and vigilant officer, under the orders which he then had."

CHAPTER XVII.

By daybreak the Rangers were within a mile of the right bank of the Schuylkill, on the Lancaster road. As soon as Colonel Gray had given up the pursuit, they had detached themselves from the body of fugitives—it being, as we have seen before, no part of their custom to accompany any main body of men in a flight—and ridden straight toward Philadelphia, intending to hover in and around the city and watch the motions of the enemy, who had approached fearfully near, and, indeed, were preparing to take possession.

Soon after they left the main body, the three Tory prisoners they had brought with them suddenly occurred to Clayton, for the first time since the attack; and he asked Bettle if he had seen them.

"No," said the latter; "I never thought of the rascals," and, riding to the rear, inquired of Frank if they were with the troop.

Frank answered in the negative.

"When did you discover their absence?"

"How?"

"When did you miss them?" said Bettle, simplifying.

"Oh! know'd it ever since we started," said Frank, who had understood the question in its previous form perfectly well, but had a perfect hatred of what he called "booktionary talk."

"Why didn't you report to the captain, then?" said Bettle, a little sternly.

"No use," said Frank, coolly; "nobody but the d—l could ha' caught 'em, with the start they had, even if there'd been time to hunt 'em. Let 'em go; can't do no harm."

Bettle was fain to be content with this, knowing that no more information would be extracted from Frank, and rode back to Clayton with his report.

"It can't be helped," said the latter; "but they may have escaped at the beginning of the attack, and, if they reach the city in advance of us, may meet some outlying parties of the enemy and give us trouble by informing them of our movements."

Nothing more was said, for none of the officers were men to waste breath in discussing matters that were inevitable, and the troop rode on in silence till they reached the spot mentioned in the beginning of the chapter.

As the day began to break, Frank and Harry had dismounted, and gone a short distance in advance to reconnoitre, the troop following at a walk, with their arms secured from rattling and jingling in the usual manner.

They were proceeding cautiously, listening for signals, when the two scouts suddenly appeared—I was going to say, breathless; but that was a condition that Frank Lightfoot and Dandy Harry did not easily get into—and, both speaking at once, hurriedly exclaimed to Clayton,—

"Close up, close up! There's eighty or a hundred British light-horse in the road, not two hundred yards off!"

"Well," said Clayton, who at the first sight of them

had silently thrown up his hand as a signal for the troop to halt, "well, are they in motion?"

"No," said Harry; "they're drawn up in the road, —I suspect waiting for us,—just around the second turn, about two hundred yards off."

"Did you get near enough to count them?" said Clayton.

"Yes; but we didn't stop to do it carefully. However, there can't be less than what we said——"

"But look'e here," interrupted Frank, "by the hokey! I seen them three rascals that got off back yonder among 'em."

"Is thee sure of that?" inquired Clayton.

"Certain; I know 'em too well to make a mistake."

"We must avoid a fight, if possible," said Clayton; "they are probably fresh, and our own men and horses are too tired to attempt such odds. At the same time, I want to reach the city if it can be done. What does thee advise, Levi?" he added, addressing Barton, who was beside him.

"I'm afraid we'll have to try and fight our way through," said the latter, speaking rapidly. "I hear them in motion now—" as the tramp of what was evidently a considerable body of horsemen, accompanied by the jingle of their arms, which they took no pains to silence, was borne past upon the fresh morning air— "they're coming. If we retreat along the road, we'll be overtaken and cut to pieces; we're hemmed in by this swampy ground on the one side, and this thicket on the other——"

"Thee's right," interrupted Clayton. "Form across the road, and give them a volley as they come up, and then charge on them; we may cut our way through."

The troop was at once formed in a solid column, filling the road from side to side, and they sat waiting in grim silence for the attack, with carbines unslung and cocked, and holsters opened ready.

About twenty yards in advance the road turned somewhat sharply around a bank, and Clayton had ordered his men to hold their fire until enough of the enemy had passed the turn for the discharge to tell upon with full effect.

By this time the enemy, who had been coming on in a sharp trot, arrived at the turn, and the next instant the head of the column had passed it, coming in full view of the Rangers.

"Ready, now; ready!" said Clayton, in a low, quick tone, and, simultaneously——

"Halt!" exclaimed the other leader, suddenly reining back his horse against the foremost rank of his men, and then holding a white handkerchief aloft. "Hold, there! don't fire on us," as he observed the carbines of the Rangers at their shoulders.

Clayton, watching him closely, motioned with his left hand to his men not to fire, and then waited to see what was to grow out of this unusual way of managing a charge of cavalry.

"May I speak a word to you, sir?" said the leader, courteously, addressing Clayton, and riding forward a few paces alone.

"Certainly thee may," said Clayton, also riding forward, until they met about half-way between their respective troops, his own men holding their carbines still cocked. "What has thee to say to me?"

"I suspect, from your language," said the other, smiling, "that I have found the men I'm looking for.

You are Captain Clayton, commanding a corps of American Free Rangers, if I mistake not."

"I am," said Clayton, quietly, though wondering to what all this was going to lead.

"Then, sir, I am happy to inform you that I have secured three runaway prisoners of yours, who informed me that I would be likely to meet you here, and who within the next five minutes will probably be in a state of profound astonishment."

Clayton was decidedly in that state himself at this moment.

"I see you are mystified, sir," said the stranger. "My name is Allen McLane, commanding very much such a corps as your own, but at this moment, for satisfactory reasons, masquerading in British uniforms. Your runaways fell in with us about half an hour ago, and, taking us for the genuine article, at once joined us for protection."

"I see, I see," said Clayton, laughing. "But why did they run the risk of coming on here, instead of joining the force that attacked us?"

"I asked them the same question," said McLane, "and they told me they did attempt to do so, but were not believed, and had to run for their lives with the rest."

A momentary glimpse of suspicion shot across Clayton's mind, for he was cautious by nature and habit, and it occurred to him that this story might, after all, be only a ruse to lull suspicion until his own men should be entangled with the others, so as to be incapable of a combined and effectual resistance.

"What does thee propose to do?" he inquired.

"To combine our forces," was the prompt reply;

"at any rate, to work in concert against the British, when they take possession of Philadelphia, as they will, inevitably. Nothing short of a miracle can prevent it; they will make it their winter quarters; and I intend to make it my business to keep in the neighborhood just as long as they stay there, and annoy them by intercepting their supplies and cutting off all who venture outside."

"Thee is not trying to deceive me?" said Clayton.

"If I were really an enemy, would I have been likely to make this parley, with a force so much your superior? I see an acquaintance among your officers, who can tell you who I am."

"Who is it?"

"Mr. Wetherill, there; will you be good enough to call him?"

Wetherill came forward in answer to a motion from Clayton, and, as he reached the spot, Captain McLane removed his cap and held out his hand to him, as he looked keenly at him, saying,—

"Have you forgotten your old friends, Mr. Wetherill?"

"Allen McLane!" exclaimed Wetherill, in surprise, grasping his hand warmly; "I'm glad to see thee, but certainly I didn't expect to meet thee in this dress: thee used to be a terrible rebel."

"I'm as bad a one as ever I was," said McLane, who then explained his disguise as he had done before to Clayton, adding, with a laugh, "and I certainly didn't expect to find men that say 'thee and thou,' with broadswords belted around their plain coats. But I wanted you to satisfy your captain that we are friends and not enemies."

"Oh, if that's all, I presume thee's satisfied, Ellis?" said Wetherill, turning to Clayton.

"Perfectly," said the latter; "and now I am free to say I'm very glad thee is not what thee seems to be, for I was really very uneasy about the prospect of a fight with thy force. My people are wearied out by a hard march and harder fighting this morning, and are in sore need of rest."

"We'll soon find a place for that," said Captain McLane, "if you'll put them in motion."

Wetherill accordingly went back to the troop, who were still standing, waiting in puzzled amazement for the issue of this strange conference, explained the true state of the case, and the whole party retraced their steps toward the city, crossed the Schuylkill, and then, striking northward, pushed rapidly toward the hills of the Wissahickon.

The astonishment of the three Tories when they found themselves prisoners again was, to say the least, profound. No explanations were vouchsafed to them, of course, and they rode in the center of the Rangers, to whom they had been transferred, in a state of pitiable bewilderment, to which were added very uncomfortable misgivings as to the unraveling of the mystery.

Now, I am not going to describe the place which the Rangers and their new friends occupied on the Wissahickon; for I know, if I do, that somebody will incontinently establish an "ice-cream and other refreshments" saloon there, and somebody else will open a lager-beer saloon, complicated with a bowling-alley and three billiard-tables, and fast young men will drive hired horses and light wagons furiously, and get very drunk on bad liquors, and picnic-parties will drive out there in double omnibuses, with a brass band in the foremost. No: I'll spare it all these abominations, by avoiding any description of it.

Suffice it to say, it was among the hills, and was used as a rendezvous until some time after the British had taken possession of the city, a constant communication being kept up with the American army, and the British worried by constant forays and surprises of stragglers and outlying parties,—enterprises in which the conduct of the Rangers so satisfied Captain McLane of the superiority of their training for their particular business, that he begged Clayton to take a portion of his own men under his command and train them.

The latter chose thirty of the best riders among them, so as to bring his force nearly up to its original number, and soon had them perfectly trained and disciplined.

In the mean time, on the 26th of September, just one month after Clayton's foray into the Hessian Camp at Turkey Point, Lord Cornwallis, better known among his own men as "Old Corn-Cob," had entered Philadelphia at the head of a detachment of British and Hessian grenadiers, leaving the rest of the army encamped at Germantown.

They marched down Second Street to their camp, which was below the city, with McLane's men hovering in their rear. Five of these, disguised as British cavalry, with the captain at their head, pounced upon a Captain Sanford* at the bridge over Dock Creek,

---

* No relation to Jenny.

and carried him and his horse off together, after having just missed the adjutant-general, with his papers, above, near Chestnut Street.

Before the British entered the city, Congress adjourned to meet at Lancaster, to which place all the archives were removed, and at the same time caused to be arrested and sent to Virginia about twenty stiff-necked individuals, among whom were several of the prominent "Friends" who had been instrumental in getting up the "Testimony" spoken of in the beginning of my narrative,—they having stubbornly refused to give, either by word or writing, any promise of allegiance to the Continental Government.

CHAPTER XVIII.

THE city was now practically in the possession of the enemy. Washington had moved down the Schuylkill from Potts Grove, where he had been encamped, to within about sixteen miles of Germantown, at which place the bulk of the British forces was still lying, and the two armies lay for some time watching each other's movements.

Howe probably supposed that when he had conquered Philadelphia he had conquered the country of which it was the capital. If he did so, he soon discovered his mistake; for he was in a very short time made acquainted—ay, and thenceforth kept acquainted, too—with the fact that he commanded precisely the area of ground which his army covered for the time, and not one foot beyond it.

The prestige which the taking of the capital was to give to the British arms, which was so much counted on, amounted to just nothing at all.

It spread no panic through the country; it brought the American forces no nearer to a surrender; Congress, when the time came, simply shifted its quarters first to Lancaster, and then to York; and, lo! Lancaster, and then York, became for the time the seat of government, and Philadelphia—simply a British encampment between the Schuylkill and the Delaware!

Nevertheless, the British encampment between the Schuylkill and the Delaware was not the most comfortable in the world, during the succeeding fall and winter.

Their supplies were anything but plentiful, and there was a very inconvenient lack of fire-wood, in particular.

True, there was no lack of willingness among the farmers in the vicinity to furnish everything that was wanted, nor any lack of efforts to furnish them; but a great deal of produce started to the city that never reached it, and a good many foraging parties went out that either came back faster than they went, or came not back at all; for there were hawks up the river and down the river and circling everywhere around the outskirts, swooping down upon farmer and forager, snapping them up or putting them to flight, and turning many a drove of sheep and cattle and many a load of grain, from their intended destination, into the hungry stomachs at Valley Forge.

But I am getting on too fast for my story. None of the British except the detachment which accompanied Cornwallis had as yet entered the city, but were, as I said before, at Germantown.

On the 1st of October, Washington, who still remained encamped near Pennibecker's Mill, was reinforced by the arrival of some troops from Peekskill and a body of militia. At the same time, Howe was weakened by the absence of Cornwallis's detachment in Philadelphia, and of a force which he had dispatched down the Delaware for the purpose of reducing Billingsport and the forts at Red Bank and on Mud Island.

Washington was aware of this, being kept posted as to all the enemy's movements by the Irregulars, whose scouts were constantly hovering about their camp; and he determined to give them battle.

His army was not in the best possible condition for service, for their ammunition was none too plentiful, and at least a thousand of them were barefooted, and, in fact, with a few exceptions, the whole army was pervaded by a general air of raggedness.

It was necessary to intercept all communication between the British and the inhabitants of the surrounding country, in order to prevent their design from being betrayed; and the Irregulars separated into small detachments, and scoured all the roads leading to Germantown and the city, from the 1st till midnight of the 3d of the month.

Washington had started for Chestnut Hill, in company with the column under the command of Sullivan and Wayne, flanked by Conway's division, at dark on the same evening, hoping to reach the place and surprise the British pickets there, before daylight. But the road was rough and difficult to travel, and when midnight came they were still miles away.

Barton's division of the Rangers, accompanied by Clayton, joined them at this point, having reconnoitred the road from near Chestnut Hill, and bringing with them a party of three countrymen whom they had intercepted, and reported himself to Washington.

The prisoners were ordered to the rear while Clayton proceeded to make his report.

"How is the road?" inquired Washington, as Clayton paused in his recital.

"Very rough; worse, if possible, than it is here."

"Did you see any of the enemy's patrols?"

"We came upon one party about three miles below, and chased them for a mile, but they escaped in the darkness by turning into the woods; we didn't pursue them any farther, being satisfied with driving them off the road."

"I am sorry they escaped you," said Washington; "I fear they will give notice of our approach."

"I think not," said Clayton. "Hardly a night has passed since we came into the neighborhood, without some such rencontre taking place between my own men or Captain McLane's, and some of the enemy's vedettes. I am satisfied that they knew us, and will not suspect the presence of any larger force until they see it."

"Where did you take the prisoners you brought in?"

"Just below, on our way hither."

"Then they have had no opportunity to communicate with the enemy?"

"None whatever," said Clayton; "I am certain that those we chased were the outermost patrol; all the other roads are in possession of my own men or McLane's."

"Do you expect to have your men together, in a body, in the battle?" inquired General Wayne.

"Certainly," said Clayton: "they have orders to fall in with Pulaski's cavalry at the first opportunity."

"Then you intend to fight under his command this time," said Mad Anthony; "I was in hopes to have had your dare-devils with me to-day, to help me in wiping out that matter at the Paoli."

"Thee may possibly have them yet," said Clayton, smiling: "we will remain with Pulaski until I think we can do better elsewhere. I think it likely, if thee should be in the part of the field where Colonel Gray is, thee will have a chance of such assistance as we can give."

"Your men are hardly adapted, from their training, for field-service, I imagine, sir," interrupted Washington.

"They have been thoroughly trained for every kind of service," said Clayton, "except artillery."

"If your Excellency had seen them at Brandywine, and the way they charged in solid column on those scoundrels at Paoli," said Wayne, "you would have no fears as to their ability for field-work."

But little more was said, and the army proceeded as silently as possible, until they reached the woods on Chestnut Hill at daybreak.

As they emerged from the woods, the vanguard came upon one of the enemy's outlying patrols, not fifty yards in advance; the latter put spurs to their horses and galloped down the road, hotly pursued by a dozen of the Rangers, with Barton at their head.

The patrol were well mounted, of course, but they would have stood no chance at all with the fleet horses that were after them, had they not come pell-mell upon a party of some fifty light-horse a short distance above Mount Airy.

They were so close upon them before they perceived them, that pursuers and pursued drew up together in a confused mass, within thirty feet of the light-horse, who had halted on hearing the clatter of hoofs coming down the road.

This confusion saved Barton and his small force; for they were so mixed and entangled with the patrol that the larger force were afraid, at first, to fire or charge on them for fear of shooting or riding down their friends, and they stood for a moment irresolute.

Taking advantage of this pause, Barton gave the

signal for retreat, and his men, wheeling their horses directly in their tracks, separated instantly, leaped the fences on each side of the road, and in a moment were skirting through the meadows, like moss-troopers, scattered, after their fashion in such cases, like a flock of partridges.

A few pistols were fired after them, and the British were about to pursue, but their leader ordered them to stand fast.

"I know those men," said he to his lieutenant: "they're Clayton's Rangers, I know by their manœuvres; we might as well chase shadows——"

"Back, back!" exclaimed the officer in command of the patrol: "the whole rebel army's within half a mile of us!"

"The d——l!" exclaimed the other, in consternation.

No more words were wasted, and the whole party rode back to the nearest post as fast as they could spur their horses, and gave the alarm.

The Fortieth Regiment, with a battalion of light infantry which was stationed at Mount Airy, immediately formed, to receive, as they supposed, the shock of the whole army; their commander sending the patrol on to the main body, which was encamped some distance below, in the middle of Germantown.

They had hardly formed, before Conway came sweeping down upon them in a furious attack, which drove them headlong into the village.

The battle was begun; it has been too often and too well described by more competent hands, to make it necessary for me to enter into its details, and I shall have but little to say about it, except so far as relates to the connection of the Rangers with it.

When the retreating columns reached the head of the village, Colonel Musgrave, the commander, threw himself, with five or six companies of the Fortieth Regiment, into the large stone house known now, wherever American history is known, as "Chew's House," and held it throughout the battle, with a stubborn bravery that deserves all praise.

While the battle was raging around this temporary fort, General Greene had come around by the Limekiln Road, routed a battalion of light infantry and the Queen's Rangers, on the right wing of the enemy, and was now hotly engaged with the left flank of the same wing, striving to enter the village. The Pennsylvania militia, under General Armstrong, also came down the Manatawny Road (now known as the Ridge Road), upon the left wing, commanded by Gray, which it was their business to attack and turn; and when they reached it, arriving in front of the German Chasseurs, on the left flank, to their imperishable glory be it said, they stood still, and never attacked them at all! Whereupon Colonel Gray betook himself, with nearly the whole left wing, to the assistance of the center, which had its hands more than full.

The Maryland and Jersey militia, under Smallwood and Forman, who were ordered to march down the York Road and attack the right flank of the right wing, executed the first half of their instructions, that of marching down the road, admirably, but arrived on the ground so late that there was nobody left for them to attack, the said wing having left the ground to go to the assistance of the center, near Chew's house.

Here was the brunt of the battle. The Rangers, in obedience to Clayton's orders, had fallen in successively, as they came up, with Pulaski's cavalry as a gathering-point. As soon as they were all together, Clayton led them off toward the house, having heard that Colonel Gray was there, and feeling a strong desire to make his acknowledgments to him in person for the affair at Paoli.

A heavy fog had fallen early in the morning, and everything was thickly enveloped in it. It was so dense that the different divisions of the two armies could not see each other, and both sides were guided in firing by the flash of each other's muskets.

Guided by the incessant rattle of musketry and cannon, which were both playing on Chew's house, Clayton pushed rapidly up the street toward the house, catching here and there dim glimpses of the battalions moving ghostily through the fog, along whose lines, ever and anon, ran the red stream of fire. Disregarding these, not looking to see whether they were friend or foe, Clayton held sternly on to seek Colonel Gray.

A company of British infantry, which had become detached from the main body in the confusion (for after the first volley or two the British loaded and fired without regard to order, and with broken ranks), wheeled into the street directly in front of the Rangers before they saw them in the thick fog.

They were greatly inferior in number, besides being on foot, and escape and resistance seemed alike hopeless. Nevertheless, the instant their captain saw the figures that loomed through the mist, distinctly enough to know that they were enemies, without stopping to see how strong they were, he ordered his men to halt, down front rank, and prepare to repel cavalry. The order was obeyed with all the marvelous promptness

nd precision with which thoroughly disciplined troops
xecute their manœuvres, and by the time the Rangers,
who kept on their steady gallop, neither hastening nor
lackening their pace, had come within thirty feet of
hem, the road was blocked by a rank of men on one
nee, with musket-butts braced against the ground and
line of bayonets bristling in front of them, while be-
ind them was another rank half crouching, with arms
resented, and behind them again another and the last
ank, standing bolt upright, with their muskets at their
houlders, leveled above the heads of those in front.

"Stand fast, men," Clayton heard the officer ex-
laim; "stand fast; don't fire, till you can see their
elts."

"Halt," said Clayton; and, as the trained horses
topped at the word, planting their fore-feet out and
hrowing themselves almost on their haunches with the
udden check, he called, riding forward alone as he
poke,—

"I should know that voice. Is that Captain Gard-
er?"

"It is," said a voice, as the speaker advanced toward
im. "Is not that Captain Clayton?"

"The same," said Clayton. "Let us pass each other
n peace, and seek strangers for enemies."

"With the greatest pleasure," said Gardner, "par-
cularly as it depends a good deal upon your forbear-
nce whether my handful of men passes at all."

"I presume it does," said Clayton, smiling; "I
would not willingly attack thee at all, and at present I
we thee a debt of kindness, for saving some of our
riends from a gang of marauding villains, the other
ay, near Brandywine."

"Oh! the women," said Gardner, with some interest. "Yes, I was just in time: did they reach you in safety?"

"Yes, they came in the next morning," said Clayton. "But we must not waste time talking here," he added. "If thee will withdraw thy men, we will push on: let us avoid each other, if possible, during the battle."

Captain Gardner nodded, and immediately ordered his men to recover their arms and march; an order which they obeyed with as much alacrity as amazement at finding themselves allowed to do so.

At this moment an officer in the American uniform spurred up to where Clayton was standing.

"What troop is this?" he inquired.

"Clayton's Rangers," was the answer. "Can thee tell how the battle is going?"

"Heaven only knows," said the officer. "I believe there are a dozen battles going on at once; there's no possibility of keeping any kind of order in this cursed fog. I was sent to tell General Sullivan to silence that battery in an orchard that lies over yonder, but I can't find him. Will you undertake it?"

"Of course," said Clayton, briefly.

"Well, at them, then," said the officer, motioning in the direction of the orchard. "I hope you'll succeed, for their fire's too hot for comfort." And away he spurred.

Clayton immediately put his men in motion in the direction indicated by the officer, guided only by the roar of the cannon and an occasional glimpse of their flash, through the smoke and fog: indeed, this was all he *could* see; orchard, cannon, and soldiers were all invisible.

Sweeping around, so as to get out of the line of fire, they pushed across the intervening meadows until within fifty yards of the battery; halting here for a moment, Clayton ordered the Mac Allan boys to dismount and steal with their rifles along the orchard fence, in advance of the troop, as near as they could get without being discovered, instructing them what to do when they had reached the point.

The ten young giants dismounted at once, knowing that their horses would keep in the ranks whether mounted or not. Stealing along the fence, crouching low, with trailed rifles, they made their way rapidly toward the battery, which was still in full play; while Sullivan's brigade, somewhere off in the fog, was keeping up a brisk but random fire, in another direction.

The fence had been leveled for several yards on each side, so as to give space for the cannon. They were placed on the edge of a kind of bank, along which the fence extended.

Arrived at the opening in the latter, and near enough to see the enemy with tolerable distinctness, five of the party crouched in the corner of the worm fence, while the other five, throwing themselves flat upon the ground, worked their way, at some distance from the edge of the elevation, across the line of fire, but so far below its level that the balls hurtled over them harmlessly, and gained the other end of the opening unperceived.

After the next discharge of the guns, as the artillerymen sprang forward to reload them, the sharp, almost simultaneous, crack of the Mac Allans' rifles was heard, and all the men at the guns but two went down, and then came the rush of cavalry, and the next moment the wild riders poured in solid column upon the flank of the body which supported the battery, before any attempt could be made to reload the guns.

Taken by surprise, having no time to display their front to repel the charge, they were broken in a moment, and the Rangers were in the midst of them. An attempt to form again was defeated by an unexpected movement of the Rangers, who—from some previously understood arrangement, apparently, for not a word was spoken—separated into four divisions, and, each taking a different direction, forced the disordered crowd apart, driving them farther and farther back. As each division penetrated the heart of the mass before it, its riders turned again, back to back, thus forming two fronts, each of which continued to force their enemies apart until they had been completely broken up into separate squads.

Then, closing again into solid column, they attacked these scattered parties in detail, riding down, shooting, sabering, in rapid succession, till all who were left threw down their arms and called for quarter.

"Where is your commanding officer?" said Clayton.

"I believe I must serve your turn for want of a better," said an officer in a lieutenant's uniform, advancing.

"Does thee surrender?" said Clayton.

The officer started, and, looking at Clayton for a moment in astonishment, muttered, "George Fox again, as I live!" and then added, aloud, "I can't help myself, that I see. I have nothing but this to give up to you," offering the hilt of his sword: "the blade parted company with it a minute ago in the scuffle."

"Keep it," said Clayton.

The officer bowed.

And now occurred the strangest and most contradictory of all the strange and contradictory things in this helter-skelter battle of Germantown. At this very time the British were practically defeated! General Howe had given up the battle, and had given orders to rendezvous at Chester. The main body, overpowered in the center of the village, had been on the point of retreating, when Gray and Knyphausen, taking advantage of the magnanimous forbearance of the Pennsylvania militia in disobeying their orders, and the very accommodating deliberation of the Maryland and New Jersey militia in coming up too late to be of any use, threw the whole left wing into the village, to the assistance of the center. This checked the Americans, who had before been gaining ground rapidly, and they were finally driven back. Colonel Gray then hurried to the assistance of the right wing, which was engaged with General Greene's column. General Sullivan, with Colonel Armstrong and General Conway, had driven the enemy into the village, when they suddenly found themselves unsupported by other troops, their ammunition exhausted, and, dimly visible through the fog, a powerful force forming on their right. At that moment some one called aloud that they were surrounded, and the Americans, in a sudden panic, one of the most unmanageable disorders to which armies are subject, broke away into a full retreat, tossing the victory out of their hands at the moment when they had only to close them upon it to make it secure.

The British commander ought to have felt deeply his obligations to the gallant militia who didn't attack his left wing; for to their disregard of their orders was owing, mainly, the turn of the battle. A great deal of precious time, however, was lost before Chew's house, owing to General Knox's opposition (which savored very strongly of what is known, since the Crimean war, as "red tape") to leaving the house in possession of Colonel Musgrave and following up their advantage outside, because " it would be unmilitary to leave a castle in our rear;" when the simple fact was that Colonel Musgrave could have done no harm while in the house, had he been only let alone, and a single regiment could have taken care of him had he attempted to sally out.

The battle was lost. The Americans retreated twenty miles, carrying all their artillery with them, to Perkiomen Creek, leaving behind them nearly seven hundred dead and wounded, besides about a hundred reported " missing," some of whom were prisoners, and some of whom had availed themselves of this capital opportunity to quit soldiering and sneak off home.

The loss of the British, as appeared by a torn report which was afterward found in a chimney-corner in Germantown and the fragments put together, was about eight hundred. Thus ended the second pitched battle in which the Rangers shared, in disaster and defeat.

CHAPTER XIX.

I LEFT the Rangers standing in the orchard, in posession of the artillery, with the troops that belonged to it prisoners. They did not remain, however, but moved off with their prisoners toward the main body of the Americans.

"Haven't I met thee before?" said Clayton to the British lieutenant, as they proceeded. "Thy face and voice seem familiar to me."

"Yes," said the other: "we have met twice before. Do you recollect the officer who let you into the Hessan camp at Turkey Point, and afterward gave the alarm when you made the night attack on it?"

"True," said Clayton, "that was it; I remembered thee, but couldn't place thee. How did thee recognize me?"

"By your language, as soon as I heard your voice, and by your face, as soon as I saw it. It is not one to be easily forgotten."

This was true enough, and the Englishman, perhaps, had the faintest possible idea that Clayton would not be displeased at being told so.

"Are your troop all Qua—no, Friends—that's the word, isn't it?"

"We call ourselves Free Quakers," said Clayton; "though most of the Society prefer to be called Friends. All my officers, and some of the men, are of the same persuasion."

"I beg your pardon," said the officer, dryly, "but has their being Quakers anything to do with making them fight like unchained devils? I thought I had seen a good deal of desperate fighting in my time, but I certainly never saw a body of troops charged into and dissected as ours was."

"I don't know that being Quakers has anything to do with it," said Clayton, smiling: "fighting, like everything else, if worth doing at all, is worth doing well, and they have been thoroughly trained to their work."

"Your horses fought, too, as savagely as their riders. It was their biting and kicking, indeed, that disordered our ranks, more even than the sabers and pistols of your men."

They had by this time reached the main street of the village, but, while crossing it, Sullivan's division, having broken, as I said before, came pell-mell up the street.

The Rangers, entangled among the broken columns, strove in vain to extricate themselves, and were carried away in the rush and separated entirely from their prisoners.

It was some time before Clayton could get his men out of the crowd and in column again; but he finally succeeded, and, leaving the discomfited army to pursue its retreat, struck off across the country toward the rendezvous near the Wissahickon.

When he reached it, and the roll was called, to seven of the names no answer was returned, and ten more were reported present, but wounded.

Among the missing was Frank Lightfoot.

"Has any one seen him?" inquired Clayton.

"*I* saw him," answered Dandy Harry, "just before that flock of frightened sheep came down on us in the village and threw us into confusion."

"He must have got separated from us then," said Clayton.

"If so," said Barton, "he is most probably taken, as I don't think he would follow that herd of runaways any farther than he could help."

"We can't spare Frank," said Captain McLane, who was present, with what was left of his own force; "we can't spare Frank. We must find out what has become of him: if they have him prisoner, we'll get him back, if we have to burn the city to do it."

"If they've got him," said Bettle, "it will puzzle them to hold him long: quicksilver isn't more slippery than Frank. Who'll volunteer to go back to Germantown and try to find him?"

Nearly every voice in the troop was raised at once.

"Softly, softly, boys," said Bettle; "we don't want to attack the army. Two or three of my own fellows will be enough, I suppose," he added, addressing Clayton, "just to scour the field quietly."

Clayton nodded, and Bettle went on.

"Harry, you and Jem Woodward and Parker had better try it. Can you disguise yourselves so as not to be suspected?"

"I have a peddler's dress that my own brother wouldn't know me in," said Harry: "Woodward and Parker, here, have nothing to do but take off their belts and other traps, to pass for farmers."

"Very well," said Clayton: "the sooner you are off, the better."

"No doubt of that," said Harry, going out at once,

while Woodward and Parker, by simply laying aside their equipments, as Harry had suggested, were at once transformed into two plain young farmers, such as might have been drawn by curiosity to see a battlefield.

In a half-hour Harry reappeared. He had certainly contrived to disguise himself pretty thoroughly; he had on a pair of old leather breeches, polished by long use, strong, ribbed woolen stockings, and heavy cowhide shoes; his head was surmounted by what had been a cocked-hat, but of which the sides now hung down around his face in such a manner as to shade it considerably. He was ordinarily quite a good-looking fellow in the face, and his form was more than usually symmetrical; but now there was an awful squint in the eyes, and a suspicious-looking redness on the nose; the shoulders were drooped forward and the back was bowed, as if with the long carrying of some kind of burden, which was now represented by the peddler's pack, under which he shambled along with a knock-kneed, lop-sided sort of gait that was certainly as far removed from Harry's usual springy movement and firm tread as anything that could possibly be imagined.

Clayton absolutely did not recognize him until he spoke.

"Thee has certainly disguised thyself very effectually," he then said; "but can thee maintain that squint for any length of time?"

"Oh, yes," said Harry, laughing; "that's a trick I learned at school. Do you think I'll pass muster?"

"No doubt of it: if I didn't know thee after a half-hour's absence, it is hardly likely thee will meet any one who will recognize thee. What plan has thee in contemplation?"

"Well, I want Woodward and Parker to keep with me till we get near Germantown, and then my plan is, to separate, they going over to the orchard to see if he's there, while I go right into the camp with my pack, and try if I can find out anything among the soldiers."

"That will do," said Clavton. "And now you had better start."

The three men accordingly started on foot on their perilous errand,— perilous, because any accidental recognition on the part of the enemy would wind up their adventure with an exceedingly short turn beneath the nearest tree that had a limb strong enough to hang them on, as spies.

Arrived at the point intended by Harry, they separated, his two companions sauntering carelessly through the village, and thence across the meadows to the orchard, gaping about them as they passed among the sad scenes of devastation which a battle always leaves. As they crossed the lawn in front of Chew's house, they saw enough fearful evidences of how severe had been the fight. Parties were already at work removing the wounded; but they did not pause to look at them, passing on across the lawn and past the house to the orchard. A careful scrutiny among the bodies lying there, however, failed to detect any one that resembled the object of their search, and they finally left the place, and, in accordance with Harry's parting suggestions, returned by a roundabout way to where the Rangers were posted.

Harry, in the mean time, shambled into the lines with

his pack, and soon contrived to mingle with a group of soldiers off duty, and to get into conversation with them.

"Hello there! Linkum Lankum," said one of these, "don't bring that 'ere conk o' yourn nigh my catridge-box, or you'll blow it up. Look out there, Billy, he's got his swivel eye on yourn!"

"Who keers if he is?" said Billy; "'tain't got nothin' but a twist o' pigtail in it——"

"Which hain't?—the conk, or the eye, or the catridge-box? Blow me if I know which you mean."

"Doan't 'ee be a chaffin' th' poor tramp," said another, with a strong Devonshire accent; "coom here, old chap, an' open thy pack an' let'n see what thee's gotten."

"Here; just light my pipe first," said the first speaker, thrusting a black "dudheen" against the red nose, which certainly looked fiery enough for the purpose, and attempting at the same time to take hold of it with the other hand.

In an instant the wrist was seized, his heels flew up, and he lay on the broad of his back, his position being thus suddenly changed by a dexterous backward trip which Harry gave him, without raising a hand except to seize the fellow's wrist.

Furious with rage at his defeat, and the jeering laughter of his companions, the soldier sprang to his feet, and, drawing his bayonet from its sheath, rushed at him with a savage oath.

Harry had, for the moment, forgotten his assumed character when he tripped the fellow, and it was too late now to mend the matter: he was in for it. However, instead of striking his assailant, he contented imself with seizing his wrist as he made a blow at im, saying, with well-affected dismay,—

"Gentlemen, will you see a poor man murdered because he didn't want his nose pulled?"

"Dom'd if we wull," said Devonshire, a fellow as tout and burly as one of his own county's shortorned bulls, seizing his comrade by the shoulders; we waen't ha' no moor stickin' work to-day. Oi oald 'ee to let un aloan. If 'ee mun foight, tak off n's co-at an' go at un loike a mon, and not loike a luidy Frencher. I'll back th' tramp agin un for half--crow-an."

"A mill! a mill!" exclaimed the reckless soldiers, all pringing to their feet. "Form a ring."

The battle was short. Harry, not wishing to disgure his opponent, and being anxious at the same ime to avoid attracting the attention of any of the fficers who might be near, brought it summarily to a lose, after parrying one or two passes, by a left-handed low on the fellow's chest which knocked the breath ut of his body, and the body itself clear out of the ing.

"There! Oi toald 'ee soa," said Devonshire. "When hee's gotten thy wind agin, thee'd betther shake honds n' be doon wi' un."

"Fight done, with the first man floored. That's air," said the others, assisting the discomfited soldier o rise. "Shake hands with him, Jack, and don't bear nalice."

"I don't bear no malice," said the latter, as soon as e had recovered breath enough to speak, "an' I hope ou don't," he added, extending his hand frankly nough to Harry; "I had no business to chaff you at first, an' I don't want no more o' your left-handers, thank'e; I'd as lief be kicked by a hoss."

Harmony being restored, together with Harry's squint, which he had dispensed with during the passage at arms, two straight eyes being none too many in boxing, all sat down again, and examined the contents of the pack which was spread upon the ground, while Harry endeavored, by cautious questions, to ascertain whether they knew anything of Frank.

Not making much progress in this way, he changed his plan for a bolder one, and, describing Frank's appearance accurately, inquired of his late opponent if he had seen such a person since the battle.

"What do you want to know for?" asked the latter, a little suspiciously.

"Why, you see," said Harry, confidentially, and lying dreadfully, "I'm sorry to say, though he's a rebel, he's my brother; and this morning, when he found there was to be a battle, what does he do but saddle his gray mare and take father's short musket an' ride off like mad afore we could stop him? I holloed after him he'd better not try fightin' his majesty's troops that way, but he said he reckoned he could pick up a sword an' pistols somewhere, and rode off, an' I hain't seen him since."

"Do'e think un's kilt?" inquired Devonshire.

"I don't know," said Harry, dolefully; "I'm afeard so; he's a dreadful obstropolous fellow when he gets a fightin', an' I don't b'lieve he'd run away to save his life. I wouldn't mind givin' a pound of pigtail I've got in my pocket to any gentleman that would help me to find out whether he's dead, or wounded, or only took prisoner."

"Just wait here," said the man with whom he had fought, who seemed to have conceived rather a liking for him, "just wait here while I go over to the guard-house an' see if he's among the prisoners. But stay—what shall I tell him if he's there?"

"Tell him his brother Harry's here from Wissahickon."

The soldier went to the guard-house, which was a short distance off, being one of the houses in the village, which had been temporarily occupied for the purpose. In a few minutes he returned, and informed Harry that his brother was there, sure enough a prisoner, but alive and unhurt.

Could he see him?

Yes, the officer in command had given permission, and he might come over at once.

Leaving his pack on the ground, Harry accompanied his quondam adversary to the place, and among the crowd of prisoners discovered Frank, leaning against the wall near the fireplace.

"There he is," said he. "May I go and speak to him?"

The soldier looked at the officer in charge, who merely nodded; Harry immediately shambled across the room toward Frank, who, after a keen glance, advanced a step or two to meet him.

"Oh, Frank, Frank!" said Harry, in a tremulous voice, throwing his arms around him, and bending his head down on his shoulder, till he had mastered the laughter with which he was almost bursting, "why couldn't you stay at home, instead of comin' out to fight against your lawful king?" And, overcome by his feelings, Harry hid his face again on Frank's neck, close to his ear, and whispered, rapidly, " Look out for us; we'll be on the track."

It is hardly necessary to say that Frank had recognized his *brother* before this; and he merely gripped the latter's arm strongly, in answer to the concluding remark.

After a great many words of admonition and consolation, interspersed with a good deal of " Oh Frank"-ing, and some pathetic allusions to his deserted father and his gray hairs, to all which Frank listened and replied—when he could edge in a reply through the torrent of words—with as sober a face as Harry's own, the latter took his departure, promising to come back with some clothes and other matters.

Returning to where he had left his pack, he first handed over the tobacco he had promised to his companion, and then drove a sharp bargain for some trinkets that had taken the fancy of two or three of the men; which bargain came to a disastrous close, owing to the fact that the price of the trinkets was two-and-sixpence, while eleven pence ha'-penny was all that could be raised by the group.

Harry would have distributed the trinkets among them, had he not feared that such unprecedented liberality might raise suspicions either of his sanity or of the truth of his assumed character.

Loading his pack, therefore, he bade them good-by, and shambled off in the direction of the Wissahickon.

CHAPTER XX.

HARRY made the best of his way to the rendezvous, and reported progress. He had been unable to ascertain when the army would remove to Philadelphia, and the only thing that could be done was to keep a sharp lookout on their movements, and be ready to act when the moment came.

Scouting-parties were sent out, which hovered around the army continually for the next two weeks, carefully avoiding observation, and refraining from molesting any of the straggling parties which they might easily have cut off.

Harry had gone back once after his first visit, with some clothes for Frank. These had been inspected before he was allowed to take them to him, to see that nothing which might aid in his escape was concealed in them. This did not trouble Harry in the least, as he had prepared himself for it by very carefully putting nothing of the kind about them.

When they were restored to him, however, he made an awkward grasp at them and let them fall upon the ground. While gathering them up he contrived, unperceived, to slip a short, broad dagger into one of the pockets, and then handed them to Frank.

On the evening of the 18th, Clayton's scouts brought in word that the army was about to move the next morning. The whole force, consisting of his own and McLane's men, was put in motion toward Germantown, about an hour before daybreak. They did not go near the village, however, but posted themselves in a wood along the road between it and Philadelphia. Patiently they waited there for five mortal hours, receiving occasional information from their scouts of the preparations of the army for departure. At last the head of the column appeared in sight, and the Rangers retired deeper into the wood, leaving Jem Woodward, and one or two others of the most active men, perched in some thick trees a short distance from the roadside as lookouts. Column after column passed, regiment after regiment, in interminable succession, as Clayton could see from his concealment, and still no signal from the lookouts.

Still the army filed along, until the rear of the last column had passed out of view, and still no signal. A moment afterward, however, Woodward slid down his tree, and, going to Clayton, told him that the prisoners were coming down the road some distance in the rear of the main army, under a strong escort.

"How many?" asked Clayton.

"Not less than three hundred, I should think," said Woodward.

"We can break that number by an unexpected attack," said Clayton, calmly, "if we know where to attack them. Could thee recognize Frank among them?"

"No," said Woodward, "they were too far off; but I could see that they are in two bodies, one in front, and the other in the rear, with the prisoners between them; there is a file of light horsemen on each flank of the prisoners, besides."

While this conversation was going on, the escort
[w]ere coming down the road slowly, and, though cer-
[ta]inly not in disorder, still, somewhat loosely, and what
[W]oodward called "squandery." The prisoners were
[en]closed as he had said, and were marching along in a
[co]nfused crowd, without much regard to order.

Harry had gone over in the morning, in his ped-
[l]er's costume, but minus his pack, to accompany his
[u]nfortunate brother" to the city, and the two were
[to]gether in the crowd. As they came near the wood,
[w]here Harry knew their friends were concealed, the
[tw]o men gradually, without attracting attention, placed
[th]emselves on the edge of the body of prisoners and
[clo]se to the file of horsemen, on the side next the
[wo]od.

The road was bordered by a tall, thick hedge, which
[ra]n along to the corner of the wood; at about forty
[ya]rds from this point there was a small gap in the
[lo]wer part of the hedge, barely large enough to allow
[a]man to pass through at the risk of a little scratching.
[A]s they came opposite this, Frank, whose keen eye
[ha]d noticed this, and whose ready wit formed his plan
[in] the instant, edged as close as possible to the horse
[by] which he was walking, stumbled, and fell upon his
[ha]nds directly in front of the beast; so close, that his
[ri]der, to keep him from tumbling over Frank, drew him
[up] with a violence that threw him upon his haunches.
[A]t the same instant, without rising, Frank leaped for-
[w]ard from all fours like a cat, pitched headforemost
[ri]ght through the gap, and then, springing to his feet,
[ra]n at full speed, sheltered by the hedge, for the wood.
Two or three pistols were fired after him at random,
[an]d several horsemen made a rush at the hedge, but

were recalled by a sharp, stern order from the officer: "Close up, there! close up! Look to the other prisoners;" and then, riding up to Harry, was beginning, wrathfully, "What does this mean, sir? Is this any of your—" when the appearance of the latter's face—one eye looking at the gap through which Frank had disappeared so unceremoniously, and the other looking at himself, the under jaw dropped, and the whole countenance divested of every expression but that of blank amazement—checked him, and, muttering, "He had no hand in it," he spurred forward to the head of the column, and detached a party in pursuit.

These galloped along the road toward the wood, in order to get around the hedge, and disappeared. Then came a crackle of rifle-shots, a sudden check in the regular beat of hoofs, and then four riderless horses came tearing down the road with dangling reins and flying stirrups, followed by a mounted horse whose rider, holding a rein in each hand, as if to steady himself, was reeling and swaying in the saddle like a drunken man. As the horse came to the ranks, he was stopped, and his rider, with a last effort to preserve his balance, dropped his chin upon his breast and lurched heavily out of the saddle into the arms of two or three of the men who started forward to catch him. They laid him on a sloping bank on the opposite side of the road from that where Frank had escaped, beneath a large chestnut-tree; but he was evidently dying.

"How did it happen, Hudson?" inquired the officer, coming up and stooping over him.

"They've—hit—me—sir," said the man, gasping out a word at a time.

"Who?"

"The—rebels—sir.—Woods—full of" They were his last words.

"Rebels! In the woods! There's treachery here. Where's that peddler? Secure him, some of you; I'll have some talk with him after awhile."

The officer then hurried to the head of his men, and the advance pushed rapidly forward toward the corner of the wood. They turned the end of the hedge, and penetrated some distance into the wood, but met nobody except the remnant of the party that had pursued Frank; the Rangers, after the single volley from the Mac Allan rifles, having fallen back, lest the report should draw the army upon them.

"Where are the rebels?" said the officer.

"Back yonder, sir, in the woods," said the man who was addressed; "they're too strong for us, without a reinforcement."

"Well, here comes one," said the officer, as a regiment came down the road at quick step and halted at the edge of the wood.

"One of our prisoners escaped just now, sir," he said, speaking to the colonel of the regiment, "and the men sent to retake him have been fired on by a party of the rebels who are somewhere in the wood here."

"We must let him go, sir," said the colonel: "it will be useless to attempt to catch these flying Irregulars, of whom the force must consist, while in the woods. How strong do you take them to be?"

"About two hundred, sir," said the trooper who had previously been speaking, in answer to a look from his officer.

"Rather strong for your force, hampered with prisoners. Close up your men, and I will remain with you until we reach Philadelphia."

The officer bowed, and, having formed his men in their original order, the whole body proceeded together along the road. When the order was given to secure Harry, he was placed on horseback, under the charge of two troopers, one of whom was our friend Devonshire, with orders that he should be instantly shot or cut down should he attempt to escape.

Harry submitted very meekly, and with as injured a look as he could assume without disturbing the usual engaging expression of his countenance. Scrambling awkwardly into the saddle, where it was a sight to see him with his round back, his loose-looking legs with feet thrust into the stirrups to the ankles, each hand, with the palm upward, grasping with the thumb and finger a rein, which hung dangling, jolting up and down with the motion of the horse as he moved along, he took his place between Devonshire and his companion, the latter being on the side of the road next the hedge.

"Don't you think it's hard, mister," said Harry, addressing Devonshire in a low voice, "to make me, a loyal subject, prisoner, just 'cause my rebel brother contrived to get away?"

"Whoy, yea," said Devonshire, "it doan't seem 'zactly right, 'case oi saw un all th' toim and oi doant think 'ee had nowt to do wi' un; but oi baent meanin' to let un git off for a' that. Doant think there's much danger, though, the way 'ee roides—tak care, there! thee'll surely toomble off and brek thy neck," seizing Harry's arm as he manifested symptoms of slipping helplessly off sideways, and pulling him straight in the saddle.

All the while Harry had been trying to judge by the *feel* of the horse beneath him—by his step and motion—of his capacity for a race, and had satisfied himself that he had both strength and speed.

Deceived by his slovenly, awkward manner of riding, and feeling sure that the first motion of his horse out of a slow trot would dismount him, they had neglected to secure him in any other way than that of merely placing him between them. He rode along dismally enough, bumping up and down with the slow but springy trot of the horse, till they came opposite the wood, which, I should have said before, was not fenced in, but lay open to the road, with a cart-way running into it.

Suddenly Devonshire's horse—perhaps moved thereunto by the instigation of a chestnut-burr which Harry had contrived slyly to place under the crupper of his saddle, in one of his own awkward lurches—first sent his heels into the air, and then went off into an exhibition of rearing and plunging, complicated with a network, so to speak, of fantastic capers, which not only gave our stout friend enough to do to keep his seat at all, but, by the infection which bad example is pretty sure to spread, set half the horses in his neighborhood capering also from sympathy.

Having thus cleverly got rid of Devonshire and drawn off the attention of the rest, Harry took his next step, which was to wheel his own horse suddenly, draw a short dirk, and, by a touch of its point in the flank, drive him with a spring full against the horse of the trooper who remained beside him, at the same time giving the man a blow with his fist which drove him bodily out of the saddle; for Harry, reckless as he was, rarely shed blood unless he thought it necessary, and therefore did not use his dirk.

Down went the horse, and away went his rider two or three yards from him, before the shock and the powerful blow; and, as the latter opened his eyes again, the first thing he saw was a horse's belly, as Harry's beast leaped clear over fallen horse and rider together. As he raised his head, he heard a voice exclaim,—

"By ——, it's that peddler rascal'! Fire at him! bring him down!"

A rattle of musketry followed, and, as the fallen trooper raised himself on his elbow,—he was too prudent to stand up right in the line of fire,—he thought at first that the fugitive had been hit; for he was hanging by the side of his horse, with one leg over the saddle and one arm over his neck, while the beast was flying down the cart-road.

"After him, men! after him!" shouted the officer. "Five guineas to the man that brings him in, alive or dead!"

Twenty or thirty of the best-mounted troopers instantly dashed into the wood in pursuit. As soon as Harry perceived that he had them between him and the fire of the infantry, to the astonishment of his pursuers, he swung himself up in his seat again, without checking his horse's speed, waved his hand to them, exclaiming, "Good-by, gentlemen: I'm going to see if I can persuade my brother back," gave his horse another prick with the dirk (having no spurs), darted off the road into the thickest part of the wood, and was out of sight among the trees and bushes in a moment.

They did not follow him any farther; it was too evidently useless,—besides the danger of falling into an ambuscade of his friends, who, they felt very well assured, were not far off.

They accordingly returned to the main road, and reported how they had lost him.

"Those are no' common men," said the officer in command of the escort. "Does any one know them?"

"Please your honor," said an old soldier, advancing and touching his cap, "I think I know 'em. The dark little chap, the one as got away first, that's Frank Lightfoot his name is, was a wagon-boy in the army when we was cut up by the Frenchers an' Injins out there at Great Meadows, by Fort Duquesne; he's now among Clayton's Rangers, an' one o' the best men in the troop."

"Well, who is the other?"

"If I'm not mistaken, it's the only other one that's equal to him. They call him Dandy Harry."

"Why didn't you tell this before?" said the officer, angrily.

"Your honor didn't ask me anything about it, an' it wasn't my place to push in my advice when it wasn't asked. Besides, Frank was a prisoner anyhow, and I didn't mistrust Harry till I seen him knock Wilson yonder and his horse, both down, an' ride over 'em."

"Well, we're a sharp-sighted set," said the officer. "I wonder who'll make fools of us next time. Close up, forward, march!" And so the army went to Philadelphia, minus two of its prisoners.

CHAPTER XXI.

"How did they take thee?" inquired Clayton of Frank, as they rode quietly toward their rendezvous.

"Why, look'e here," said Frank "I got mixed up with our prisoners when them fellows run through us there in Germantown. You know they got squandered away, an' blamed if they didn't carry me off right in the middle of 'em. I tried my best to git out o' the muss, but couldn't, for they were all round me, an' some of 'em, I found, know'd me, an' kep' too sharp an eye on me to give me any chance. Then we come up with a ridg'ment, an' they fell in with it, an' I had to give it up."

Frank was a man of few words, and this was all the account he gave of his adventure.

Harry, however, made amends at the camp-fire that night, by giving a full and ludicrous account of his own and Frank's adventures in the British camp, and wound up by a descriptive ballad which he improvised for the occasion: it was never reduced to writing, and therefore I am unable to give it.

The season passed on without anything of note having taken place in which the Rangers were immediately concerned.

Count Donop, with twelve hundred picked Hessians, had attacked the American defenses, garrisoned by four hundred men, at Red Bank, in pursuance of General Howe's determination to sweep away the whole of the American defenses on the river, and had sacrificed his own life and that of some four hundred of his men in the vain attempt.

The men-of-war had thundered away at Fort Mifflin, on the opposite side of the river, to no purpose, having achieved nothing but the loss of a number of men and of two ships, the Augusta and Merlin, which took fire and blew up.

The attack had been renewed, the garrisons compelled to abandon their defenses by the overwhelming force which was sent against them, and the river below the city, to the ocean, was in command of the enemy.

Lydia Darrah, the brave Quaker woman, had saved the American army from surprise and defeat, by her walk through the snow to Whitemarsh to give notice of the intended attack.

The British had marched out in the dead of the succeeding night, very slyly indeed, reached Whitemarsh unperceived, and—found the army drawn up, cannon mounted, and all so prepared to receive them that, after dancing distractedly around them for three days, on the fourth they scampered back, as one of their officers expressed it, "like a parcel of fools."

It is a sight to be remembered, by us who can call it up in vision, that small, weak, sickly figure, clad in plain Quaker garb, urging its solitary way on foot through the cold December dawn, ankle-deep in the falling snow, to save an army from destruction.

That woman walked, altogether, twenty-eight miles in the dismal weather, on that day, carrying with her, over the last five miles, from Frankford, a bag containing twenty-five pounds of flour, the necessity of procuring which had been her excuse for leaving the city; and General Howe had furnished her with a pass! I rather think it was Lydia who "made fools of us next time."

Then there was a lull in the storm of war; the two great clouds had rolled asunder, and lay grumbling and growling at each other twenty miles apart, one along the hills of the Schuylkill at Valley Forge, the other along the shores of the Delaware at Philadelphia.

But the British, as I said before, had not a time of uninterrupted comfort in Philadelphia, by reason of the very improper and unseasonable restlessness of the two bodies of Irregulars who had taken upon themselves to beleaguer the city.

They caused so much annoyance by intercepting supplies, cutting off foraging-parties, and playing all manner of mad pranks generally, that the British commander got out of all patience, and at last detached Captain Gardner, with a considerable force, to scour the country and drive these pestilent marauders away.

The captain had no trouble in fulfilling his instructions to the letter; not the least: the only difficulty was that the "marauders" did not *stay* away, not seeming to understand that they were defeated. In fact, they led him as uneasy a dance among the rocks and hills of the Schuylkill and Wissahickon as David led King Saul over the mountains of Judea.

He would hear of them somewhere, and sally forth to capture or disperse them; when he arrived at the place, behold, they were gone! By the time he had got comfortably over the fatigue of his march, word would come that they were up again in some other quarter, and away he would go, only to come back again with the same report,—"left the place." Now it was Clayton's Rangers who were at work, now it was McLane's men, now the two together, now both up at once in different places, till both the general and the captain were half distracted by the ceaseless activity of this intangible swarm of hornets.

It was an easy enough matter for both Clayton and Captain McLane to avoid these scouring-parties when they chose, having always timely notice given by their scouts of any movement against them.

They did not always choose to escape, however; and two or three sharp skirmishes among broken ground and trees, and from which he was obliged to retreat with some loss, convinced Captain Gardner not only that the Rangers understood their own way of fighting better than he did, but that he was likely to have his hands full at any kind of fighting. He learned to appreciate better the various and thorough training of Clayton's force particularly.

The duty he was engaged in, so far as the Rangers were concerned, was irksome to him, besides, from personal reasons. His life had been spared, by Barton's forbearance, at the spring below New Castle, under circumstances which would have warranted him in taking it; he had been treated with the utmost kindness while among the Rangers, during the few days he remained among them, had formed a very pleasant acquaintance with the officers, and had been released upon his parole after a very short detention. More recently, he had been treated with rare courtesy and consideration by Clayton, who, as has been stated, allowed him to pass with a much inferior force, when he might have captured him with ease.

On these accounts, the service he was performing was very unpleasant to him, and he had made two or three ineffectual attempts to be relieved from it and have some other officer employed in his place.

While the Irregulars on the one side, and the Regulars on the other, were leading each other this kind of contra-dance, the female department of the Free Quaker church were not idle; and their activity found vent—as I suppose that of most women who have not discovered that they have a "mission" does, naturally—in needles and thread.

On a crisp, clear afternoon in January, a party of them were assembled in the large parlor of a house on the west side of Water Street. The room looked out over an open lawn to the river; for the unsightly warehouses which now lumber the bank were not then in existence, and the view was unobstructed, except by the trunks of two or three large and now leafless trees which stood upon the lawn. Before it spread the noble river, its broad bosom sheeted with ice, bound in which lay the black hulls of the men-of-war, and beyond lay the low, beach-like Jersey shore, rising gradually to the northward into rolling ground as it receded from the water.

The wind was high, and the leafless trees rocked and groaned and rattled their bare arms together in the blast which came shrieking from the distant ocean, through the moaning pines of mid-Jersey and across the frozen surface of the river. It was cold, bitter cold, and the streets were almost deserted. The Hessian sentry, with his musket clasped to his side by his arm, blew his aching fingers through his ice-fringed mustache, as he paced up and down his beat, stamping along as if trying what kind of sewing his Majesty's contract-shoemakers had put into his brogans. The woodsawyer stopped as the last section of each stick fell from his saw-horse, and thrashed his arms across his breast, with a "whew!" at each blow of his heavy arms, as if it had knocked the breath out of him. Their noses, as well as those of the few passengers who were in the street, were each ornamented by a pendent jewel at the end thereof, which hung there undisturbed, for it was too cold to think of taking hands out of pockets to use either handkerchiefs or fingers. Here and there was a poor, thinly-clad, shivering form, stealing along in search of chips to make a scanty fire for other poor squalid little forms to cower over; for firewood was scarce, even for those who had means to buy it, and but little was left to be gleaned by those who had not.

While all was thus bleak and dreary outside, the scene within the large room in which the women were assembled was bright and cheerful. True, the walls, instead of being covered with the wonderful specimens of machine-produced art with which paper-hangers so liberally cover walls nowadays, were painted a sober drab, and the ceiling was not as high by a couple of feet as we think it necessary to have them now; but the floor was carpeted, in itself an evidence of some wealth, and a bright wood-fire, plentifully supplied, was burning in the large Franklin stove, whose brass mountings and those of the fender in front of it shone with all the luster which powdered brick-dust and flannel, applied with all the vigor of a sturdy housemaid's arm, could produce. In front of the fender was spread a large bear-skin rug, on which lay a plump gray-mottled cat, evidently a privileged pet, basking in the heat of the fire, and purring dreamily.

In short, the gathering was what is now called a "sewing-circle," at which, as is well known, there is always, nowadays, an immense amount of work done, with a very small amount of talk and tea-drinking.

The party with whom I have to do at present were not working, however, for the natives of Booriobhoola Gha; neither were they making flannel shirts to keep warm the other sans-culottes gentlemen in Africa, who eschew all clothing except a breech-cloth and a general smearing over with rancid cocoanut oil; nor were they working for the Greeks, nor for anybody else out of sight and hearing across the ocean; for, as the splenetic John Randolph once told a lady who was commiserating the sufferings of the Greeks during their revolution, and lamenting that she was not among them to relieve them, "Madam, the Greeks are at your door."

There was suffering enough within twenty miles, in the rude slab huts imbedded in the snow among the hills of Valley Forge, to absorb all the spare sympathy, as well as the spare time and money, of any given number of philanthropists; and it was to do what they could toward relieving this suffering that they were met together on this clear, crisp January afternoon.

There was a sprinkling of the gayer dresses of the "world's people" among the party; but most of them wore the unmistakable, plain garb of the Friends.

Across one end of the room was spread a quilting-frame, on which was stretched a quilt about half finished; around it were about a dozen elderly ladies, who were busily stitching along the white chalk-lines with which its surface was latticed. These were all stout, comfortable, grandmotherly-looking dames, ranging from fifty to sixty, well preserved, with complexions still fresh and ruddy, and some of them hardly more wrinkled than their granddaughters.

Around a circular table which stood about the middle of the room, in front of the fireplace, was another group, of younger ladies, some of them the daughters of those around the quilting-frame, and employed quite as industriously as their mothers, in cutting out and sewing strong coarse cotton shirts, and—some of the older ones—knitting heavy woolen stockings.

At the other end were four or five girls, of perhaps from sixteen to twenty years of age, seated on the carpet, around a flag which they had just finished embroidering and had spread out upon the carpet to admire. It was not large, being only about two feet square, but large enough for the purpose it was intended for, —a cavalry pennon.

It was not a very unusual employment for a party of ladies in those days; but in the present instance there was a curious contrast between that battle-flag, with its deep-blue ground and border of crimson silk and gold, and the plain dresses of the girls around it, from which every warm or bright color, every appearance or suggestion of ornament, had been studiously banished.

If the dresses were plain, however, the faces above them were not; for young Quakeresses then were as pretty as young Quakeresses are now; and no ungracefulness of dress or soberness of color can entirely neutralize the beauty of the delicate, regular features, the smooth, glossy hair, and the fresh complexions—

when their bonnets are off. I have not a word to say in mitigation of the "regulation" Quaker bonnet, which would eclipse the face of—I won't say Venus, for I consider it an insult to a modest woman to liken her to that Queen Light-o'-love, but of—well, say—Hebe.

"Isn't it beautiful, Mary?" said one of them, addressing a girl of about twenty, who sat opposite her, a tall, slender, queenly-looking blonde. "I wish Captain Clayton was here to see it. What does thee intend to say when thee gives it to him? Thee must make a speech, and he must make another in answer."

"I'm afraid," interposed one of the ladies at the table, "that it won't be so beautiful after it has been carried a year, and gone through the battles of that time, daughter Sarah. Gunpowder, smoke, and bullets make sad work with fine clothes."

"Well, I hope it won't get spoiled; don't thee, Mary?" said Sarah.

"No; I hope to see it come home riddled with bullet-holes," said Mary, spiritedly.

"Mercy!" said the younger girl, raising her hands in affected horror, "and spoil all our beautiful work! I hope it won't be Sam that carries it, for fear he might come home riddled too——"

"Sarah—Sarah Wheeler!" said one of the elderly ladies at the quilt, who overheard her, "thee should not jest on such grave subjects. If thy brother should be brought home wounded or dead, thee would never forgive thyself for this trifling."

The girl colored under the rebuke, and said no more. She was a sister of Wheeler, whom I have mentioned several times; while the queenly-looking blonde was the only sister of Wetherill, and the only—something else, which brought the rich blood over her transparent face and neck when his name was mentioned—of Clayton.

I am a terribly poor hand at describing love-passages, and, having Bettle's affair on my hands, I have spared myself and you the bore of following a second trail of this kind, step by step. In this instance, therefore, I will only give results.

Clayton and Mary Wetherill had been "engaged" since about a month before the flare-up in the Society to which they both belonged, and she was naturally one of the first of his friends whom he had consulted previous to taking the important step which had so changed the current of his life.

Some of these friends had given him their opinion in a way that was as non-committal as a judge's charge, and which might be taken either way; some had fairly turned their backs upon him; but Mary Wetherill never faltered.

"Thee is right, Ellis," she said, promptly, when he mentioned his "concern" to her; "thee is right. If it is the duty of Friends to side in opinion with the Congress and the army, it is their duty to side with them in person too. He has no right to assist by counsel who is not ready and willing to assist with the sword."

"I knew thee would think so, Mary," said Clayton, "but I wanted to hear it from thy own lips. My own convictions of duty in this matter are clear and decided; and I shall carry them out with all the vigor of body and soul which my Maker has given me."

So they parted for the time. Clayton set to work, as I stated in the beginning of my narrative, to raise his troop, succeeding as I have already stated.

22*

She had parted with him again on the morning of the 4th of August, an hour or two before he wheeled into the line of the American army opposite the State-House, at the head of his troop, and from that time had never seen him, nor, but once, heard directly from him, though she had heard a good deal of him in the flying rumors which chased each other ceaselessly through that busy summer and autumn.

Her love for Clayton was fully as deep and strong as Jenny Sanford's was for Bettle, but it was as different as her nature was. Strong and self-reliant, her husband must be one by whose side she could stand like a palm-tree by its mate; to whom she could be counselor, companion, friend.

Jenny's nature was very different from this. Though about the same age as Mary, she was much younger in character. She was child-like, more frank and impulsive, without a touch of the pride which was a predominant trait in Mary's character, plain Quaker though she was; entirely free from anything like queenly dignity and reserve, but simply a tender, warm-hearted, lovable girl, who would cling to the man she loved, as the ivy clings to the strong tower, enveloping it gradually in its warm, ever-growing mantle.

When the storm should sweep down the palm-tree, his mate would stand and wave her plumed head over him in grand, majestic grief. When the earthquake should hurl down the tower, the ivy would go down with him and—die.

Such was the difference between the two girls. The idea of the flag had been first suggested by Sarah Wheeler, and had been seized upon with avidity by the other girls, and they had for some time been busily engaged at it. It was now finished, and the next thing was to present it.

This was not such an easy matter, inasmuch as they, the donors, were cooped up in the city, without much chance of getting out, even if any of them had known where to look for the donees in their eccentric wanderings.

"Now, won't it be too bad," said Sarah Wheeler, "if, after all the trouble we've had, we can't catch one of these Jack-o'-lanterns of Rangers to hand it to? This would be such a nice time, when we are all here, to give it to Captain Clayton."

"Thee should say Ellis; not captain, Sarah," said her mother, reprovingly. "I wish thee would get out of that way thee has of giving vain titles."

"Why, mother," interrupted Sarah, "he *is* a captain, isn't he? And why shouldn't I call him so? Didn't we call James Pemberton clerk of the meeting, because he *was* clerk? And why shouldn't we call Ellis Clayton captain of the Rangers, when he *is* captain? I don't see that one is a vain title more than the other."

What answer her mother would have made to this style of argument, it is hard to say; for at this moment the door opened, and in walked the subject of the discussion, accompanied by Harry.

"Why, here's the man himself," said Sarah Wheeler, joyfully, springing forward, and seizing him by the hand. "Come in, thou man of peace: we were just talking about thee."

"Thee is welcome, friend Ellis," said the mistress of the house, coming forward. "Come near the fire, thee and thy friend: you must be cold this bitter day."

Clayton and his companion drew near the fire with

manifest enjoyment of its heat, while Mary placed herself by his side, having been the second — Sarah Wheeler having sprung forward ahead of her — to greet him. She did this pleasantly, even warmly, but still with an indescribable something of dignified reticence strongly in contrast with the frank, open demonstration of delight which Sarah had shown. Considering how long they had been separated, any one not knowing the actual circumstances would have reversed the real position of the two girls toward him.

There was no lack of feeling on Mary's part, as Clayton knew right well; but that dominant pride of hers kept down any manifestation of it in the presence of others. He himself was no more demonstrative than she, though feeling quite as deeply; but with him it was the effect of a grave, impassive temperament, to which a demonstrative display of any kind would have been unnatural, rather than of any effort of pride to keep it down. On the whole, they were admirably suited to each other.

"But what brought thee here among the Philistines, Captain Clayton?" said Sarah, with a slight emphasis on the word captain and a sly glance at her mother. "Ain't thee afraid they'll catch thee and serve thee as their ancestors did Samson? If thee could only pull down the walls of that temple of Dagon, the Walnut Street Prison, and bury its high-priest Cunningham in the ruins, it might be——"

"Sarah, Sarah!" interposed her mother, holding up her finger reprovingly.

"I can't help it, mother," said she: "when I think of the way our poor prisoners are treated there, I get out of all patience, and only wish I were a man, to punish the villain."

"Well," said her mother, "there's no use in trying to bridle thy tongue. I believe thee's incorrigible."

"My errand here to-day," said Clayton, "had reference to the very place thee speaks of. Three of my own men were taken prisoners in that unfortunate affair at Germantown, and I came in to gain some tidings of them."

"Did thee succeed, Ellis?" said Mary.

"Only too well, Mary. They are dead,—literally starved to death. May God forgive their murderer as I *try* to do, and show him more mercy than he ever showed to any who were in his power!"

"I suppose we ought all to say the same thing," said Sarah; "but I must say I don't feel exactly clear in my own mind about it. How does thee feel?" she added, suddenly turning to Harry. "Does thee try to forgive him, too?"

"Oh, no," said Harry, quietly, in his soft, musical voice, and shaking his head gently: "*I* don't forgive him; and I'm afraid he'll need a great deal of mercy if he ever falls into the hands of our men or Captain McLane's."

"What would they do with him?" inquired one of the elderly ladies at the quilting-frame.

"Hang him," said Harry, placidly.

"Hang him, eh?" said a voice, as the door swung open, and three or four men in British uniform, with an officer at their head, strode into the room. "Then we had better get two of the hangmen out of the way. Madam," added the officer, addressing the mistress of the house, "I beg your pardon for this intrusion, but I am sent to apprehend a desperate rebel who is here in disguise. Captain Clayton, you and your companion are my prisoners."

CHAPTER XXII.

The door remained opened, no one, in the general consternation caused by this announcement, having thought of shutting it, and the four soldiers stood abreast, between it and the two Rangers, with muskets presented and fixed bayonets.

"You had better surrender quietly, gentlemen; resistance will only involve bloodshed, which I would much rather spare these ladies the sight of."

Clayton had calmly folded his arms while the other was speaking, and stood, with Mary close beside him, looking him straight in the eyes, with perfect calmness and self-possession.

The last word was on the officer's lips, when Harry suddenly, without the slightest warning, sprang, with a leap like a panther's, right over the bayonet of one of the soldiers, driving his heels against the fellow's breast with tremendous force and felling him like an ox, and was through the door and out of sight before the others fully comprehended what had happened.

The officer uttered a sudden exclamation, rather more terse and emphatic than he was in the habit of using before ladies, while his men, recovering from their momentary astonishment, rushed through the door, without waiting for orders, in the blind instinct of pursuit.

At the same instant, while the officer's attention was diverted, Clayton drew a pistol from his bosom, cocked it, and, laying his hand with a quiet but firm gripe upon the officer's shoulder, held the muzzle within an inch of his face, and said, in that calm, grave tone of his that nothing ever disturbed,—

"Thee labors under a mistake in calling me thy prisoner: I have no intention of being any one's prisoner. I don't wish to have bloodshed here, any more than thee does; and thee will therefore see the wisdom of requiring thy men to behave civilly and molest *no one* here. Leave thy sword where it is," he added, as the officer made an attempt to seize the handle: "if thee attempts to draw it or move away, or if thy men" —who had now returned—"come beyond the door, thee will be carried home. Order them to halt."

The officer did so, perforce, and the men stopped just within the door, while Clayton went on in the same cool, unimpassioned tone:

"Did thee suppose I was weak enough to thrust my head into the lion's jaws without having the means at hand of breaking his teeth if he attempted to close them?"

"Indeed!" said the officer; "and pray, sir, what means may you have of breaking the lion's teeth, as you phrase it?"

"I will show thee," said Clayton, giving a low whistle. It was answered immediately from the grounds in the rear of the house, and the next moment the tramp of feet was heard in the hall, and then twenty of the Rangers, with Frank and Harry among them, armed to the teeth, poured into the parlor.

"Thee sees," said Clayton. "Now order thy men to lay down their arms. If they stir for anything else, they are dead men."

The officer stood silent. It was quite an impressive tableau. He and Clayton stood in their original position, about the middle of the room, the latter's hand still upon his shoulder, and the cocked pistol, which had never wavered for a moment, still poking its muzzle within an inch or two of his face; the Rangers, who had stationed themselves between the two men and the soldiers, who remained by the door, stood there with pistol in each hand, holding the soldiers covered by the leveled pistols, and almost touching the bayonets of the "presented" muskets of the latter as they stood stolidly waiting for orders; the women, with the exception of Mary Wetherill and Sarah Wheeler, who kept their position near Clayton, were huddled in the corners, with their hands to their ears, waiting in terror for the explosion, which they thought, of course, was coming; while the gray-mottled cat, startled from her doze before the fire by the fall of the soldier whom Harry had kicked over, still stood upon the rug, with her back and tail arched, spitting and swearing in feline language furiously.

"Thee sees the odds against thee," said Clayton.

"Yes," said the officer, through his clinched teeth, "I see. I surrender, sir. Order arms"—to his men, who obeyed the order with pardonable alacrity "If it hadn't been for the mountebank trick of your follower there," he added, glancing wrathfully at Harry, "there might have been a different tale."

"Possibly," said Clayton; "but thee sees thee was mistaken in calling us prisoners. Now, I don't wish to be harsh with thee, and if thee will promise me upon thy honor that this family shall receive no further molestation, after we leave, I will release thee and thy men as soon as we are clear of the city"

"I'll promise that very willingly," said the officer; "though I had no intention of molesting them at any rate."

They now prepared to take their departure. In the mean time, Sarah Wheeler had been nudging and making faces at Mary, and pointing to the flag, which still lay upon the floor ; but the latter shook her head.

"Well," said Sarah, at last, "if thee won't, I will;" and, picking it up, she advanced with it toward Clayton, and handed it to him, saying, "Now that thy little affair with these friends is satisfactorily settled, I'll tell thee why we wanted to see thee. We want thee to take this piece of 'fine clothes,' as mother there calls it, to be the standard of thy troop, never to be lost, never to be given up, except to those who made it."

Clayton took the flag, and was about to reply, when she cut him short:

"There, now! thee needn't make a speech about it; we know by heart what it would be proper to say."

"Very well," said Clayton; "but will thee allow me to give it in charge to my standard-bearer now?"

"By all means," said she. "Who is he?"

"Here he stands," said Clayton, handing the flag to Harry.

"Thee will never disgrace it, I know," said Sarah, turning to Harry with a bright smile and a glance which brought the blood to his cheek, cool young gentleman as he was.

"I may die with it in my hand; it shall never leave me in any other way," said he, briefly, folding it up and placing it in his bosom.

At this moment Frank, who, with his habitual caution, had been keeping a sharp lookout on the river through the front windows, paying very little attention to this exceedingly informal flag-presentation, came up to Clayton, and whispered in his ear,—

"Marines puttin' off from one o' th' ships. Be quick."

Clayton instantly put his men in motion, gave a single pressure of Mary's hand, placed his prisoners in front, and in another moment the whole party had passed out at the back of the house, leaving the inmates in the utmost surprise at their sudden departure.

When fairly out, he stopped, and said to the Englishman,—

"There is a party of marines coming from one of the ships toward the house. We can fight them if necessary, but I don't want to fight here; we can escape and carry thee and thy men with us without difficulty; but I don't wish to leave the women alone to meet those who are coming. Will thee promise, as an officer and a gentleman, that thee will remain here till they come, and prevent any annoyance or insult to those in the house, if I release thee now?"

The officer hesitated a moment.

"If not," said Clayton, calmly, "we will remain and fight it out; but thee and all thy men will be the first victims, whoever else may fall. My object is to avoid strife and bloodshed here; thee may send them after us if thee chooses, and they may take us, if they can. There is no time to lose."

"I promise," said the officer, "with that understanding. Those in the house shall not be molested; but I shall lead the marines directly after you, I tell you candidly."

"Thee is at liberty," said Clayton; and, leaving them to return into the house, he moved rapidly with his men across the grounds which opened upon Front Street, passed into the street, crossed it, passed through an alley which led off from it, thence through another and another, zigzagging along until they reached the edge of Dock Creek, where he found the rest of the troop waiting impatiently for them, having become alarmed by their delay.

The bitter cold of the weather, as I said before, had almost emptied the streets of passengers; and, having nothing unusual about their dress, their arms being all carefully hidden beneath their coats, the Rangers had attracted very little attention from the few they met.

Mounting their horses at once, they formed upon the bank of the creek and awaited the approach of the marines. The latter, who had been tracking them faithfully, halted as soon as they came in sight of the powerful force drawn up to receive them.

I have no fight to describe in this instance. There would have been, however, if the peppery old marine officer could have had his way; for, with a force of twenty-five men, all told, he at first "pooh-poohed" the suggestion of the other officer that it might not be altogether safe or prudent, with so small a force, and on foot, to attack a body of eighty or ninety, admirably mounted, as they could see, even though they were "Yankees."

"Why, sir," said the marine, "do you mean to say that twenty-five of his Majesty's picked men could be made to turn their backs on that gang of clod-hoppers, mounted though they are? You must excuse me, sir, but I can't conceive the possibility of such a thing."

"Those are not clod-hoppers, as you call them, sir," said the other, "but a band of picked men, against whom our small force would stand no more chance than a handful of chaff before a gale. Do you know that they are the men who stormed the orchard battery at Germantown, and tore the companies supporting it to fragments, as if a magazine had blown up among them? We will do very well if they let us go back at all."

After some further discussion, and a good deal of grumbling on the part of the old marine at the disgrace of his Majesty's troops turning their backs upon any number of rebels, the order was given to retreat.

It was conducted in good order, the Rangers not interfering; for Clayton did not wish to be troubled with prisoners he had no convenient means of disposing of, and was very well satisfied to avoid a conflict in the city, where he might have been hemmed in: so, as soon as he saw the enemy fairly on their retrograde march, he put his troop in motion in the opposite direction, and made his way as rapidly as possible from the dangerous neighborhood.

As soon as they were in the open country, Harry raised the flag upon his carbine, securing it between the ramrod and the stock, for want of a better flag-staff, thus diverting the attention of a few of the men who were inclined to grumble at having been prevented from attacking the marines; which was Harry's principal reason for showing it at that time.

I cannot do justice to the rage of General Howe when he learned what a prize had walked into his grasp, and the cool manner in which it had walked out of it again.

CHAPTER XXIII.

Month after month passed on. The British were still in Philadelphia, leading the sober and moral life which armies are accustomed to lead in a garrison town.

The American army still lay at Valley Forge, enduring with stern patience their unparalleled sufferings. Washington was occupying a little low-browed room in old Isaac Potts the Quaker preacher's house, as his head-quarters, with a hole cut under the window-seat for a fire-proof safe in which to keep his private papers. Old Baron Steuben was there, drilling the barefooted troops in the snow, cheerful and lively on the scanty fare, in the luxury of which the officers shared as well as the men,—so scanty that, as the old baron afterward told, his cook left him, saying, by way of justification, that "where he had nothing on which to display his art, it was of no consequence who turned the string" (of the spit).

The memorable and never-to-be forgotten "Battle of the Kegs" had been fought and won by the persistent and stubborn gallantry of the British, who lined the wharves and kept up a fire upon every stick that floated past, throughout the whole of a January day. In the words of an old letter published in the "American Museum" of 1787, "Both officers and men exhibited unparalleled skill and prowess on the occasion, while the citizens stood gaping as solemn witnesses of this dreadful scene. In truth, not a chip, stick, or drift-log passed by without experiencing the vigor of the British arms. The action began about sunrise, and would have terminated in favor of the British by noon, had not an old market-woman, in crossing the river with provisions, unfortunately let a keg of butter fall overboard; which, as it was then ebb tide, floated down to the field of battle. At sight of this unexpected reinforcement of the enemy, the attack was renewed with fresh force; and the firing from the marine and land forces was beyond imagination, and so continued until night closed the conflict. The rebel kegs were either totally demolished or obliged to fly, as none of them have shown their *heads* since. It is said that his excellency Lord Howe has dispatched a swift-sailing packet with an account of this signal victory to the Court of London. In short, Monday, the — of January, will be memorable in history for the renowned Battle of the Kegs."

The Rangers still hovered around the city, pouncing on straggling vedettes and foraging-parties, and sending them home empty and disarmed (for they never troubled themselves with prisoners), or following them helter-skelter up to the very lines of the enemy, drawing out the guards in bootless pursuit, carrying off their plunder under their very noses, perambulating the city in disguise and picking up information of their plans, which they then diligently thwarted, and keeping the British in a constant fever of excitement with their mad pranks. But "the pitcher that goes often to the well gets broken at last."

One afternoon in March, Clayton's scouts brought in word that a strong party was out in the neighborhood of Frankford, coming toward the city, with a number of cattle which they had seized.

He immediately started to intercept them, at the head of Bettle's and Wetherill's divisions, and some others, amounting, altogether, to about sixty men. Coming up with the enemy in the Frankford road, about half a mile above the city, he attacked them. The latter, though fully as strong as his own party, immediately broke before the charge, and, abandoning their booty, retreated in confusion toward the city. Ordering Wetherill, with some half-dozen men, to take charge of the cattle and drive them to the rendezvous, he followed with the balance of his force in hot pursuit.

The two parties rushed together pell-mell down the road, when, as they entered a kind of defile, formed by a deep cut, hedged in by woods on each side, a shower of musket-balls from the thick undergrowth of bushes on the edge of either steep bank poured down upon the Rangers like a hailstorm. At the same instant Clayton saw that the road was blocked up in front by a solid body of infantry, certainly not less than two hundred strong, which had opened its ranks to let the fugitives pass through, and then instantly closed again.

They were betrayed! Not, however, by their scouts, who had neither seen nor suspected the presence of any stronger force than the escort which had been first attacked, and which had in reality only acted as a decoy to lead them into the trap.

Before they had recovered from the momentary surprise of the first double volley, which had emptied nearly half the saddles in the troop, another storm of balls from the strong force in front swept through them.

Reeling under the deadly fire, their movements hampered, in the confined space in which they were crowded, by the bodies of fallen men and horses, disordered by the frantic kicking of some of the latter, which lay wounded and entangled among the legs of their own horses, the surviving Rangers wavered for a moment, and seemed upon the point of breaking away in a headlong panic.

It was only for a moment. Restored to order by the calm but powerful voice of Clayton and the fiery orders of Bettle, the few remaining men backed their horses rapidly but steadily a few paces to clearer ground, wheeled suddenly, firing as they turned, and dashed up the road toward Frankford, scattering the foragers, who had taken advantage of the momentary pause to steal around to their rear, like dead leaves before a gale.

Wetherill, with his half-dozen men and the cattle, had not got more than a quarter of a mile away, when the volleys were heard in quick succession.

He ordered a halt at once; for his practiced ear told him that the fire was too heavy for the party they had chased.

"They're in a trap," said he, "as sure as—Woodward, thee has the swiftest horse. Ride for life, and bring up all the men; McLane's and all. There's half an army at Clayton."

With these hurried words, Wetherill, leaving the cattle to take care of themselves, turned back toward the fight with his companions, while Woodward, before his officer had more than half finished his order, was skimming across the fields, over hedge and ditch and fence, his light-heeled mare clearing everything like a wild deer.

When Clayton broke through those in his rear, a strong body of light-horse dashed out of the woods on each side of the road in pursuit. They kept to the fields, and continued the pursuit in this way, with the Rangers a little in advance, but exposed, thus, to a raking fire from each side.

The latter pushed on, keeping up a sharp fire, however, from their carbines as they ran, until the superior speed of their horses had put them sufficiently in advance to give them room to turn off the road to the left and gain the large open meadow which lay beside it, crossing the front of the body of horsemen on that side, and bringing them between them and the others.

Once on open ground, with room enough for the purpose, the Rangers scattered in their usual fashion when in conflict with a much superior force, thus separating and distracting their fire.

The two bodies of light-horse had now united, and the Rangers still retreated, slowly, wheeling and circling in their hawk-like movements, not widening the space between them and their enemies materially, but keeping nearly the same relative distance—about a hundred yards—never offering for an instant a stationary mark to fire at, while nearly every ball from their carbines and pistols told on the solid column which was steadily pursuing them.

In the mean time, the commander of the infantry at the defile, who had seen the Rangers in action before, suspecting that they would take to the fields as soon as possible, and make for the Wissahickon, had taken advantage of a bend in the road, pushed as rapidly as possible through the wood, and now emerged from it with his whole force a little in advance of the Rangers, —on their flank, I was going to say; but they had no flank, properly speaking; but in a position which was parallel to their general course.

As they appeared, the Rangers, without closing their ranks, at a whistle from Clayton, abandoned their wheeling movements, and all but Clayton and Bettle, who remained upright in their saddles, dropping by the sides of their horses as Harry had done when he escaped, darted forward in a straight line for a couple of hundred yards or so, until they had left this danger in their rear also.

They received a volley from the whole line as they passed; but the Regulars fired high, and no damage appeared to have been done.

As they slackened their pace again, a small flag appeared above a roll in the ground about a quarter of a mile off, and the next moment Harry appeared on the crest of the hill, waving the blue flag, and followed by the whole remaining force of the Rangers and McLane's men combined.

"There they come," said Bettle, turning to Clayton, beside whom he was riding. "Now we'll—But what's the matter?" he exclaimed, interrupting himself in alarm, as he saw Clayton's face ghastly pale, and his hand pressed against his side.

"I'm hit," said Clayton; "badly, I fear; but don't tell the men; I'll stay in the saddle as long as possible," and then added, in an undertone, as though speaking to himself, "Oh, Mary, Mary, this will be sad news for thee." He spoke with difficulty, as if the effort gave him pain, and said no more. Once or twice he swayed slightly in his seat, but immediately recovered himself, and sat there sustained by the indomitable spirit within him, to all appearance the same calm, strong man he had always been.

By this time the others had come up and thrown themselves between the wreck of their companions and their pursuers, covering their retreat and holding the light-horse at bay, the infantry having been left by this time at a distance, which removed all apprehension of danger from them.

Calling Wetherill to take his place by Clayton's side, to be ready to support him if he grew too weak to keep his seat, Bettle spurred back to Captain McLane and told him the circumstances.

"Who's with him?" said McLane.

"Wetherill."

"Tell him to take half a dozen men and get Clayton away to the rendezvous as fast as possible. I'll take care of these scarlet gentlemen here."

Bettle hurried forward again to give the order, and the fight went on.

The Americans, being now more nearly equal in numbers to the enemy, changed their tactics, and, forming in solid column, charged headlong upon them. By this time the fact of Clayton's wound had spread through his own troop, and, instead of dispiriting them as he had feared, it had only set them mad with rage. Pressing forward in advance of the column, in spite of the efforts of Bettle and the other officers to restrain them, they hurled themselves upon the enemy with a reckless fury that no discipline could withstand, driving back their front ranks upon those behind them in a confused, huddled-up mass, and disordering their whole column.

Before they could recover, McLane with his steadier force was upon them, pushing the advantage thus gained. Their ranks disordered, those savage Rangers in the midst of them, fighting, men and horses, with the blind, reckless ferocity of wounded tigers, McLane's iron column pressing them steadily back, the infantry which could have supported them out of reach, they broke into a disorderly flight toward the main body. McLane's men stopped at once without pursuing, for to have followed them to the main body would have been running into the jaws of death; but the Rangers clung to them like leeches, paying no attention to their officers' repeated orders to halt, until Bettle seized the bridle of the foremost and backed his horse by main force upon the rest, with his sword-point at the rider's throat.

CHAPTER XXIV.

The men in charge of Clayton hurried to the rendezvous, Wetherill and another one supporting him in the saddle for the last half-mile.

When they reached the place, he dismounted, with their assistance, and walked between them into the house, where he at once lay down, overcome with weakness.

The rest of the force followed as rapidly as possible, after they had driven back the enemy and discipline had been restored among the half-demented Rangers.

There had been almost a mutiny among them before this could be done; and Barton had actually drawn the trigger of his pistol at the face of one of the men who attempted to force his way past him. Fortunately for the fellow, the pistol snapped, and, brought to his senses by this sharp reminder, and by observing that Barton had recocked it, he slunk back to his place.

"Is there any one else who would like to disobey my orders?" said Barton, slowly and sternly. "For shame, men! shall it be said that Clayton's Rangers, with all their discipline, broke into mutiny as soon as their captain was wounded? For shame!"

"But, lieutenant," said another of the men, "we only wanted to revenge the captain, and all the boys that were murdered by them cowards awhile ago."

"By sacrificing the balance of the troop! Do you know there are not less than three hundred infantry yonder, and that another minute would have brought you right among them? We have nothing to do with vengeance; leave that where it belongs,—to your Maker. Back to your place and obey your orders, if you want to please the captain."

Order being restored, the whole party marched together toward the Wissahickon.

"How did you happen to come up so early?" said Bettle to Captain McLane, as they rode on together. "Woodward certainly hadn't time to reach the creek and bring you from there, when you came up."

"We were on the march," said McLane. "One of my scouts discovered the ambuscade and brought me word at once; and, fearing you might fall into the trap, we pushed out immediately to support you. We heard the firing, and were coming up at full speed, when Woodward reached us, about half a mile from where we first came in sight."

When they arrived at the rendezvous, they found Clayton lying upon a rude couch, with Wetherill standing beside him. He was quiet, and apparently free from suffering, but pale and exhausted.

His eyes had been closed, but the noise of their arrival had roused him.

Turning his head toward the door as McLane and Bettle entered, with a calm, grave smile, he beckoned the latter to him.

"William," he said, "the end has come: I shall never draw sword more."

"Oh, yes, you will, Captain Clayton," said McLane, cheerfully. "Wait till we get you into the city, where you can be properly cared for, and we'll see you in the saddle again in a month."

Clayton shook his head with the same calm, grave smile.

"I'm going to send a flag to Howe, to ask leave to have you taken in. You can't have proper treatment here."

"It is useless," said Clayton : "I could not bear the journey, and I wish no better care than my own wounded men have had. Let me meet death where it has found me,—among them."

"Would thee like to see Mary?" whispered Wetherill, stooping over him.

Clayton's eyes brightened.

"It is the dearest wish I have left," said he; "but I must give it up."

"No, thee *shall* see her," said Wetherill; "I'll bring her here to-night."

In a few minutes more, Wetherill was on his way to the city with a flag. After some delay, he was admitted within the lines, and conducted to Howe's quarters, where he stated his errand.

The general gave him the order, remarking,—

"It is not the safest time for a lady to travel; but, if you choose to take the risk of falling in with any of the marauders who are prowling around the city, you can do so."

"We will have to take the risk," said Wetherill.

"If your excellency will allow me to accompany them with an escort," said an officer who was in the room, "I will esteem it a special kindness. I know Captain Clayton personally, and would be glad to do him this service, as a requital of the courtesy I received from him and his officers when a prisoner among them."

"You may do so if you wish, Captain Gardner," said Howe. "You have hunted him faithfully, very much against your will, as I know: it is but fair that you should have the opportunity to do him a favor."

"I thank your excellency," said Captain Gardner (for it was our old acquaintance of the spring): "it is a kindness I will remember gratefully."

So saying, he took Wetherill's arm, and they left the house, the British captain in his gay uniform arm-in-arm with the Quaker lieutenant in his sober drab suit.

In the course of half an hour more they were on their way to the Wissahickon, under the promised escort; Mary, her mother, and Sarah Wheeler, whom Mary had requested to accompany her, in Mrs. Wetherill's carriage, and Wetherill himself and Captain Gardner on horseback riding beside it.

They reached the place about midnight.

As they approached the door, it was opened from the inside by Bettle, who had heard them coming. Placing his finger on his lips, he led them quietly into the room where Clayton was lying with his eyes closed, breathing heavily.

"How does he seem?" whispered Mrs. Wetherill to Bettle.

He shook his head.

"He's sinking; he has been sleeping a little at intervals until about half an hour ago, when a stupor seemed to come over him——"

Captain Gardner touched Bettle on the shoulder.

"Excuse me," said he, "for interrupting you; this gentleman, Mr. Lawrence," beckoning to a gentleman in an army surgeon's uniform, who had come in with him, "is the surgeon of our regiment. I have brought him with us to see if anything can be done to save Captain Clayton."

Bettle pressed the surgeon's hand silently, and led him to the rude couch on which the captain lay.

He looked at him for a moment, felt his pulse, applied his ear to his chest, and then turned to Bettle and Captain Gardner, who were watching him with anxious faces, and shook his head gravely.

"Nothing can save him," he whispered. "He is bleeding to death internally. Is there any wine or brandy at hand?"

"I have both in the carriage," said Mrs. Wetherill; "I will bring them in."

Pouring out a glass of brandy, the surgeon raised Clayton's head upon his arm and applied it to his lips. Partially aroused by the motion, and the pungent smell of the brandy, Clayton opened his eyes again and looked dreamily around him.

"Drink," said the surgeon.

Clayton obeyed, mechanically, and in a moment afterward, revived by the powerful stimulant, raised himself on his elbow and looked around him again, still dreamily, but with more apparent consciousness than before.

"Where's Mary?" said he: "I thought Wetherill brought her here."

Bettle silently beckoned to her, and she came forward and knelt by her lover.

"I am here, Ellis," she said, as she bent over him, and, pushing back the damp locks from his forehead, kissed it tenderly. What cared she that others were standing by? So far as any consciousness of the presence of others was concerned, she and Clayton were the only occupants of that lonely house. She saw nothing but the pale face that was now resting against her breast; she felt nothing but the faint pressure of the hand in which her own was grasped; she heard nothing but the low murmur of his voice as he strove, forgetful as ever of himself, to console *her* and strengthen her to bear the great sorrow that had come upon her.

"Has he a mother?" asked McLane of Bettle, as they stood looking sadly at this spectacle.

"No," said Bettle: "his parents are both dead. I am the only relative he has living, that I know of."

At this moment Mary pointed to the glass which was standing near, with a spoonful of brandy in it.

It was handed to her, and she put it to his lips; he swallowed a little of it, and, raising his head again from Mary's breast, beckoned the others to him.

"I have not taken the sword for fame or glory," he said, as they gathered around him, "but that I might do my duty. I have striven to do it faithfully, as I understood it. When I am dead, let me be buried by my father, if possible, without any show or parade, according to the custom of my people. Let such of my men as wish, or are permitted, attend, unarmed, and as private citizens. Call in Frank and Harry."

They came in.

"I have sent for you," continued Clayton, "to bid you farewell. We have fought our last battle together; and I want to leave you a last charge. Do not attempt —let no one attempt—to revenge my death. Tell the men so; and tell them to obey their officers as well as they have always obeyed me. These are their captain's last orders. Farewell."

The two men each grasped their captain's hand with a silent pressure, and then walked sadly away.

Clayton ceased speaking, and his head sank back upon the pillow. He lay thus for some time, with his eyes closed, in silence, Mary still kneeling beside him, with his right hand clasped in both of hers, looking at the pale face in dumb, tearless agony; while Sarah Wheeler bent over him, gently wiping away the cold damps which gathered over the forehead.

Bettle stood close beside him, his arms locked tightly across his chest, and his features working convulsively as he watched the face of the surgeon, who, with one hand thrust into the breast of his coat, and the other on the dying man's wrist, stood watching his countenance with the calm gravity of his profession.

They remained thus for some minutes, when the surgeon, turning to Bettle, who was standing nearest him, said, in a low voice, "It is coming!"

There were a few of those long, deep, awful inhalations, which he who has seen never forgets; they grew fainter and fainter, and at last Mary's face, which had been directed fixedly toward Clayton's, dropped upon his breast; the surgeon gently laid down the hand he held, and all that was left of Ellis Clayton lay there motionless and still.

CHAPTER XXV.

It was the third day after the death of Clayton, and Captain Gardner had obtained permission to have him brought to the city and laid beside his father, as he had requested. Permission was also given to his troop and that of McLane to attend the funeral; and they were all there,—the wild, bronzed Rangers standing around the grave in solemn silence, with heads uncovered, as the body of their commander was lowered to its last resting-place by Frank and Harry with their lariats.

It was a privilege the latter had asked of Wetherill, that their hands should be the last employed about the person of their captain.

They did not withdraw the lariats, but, gathering togther the leaden balls with which the ends were armed, Harry drew the flag from his bosom, and, wrapping them in it, dropped it upon the breast of Clayton.

The two men then stepped aside, and Bettle led Mary forward to the trying ordeal, which custom still preserves, of taking her last look into the grave.

She shed no tears. She could not. Her face wore the same look of dumb, tearless agony it had shown when she knelt by him as he was dying. But it was wan and haggard; there were lines upon it that told of years of suffering crowded into those brief three days, and she shook as with deadly cold.

Her mother then came forward, leaning upon her son's arm, followed by Sarah Wheeler and her brother, and then by the numerous friends who had attended.

When all had given their last look, and turned away, with tears flowing plentifully, and taken their departure from the ground, Captain Gardner, who had stood beside Barton, stepped forward, and, taking a handful of earth, leaned over the grave and dropped it in. His example was followed by the other officers present, and by the troopers, one by one, as they filed past the grave and so marched slowly away.

"Your cause has lost one of its best and bravest men, and earth one of her great souls, in him who lies yonder," said Captain Gardner to Barton, as they parted near the gate.

"It may be," said Barton. "I know that *I* have lost the best and noblest friend I ever had."

So saying, he bent down his head and walked silently after the troop.

I have not much more to tell. The history of the Rangers, in their distinctive character as an independent corps, ceases here. They did not disband, nor did a man withdraw from the work to which they had devoted themselves. But with Clayton the vital power of the troop, in its peculiar organization, had departed. Barton, unquestionably the nearest like him in character of mind, was still far inferior to him in the prompt readiness to meet all emergencies, the unfailing self-command, the fertility of resources, and the iron fixedness of purpose, which were Clayton's distinguishing characteristics. Fully conscious of this, he would not assume the responsibility of taking his place. After some consultations with the other officers, therefore, at Bettle's suggestion, which was seconded by the rest, and acquiesced in cheerfully by the men when they found that neither Barton nor either of the other lieutenants would assume the command, the troop was placed under the command of Captain McLane (with the exception of Long Johnny Mac Allan's boys, who, becoming a little tired of cavalry service, which was not their forte, attached themselves to Morgan's riflemen), and remained so, acting entirely under his orders as part of his corps, so long as they remained before the city. Their sojourn there terminated with the Meschianza, that stupendous piece of gorgeous folly with which the British officers disgraced the last month of their residence in Philadelphia. I have neither time, space, nor inclination to describe it. It was got up mainly by Major André, whose principal forte seems to have lain in the direction and management of private theatricals, and whose achievements, so far as history has recorded them, appear to have consisted chiefly in writing doggerel verses in ridicule of better men than himself, scene-painting for the aforesaid private theatricals, sketching designs for ladies' head-dresses, getting up balls and dancing gracefully at the same, and occupying his time in an industrious display of these and similar small accomplishments.

I am afraid, if Arnold's cunning in making a cat's-paw of him had not brought upon him the fate which should have been his own, that Major André would have occupied a very different and much smaller niche in the world's history than he does; and there would have been one monument less in England's Walhalla, Westminster Abbey. Where stands the tomb of Nathan Hale, among *our* national monuments?

While this gigantic farce of a Meschianza was in what somebody calls "the full tide of successful experiment," Captain McLane, with his whole force, armed with camp-kettles full of combustibles, somewhat after the fashion of Gideon of old with his pitchers and lamps therein, approached the line of abatis which extended along the Delaware south of the city, touched off their combustibles, fired the whole abatis, and then skurried off by the light to the hills of the Wissahickon, and thence leisurely to Valley Forge; leaving the Neck all alive with guards, turning out at the roll of the drums, officers hurrying to their posts, and alarm-guns banging away across the peninsula from river to river, and raising such a clatter around the Wharton House that it required the most strenuous exertions of the officers at the fête, backed by an infinite number of fibs, to persuade the ladies present that there was really nothing at all the matter, and that all this hideous noise was only a part of the performance.

This was the last prank that was played upon the British during their occupation of Philadelphia, McLane, as I said before, having immediately proceeded to Valley Forge, where he remained until the army marched to the city, on the 18th of June, entering it close on the heels of the retiring enemy,—so close, indeed, that one of their officers, "The Honorable Cosmo Gordon," being perhaps addicted to late hours, slept so late in the morning that the family on whom he was quartered thought it but kind to rouse him and tell him that "his friends the rebels" were in town.

"The Honorable Cosmo" dressed himself with marvelous speed, and, after a great deal of trouble, succeeded in hiring a boat, in which he was put across the river just as "his friends the rebels" marched into the city.

Philadelphia was once more in the hands of its rightful owners; and nothing remains now but to gather up the few scattered threads of my story, knot them together, and leave them and it in your hands.

As soon as the American army was comfortably settled in the city, Bettle obtained leave of absence for a short time, which he improved by going straightway to Brandywine. He found the Sanfords quietly settled in the old house, everything prosperous around them, all glad to see him, Jenny very manifestly so.

Bettle had intended to surprise them, but was defeated by Mike, who caught sight of him coming along the road, and at once left his work and burst uproariously into the house, shouting,—

"Whirra-r-r-r-oo! but it's meself's got the news for yeez. He's comin'; I seen 'im wid me own two eyes a-comin' along the road."

"If thee can come to thy senses without too much trouble, and tell us who it is thee means," said Thomas Sanford, "we'll be obliged to thee."

"Och, now," said Mike, "an' didn't I tell yees who it was? Annyhow, it's always puttin' the horse before the cart I am—no, puttin' the cart behind the horse, it is—blur an' ages! but I mane puttin' the cart in the horse—tunder and turf! I don't know what it is, only it's Misther Bettle."

"I'm glad thee's found out at last what it is," said John Sanford, dryly, as they all rose from the supper-table at which they had been seated, and hurried to the door.

In a few minutes more, Bettle was seated in the old-fashioned kitchen, with the family around him, with the exception of John, who had taken Roland to the stable, Mike having "respectfully but firmly" declined to go within ten feet of him.

"I bring good news in general," said Bettle, "but sad news, in one respect, to me, and I think to you also. We are masters of Philadelphia again; but Clayton is dead."

"Clayton dead!" said Thomas Sanford. "That is sorrowful news indeed. How did he die?"

"In battle. We were decoyed into an ambuscade by a party of foragers, and the troop was almost cut to pieces before we could get clear; Clayton was shot, in the retreat."

"Did he die on the field?" asked Jenny.

"No," said Bettle: "He was able to keep on his horse at first, and we held them at bay, with the assistance of Captain McLane, till he reached a place of safety. He died in a few hours afterward, however."

Bettle then gave a short history of all that had taken place since the troop left the Brandywine, occupying the rest of the evening in his narrative.

He remained in his present quarters about ten days, in the course of which he visited old 'Riah Woodward, and delivered some messages from his three sons, concerning, among other things, the desirableness of some remittances of clothing, their joint stock consisting of two ragged coats, one horse-blanket doing duty as a coat, one pair of breeches in tolerable condition, two ditto dilapidated, one shirt and a half, and three stockings.

He also took an opportunity of whispering to Mary Woodward a message from Harry, at which she tossed her head saucily, and said—not exactly as if she meant it—that he was an impudent fellow, and what business had he to be sending messages to her, indeed?

Somehow or other, nevertheless, when Bettle returned, he was charged with a message to Harry. I don't know what it was; something about his impudence, probably. Be that as it may, at the close of the following autumn there was a wedding at the old miller's house, in which the principal performers were Harry Darlington and Mary Woodward.

Bettle also visited Mac Allan, whom he found, with his family, domiciled in a comfortable log house, very much like the old one which had been burnt, and, for the rest of the day, kept the old man and his family in a state of delight with his accounts of the doings of the troop, and particularly with the high praise he bestowed upon the boys for their skill and daring. When he described the taking of the battery at Germantown, and told him how much of their success was owing to the cool and effective way in which the boys had cleared the ground for the charge upon the guns, the old man's feelings fairly overcame his discretion, and, springing to his feet, he waved his huge arm over his head, and gave them vent in a prodigious hurrah!

Relieved by this, he sat down again, and listened quietly to the rest of the narrative, only remarking, when told that the boys had joined Morgan,—

"Ay, ay! that's the place for 'em; they're used to

that kind o' sarvice. I was a little dubersome about how they'd git along in the stirrups; though they've done better than I thought they would."

Bettle also told of the death of Clayton, but did not dwell much upon it; for it was a subject on which he could not trust himself to speak much, as yet.

The ten days of furlough passed all too rapidly; but before they had passed by, Bettle had broached the subject nearest his heart to Thomas and Martha Sanford.

"We have expected it," said Thomas; "and thee is the one we would have chosen of all others to intrust our daughter with. She is a good girl, and has always been a dutiful child to us; I think she will make a good and dutiful wife to any one she is attached to, as I think she is to thee. But there is no hurry"— (why do fathers *always* say "there's no hurry"? They didn't think so when *they* wanted to be married)—"she's very young yet, and while thee will have to be away from her so much during this war, at any rate, wouldn't it be better for her to stay at home with us?"

"Perhaps reason would say yes," answered Bettle, "but I don't feel reasonable on this subject. Did thee, under the same circumstances?"

"I don't suppose I did," said Thomas. "Nevertheless, Martha and I waited for each other for four long years, and didn't get tired of waiting, either; did we, Martha?"

"No," said Martha, "we did not; though," she added, with a quiet smile, "one or two of thy friends tried to persuade me that *I* ought to be tired of it. No, William, it will do no harm to either of you to wait. Jenny is too young to marry yet.; thee must let us keep her for a year or two longer, till we see what are the prospects of peace. When the war is over, we will give her to thee. I think we can trust thy affection, I *know* we can trust Jenny's, not to wear out by a little delay."

A momentary feeling that this talk was a little cold-blooded, flashed across Bettle, but he dismissed it at once, for he could not help feeling its prudence and sound judgment. He saw the force of what was said about his unavoidable absence from her during the war, and hoping, as did every one else, that it would soon be at an end, he acquiesced, as cheerfully as he could, in the decision. Had he suspected that nearly six long years more lay between him and his crowning happiness, I doubt if he would have been half so strongly impressed with the force of the arguments that were used.

The furlough had expired, and Bettle returned to his duty. The war went on with varying success, from Monmouth, where humble Molly Pitcher earned for herself a place, in the annals of female heroism, beside the Maid of Saragossa, to Yorktown, where the long, sore struggle between might and right ended as, sooner or later, in God's good providence, it always has ended, and always will, till the flame of His final Judgment shall have swept away all evil from the earth.

The Rangers followed the war to its close, fighting well and faithfully, wherever their duty led them.

In the spring of 1784, following the treaty of peace, Bettle and Jenny were married, and took up their abode in Philadelphia, where, in as short a time as could reasonably have been expected, Mike, who, on Bettle's marriage, had installed himself as his coachman, wages or no wages, might have been seen carefully leading a horse to water—not Roland, he had been killed, poor fellow, in one of the frequent skirmishes his master had been engaged in—on which was mounted, bare-backed, a sturdy boy of some three years old, with his heels kicking gleefully against the horse's sides, while his fat, chubby hands were half buried in the mane to which he clung.

Frank and Harry returned together to the Brandywine. The former went to his old post at Thomas Sanford's, where he remained about a year, and then departed for what was then known as the "backwoods," not far from the scene of his first experience in battle, taking with him Jemima Mac Allan, and settled down as one of the band of hardy pioneers to whom our country owes so much of its early greatness.

Harry went back to the mill of 'Riah Woodward, of which he took charge, the old man saying he had worked long enough, and now meant to play. He had settled his sons around him, on farms of their own, and occupied his time, when not *playing* in the mill, with circulating around among them, giving them all, in turn, the benefit of his experience in their farming operations, and always turning to, from old habit, whenever any work was to be done, and doing his share as industriously as anybody—all in the way of rest and play, he said.

The Mac Allan boys scattered through Western Pennsylvania and Eastern Ohio, and became mighty hunters of deer and "varmint," such as bears, panthers, wild cats, etc.

Bettle and his wife made an annual visit to the old homestead with their children, and never failed to climb to the summit of old Deborah's Rock. Year after year they told their children—they never tired of hearing it—the story of the siege there, and how they had driven the Tories down the bank, and how he, by whose grave they stood, had lost his life to save the mother to whose low, sweet voice they listened.

Mary Wetherill never married. She might have done so, but her first love had been given to Clayton; and a nature like hers had no second love to bestow.

"It cannot be," she said to Captain Gardner, whose sympathy for her had ripened into strong affection. "My heart is dead to all earthly love."

So the Palm stood on, alone in its desolation.

Sarah Wheeler never married. She had opportunities enough, but she said that now the country had obtained *its* independence, she didn't see why she should throw away *hers*.

They are all gone, now, the actors in my story. But the old Rock still heaves up its craggy breast beside the quiet stream; the trees still wave their leafy crowns around it; the old house still looks toward it, across the broad, low meadows, through which the little stream trickles from under the rude bridge, the scene of Bettle's early reverie; and the Brandywine Hills still roll off to the horizon in the same matchless beauty, sleeping in the sunlight, with the shadows of the summer clouds flitting over them.

THE END.

ENTERTAINING NEW BOOKS

Published by J. B. LIPPINCOTT & CO., Philadelphia.

Will be sent by Mail, post-paid, on receipt of price.

THE WHITE ROSE.
A Novel. By G. J. WHYTE MELVILLE, author of "Cerise," "Digby Grand," "The Gladiators," etc. 12mo. Cloth. $1.50.

"The book abounds in beautiful sentiments, beautifully expressed, and its moral tone is undeniably good. We take pleasure in commending it to the public."—*Phila. Ev. Bulletin.*

THE OLD MAM'SELLE'S SECRET.
A Novel. After the German of E. Marlitt. By MRS. A. L. WISTER. 12mo. Fine cloth. $1.75.

"A more charming story, and one which, having once commenced, it seemed more difficult to leave, we have not met with for many a day."—*The Round Table.*

"Is one of the most intense, concentrated, compact novels of the day. And the work has the minute fidelity of the author of The Initials, the dramatic unity of Reade, and the graphic power of George Elliot."—*Columbus (O.) Journal.*

THE VOICE IN SINGING.
Translated from the German of EMMA SEILER by a Member of the American Philosophical Society. One vol. 12mo. Tinted paper. Fine cloth, beveled boards. $1.50.

"We would earnestly advise all interested in any way in the vocal organs to read and thoroughly digest this remarkable work."—*Boston Musical Times.*

ABRAHAM PAGE, ESQ.
A Novel. "Pity the sorrows of a poor old man." 12mo. Tinted paper. Cloth. $1 50.

FIGHTING THE FLAMES.
A Tale of the Fire Brigade. By R. M. BALLANTYNE, author of "The Wild Man of the West," "The Coral Islands," "The Red Eric," etc. With Illustrations. 12mo. Cloth. $1.50.

"An interesting and spirited little work. Mr. Ballantyne is well known as a popular writer for youth, and his present work does not detract from his reputation."—*Phila. Ev. Telegraph.*

OLD DECCAN DAYS;
Or, Hindoo Fairy Legends current in Southern India. Collected from Oral Tradition By M. FRERE. With an Introduction and Notes by SIR BARTLE FRERE. Illustrated. 12mo. $1.50.

SILVER LAKE;
Or, Lost in the Snow. By R. M. BALLANTYNE, author of "Fighting the Flames," "The Coral Islands," etc. Illustrated. $1.25.

VALUABLE AND INSTRUCTIVE WORKS
RECENTLY PUBLISHED BY
J. B. LIPPINCOTT & CO., Philadelphia.

FIVE YEARS WITHIN THE GOLDEN GATE.
By ISABELLE SAXON. Crown 8vo. Fine stamped cloth. $2.50
"This volume is instructive and entertaining."—*The Press.*

A SUMMER IN ICELAND.
By C. W. PAIJKULL. Translated by M. R. BARNARD, B.A. With map and numerous illustrations. 8vo. Cloth. $5.00.

AMONG THE ARABS.
A Narrative of Adventures in Algeria. By G. NAPHEGYI, M.D., etc., author of "The Album of Language," "History of Hungary," "La Cueva Del Diablo," etc. With Portrait of Author. 12mo. Tinted paper. Fine cloth, beveled boards. $1.75.

"The author describes a journey in Algeria, in which he had peculiar facilities for observing and studying the habits, customs, and peculiarities of the people of that land—of whom but comparatively little is known. He has made one of the most interesting books of travel which have been issued for a long time."—*Boston Journal.*

MORTE DARTHUR.
SIR THOMAS MALORY'S Book of King Arthur and his Noble Knights of the Round Table. The original Edition of Caxton revised for modern use, with an Introduction by SIR EDWARD STRACHEY, Bart. THE GLOBE EDITION. Square 12mo. Tinted paper. Cloth. $1.75.

CURIOUS MYTHS.
Curious Myths of the Middle Ages. By S. BARING GOULD. Second Series. 12mo. Illustrated. Tinted paper. Fine cloth. $2.50.

LIVES OF THE ENGLISH CARDINALS,
Including Historical Notices of the Papal Court, from Nicholas Breakspear (Pope Adrian IV.) to Thomas Wolsey, Cardinal Legate. By FOLKESTONE WILLIAMS, author of "The Court and Times of James I.," etc. Two vols. 8vo. Cloth. $12.00.

AB-SA-RA-KA, HOME OF THE CROWS.
Being the Experience of an Officer's Wife on the Plains: marking the vicissitudes of peril and pleasure during the first occupation of the Powder River route to Montana, 1866-67, and the Indian hostility thereto; with outlines of the natural features and resources of the land; tables of distances, and other aids to the traveler. Gathered from observation and other reliable sources. 12mo. Illustrated with maps and wood engravings. Tinted paper. Fine cloth. $2.00.

For sale by all Booksellers, or will be sent by mail, postage free, on receipt of price by the Publishers.

VALUABLE WORKS
Published by J. B. LIPPINCOTT & CO., Philadelphia.
Will be sent by Mail, post-paid, on receipt of price.

THE AMERICAN BEAVER and his WORKS.
By LEWIS H. MORGAN, author of "The League of the Iroquois." Handsomely illustrated with 23 full-page lithographs and numerous wood-cuts. One vol. 8vo. Tinted paper. Cloth extra. $5.00.

"We have read Mr. Morgan's elaborate but most lucidly written volume with intense delight and full satisfaction."—*Boston Ev. Transcript.*

DIXON'S SPIRITUAL WIVES.
By W. HEPWORTH DIXON, author of "New America," "William Penn," "The Holy Land," etc. SECOND EDITION. Complete in one crown 8vo. volume. With Portrait of Author from Steel. Tinted paper. Extra cloth. $2.50.

"The subject of 'Spiritual Wives' is at once sensational, appalling, and full of deep interest. If we look at it simply as a system, it is replete with scenes which cannot be surpassed even in fiction."—*London Morning Post.*

U. S. CHRISTIAN COMMISSION.
Annals of the United States Christian Commission. By REV. LEMUEL MOSS, Home Secretary to the Commission. In one vol. 8vo. of 752 pages. Handsomely illustrated. Tinted paper. Cloth extra. $4.50.

LETTERS FROM THE FRONTIERS.
Written during a period of Thirty Years' Service in the U. S. Army. By MAJ.-GEN. GEORGE A. MCCALL, late Commander of the Pennsylvania Reserve Corps. One vol. crown 8vo. Toned paper. Fine cloth. $2.50.

"His letters in the volume before us include a period of over thirty years of active service in Florida, the West, the Mexican War, and New Mexico. They are admirably written—easy, familiar, graphic, anecdotal, descriptive, and full of information. It seems as if the gallant writer was as much master of the pen as of the sword."—*Phila. Press.*

BAKER'S ABYSSINIA.
The Nile Tributaries of Abyssinia, and the Sword Hunters of the Hamran Arabs. By SIR SAMUEL WHITE BAKER, author of "The Albert Nyanza." With Maps and numerous Illustrations, drawn by E. Griset from Original Sketches by the Author. Superfine paper. One vol. crown 8vo. Extra cloth. $2.75.

. . . "We have rarely met with a descriptive work so well conceived and so attractively written as Baker's Abyssinia, and we cordially recommend it to public patronage. . . . It is beautifully illustrated, and contains several well executed maps of great value."—*N. O. Times.*

OUIDA'S WORKS.

Novels. 12mo. Price $2.00 each.

TRICOTRIN, The Story of a Waif and Stray. With Portrait of the author from an Engraving on Steel.

"Tricotrin is a work of absolute power, some truth, and deep interest."—*N. Y. Day Book.*

GRANVILLE DE VIGNE; or, Held in Bondage. A Tale of the Day.

"This is one of the most powerful and spicy works of fiction which the present century, so prolific in light literature, has produced."

STRATHMORE; or, Wrought by his own Hand.

"It is a romance of the intense school, but it is written with more power, fluency, and brilliancy than the works of Miss Braddon and Mrs. Wood, while its scenes and characters are taken from high life."—*Boston Transcript.*

CHANDOS.

"It is a story of surpassing power and interest."—*Pittsburg Ev. Chron.*

IDALIA.

"It is a story of love and hatred, of affection and jealousy, of intrigue and devotion. . . . We think this novel will attain a wide popularity, especially among those whose refined taste enables them to appreciate and enjoy what is truly beautiful in literature."—*Albany Ev. Jour.*

UNDER TWO FLAGS. A Story of the Household and the Desert.

"No one will be able to resist its fascination who once begins its perusal."—*Phila. Ev. Bulletin.*

NOVELETTES.

Each of these volumes contains a selection of "Ouida's" Popular Tales and Stories. 12mo. Price $1.75 each.

First Series.—CECIL CASTLEMAINE'S GAGE.
Second Series.—RANDOLPH GORDON.
Third Series.—BEATRICE BOVILLE.

"The many works already in print by this versatile authoress have established her reputation as a novelist, and these short stories contribute largely to the stock of pleasing narratives and adventures alive to the memory of all who are given to romance and fiction."—*N. Haven Jour.*

The above are all handsomely and uniformly bound in Cloth, and are for sale by booksellers generally, or will be sent by mail, postage free, on receipt of price.

J. B. LIPPINCOTT & CO., Publishers,
715 & 717 Market St., Philadelphia.

LIPPINCOTT'S MAGAZINE
OF
LITERATURE, SCIENCE, AND EDUCATION.

SHORT PROSPECTUS.

UNDER the head of *Literature*, will be included an original *Novel*, by a writer of high reputation and acknowledged talent; and numerous shorter *Tales, Sketches of Travel, History and Biography, Essays, Papers of Wit and Humor, Poetry,* and *Miscellanies.*

Articles will be given, presenting in a clear and popular style the latest discoveries in various branches of *Science.*

Education, a topic of the highest importance in a country like the United States, will receive special attention.

It is not proposed to engage in partisan or sectarian warfare, but vital questions of the day will not be neglected; and the *Financial and Commercial* condition of the country will be handled by an able writer.

Each number will contain a paper entitled *Our Monthly Gossip*, in which Notes and Queries, Answers to Correspondents, Anecdotes, and Miscellanies will find a place. The *Literature of the Day* will also receive attention.

OPINIONS OF THE PRESS.

"It has, from its first appearance, entered the front rank of our monthlies. We commend it heartily."—*N. Y. Independent.*

"Not only confirms the favorable impression produced on its first appearance, but continues to improve upon acquaintance."—*Presbyterian Banner.*

"It has no superior."—*New Haven Register.*

"Worthy to be classed with the best literary monthlies of England and this country."—*Philada. Ev. Bulletin.*

"We pay it the highest compliment when we say that its contents and editorial management are in harmony with its rich-toned paper and varied typographical excellencies."—*Albany Ev. Journal.*

TERMS OF LIPPINCOTT'S MAGAZINE.

YEARLY SUBSCRIPTION. — Four Dollars. SINGLE NUMBER. — Thirty-five cents. CLUB RATES.—Two copies for $7; Five copies for $16; Ten copies for $30; and each additional copy $3. For every Club of Twenty Subscribers an extra copy will be furnished GRATIS, or Twenty-one copies for $60.

SPECIAL.—The publishers have prepared a list of valuable Standard Books, which they offer as Premiums for Subscriptions. A copy of the list, with terms, will be sent on application. SPECIMEN NUMBER sent to any address on receipt of 35 cents. SUBSCRIBERS will please be careful to give their Post-office address in full.

Address **J. B. LIPPINCOTT & CO., Publishers,**
715 and 717 Market St., Philadelphia.

THE SUNDAY LIBRARY
FOR HOUSEHOLD READING.
NOW READY.

Vol. I. THE PUPILS OF ST. JOHN THE DIVINE. By the author of "THE HEIR OF REDCLYFFE." Illustrated. 12mo. Extra cloth. $2.00.

Vol. II. THE HERMITS. By REV. CHARLES KINGSLEY. Illustrated. 12mo. Extra cloth. $2.00.

Vol. III. SEEKERS AFTER GOD. The Lives of Seneca, Epictetus, and Marcus Aurelius. By REV. F. W. FARRAR, M.A. Illustrated. 12mo. Extra cloth. $2.00.

Vol. IV. ENGLAND'S ANTIPHON: a Historical Review of the Religious Poetry of England. By GEORGE MACDONALD, M.A. Illustrated. 12mo. Extra cloth. $2.00.

Vol. V. LIVES OF ST. LOUIS AND CALVIN. By M. GUIZOT. Illustrated. 12mo. Extra cloth. $2.00.

The projectors of "*The Sunday Library for Household Reading*" feel that there is a want of books of a kind that will be welcome in many households for reading on Sundays, and it will be their aim to embrace in this series volumes that will supply this want.

EACH VOLUME SOLD SEPARATELY.

THREE VALUABLE BOOKS FOR
EVERY WIFE AND MOTHER.

I. ADVICE TO A WIFE on the Management of her own Health, and on the Treatment of some of the Complaints incidental to Pregnancy, Labor, and Suckling; with an Introductory Chapter especially addressed to a Young Wife. By PYE HENRY CHAVASSE, M.D. Eighth edition, revised. 16mo. Neatly bound in cloth. Price $1.50.

II. ADVICE TO A MOTHER on the Management of her Children, and on the Treatment on the moment of some of their more pressing Illnesses and Accidents. By PYE HENRY CHAVASSE, M.D. Ninth edition, revised. 16mo. Neatly bound in cloth. Price $1.50.

III. MATERNAL MANAGEMENT OF INfancy. For the use of Parents. By F. H. GETCHELL, M.D. 16mo. Cloth. 75 cents.

For sale by all Booksellers, or will be sent by mail, postage free, on receipt of price.

Published by J. B. LIPPINCOTT & CO.,
715 & 717 MARKET ST., PHILADELPHIA.

THE STANDARD LIBRARY EDITION
OF
THACKERAY'S WORKS.

ELEGANTLY ILLUSTRATED.

To be completed in about Twenty Volumes, large Crown 8vo., printed in Large Type on Superfine Tinted Paper, and handsomely bound in fine Cloth Gilt, beveled boards. Price $3.50 per volume. Fine Cloth, Gilt Top, $3.75 per volume. Half Turkey Morocco, $5.50 per volume. Half Calf Gilt, $5.50 per volume.

NOW READY.
EACH COMPLETE IN TWO VOLUMES.

1. **VANITY FAIR**
   With 40 Steel Engravings and 150 Wood-cuts.
2. **PENDENNIS.**
   With 46 Steel Engravings and 120 Wood-cuts.
3. **THE NEWCOMES.**
   With 46 Steel Engravings, and 118 Wood-cuts by RICHARD DOYLE.
4. **PHILIP.**
   Prefixed by a Shabby Genteel Story. With numerous Illustrations.
5. **THE VIRGINIANS.**
   With 47 Steel Plates and numerous Wood-cuts.

IN ONE VOLUME.

6. **HENRY ESMOND.**
   With numerous Illustrations.
7. **THE PARIS SKETCH BOOK.**
   With 17 Steel Plates and numerous Wood-cuts.

THE REMAINING WORKS WILL BE ISSUED IN MONTHLY VOLUMES.

FOR SALE BY BOOKSELLERS GENERALLY.

PUBLISHED BY
J. B. LIPPINCOTT & CO.,
PHILADELPHIA.

PUBLICATIONS OF J. B. LIPPINCOTT & CO., Phila.
Will be sent by Mail, post-paid, on receipt of price.

THE PEOPLE THE SOVEREIGNS.
Being a Comparison of the Government of the United States with those of the Republics which have existed before, with the Causes of their Decadence and Fall. By JAMES MONROE, Ex-President of the United States. Edited by SAMUEL L. GOUVERNEUR, his grandson and administrator. One vol. 12mo. Tinted paper. Extra Cloth. Price $1.75.

A HISTORY OF SACERDOTAL CELIBACY.
An Historical Sketch of Sacerdotal Celibacy in the Christian Church. By HENRY C. LEA. In one octavo volume of nearly 600 pages. Extra Cloth. Price $3.75.

. . . The work has been laboriously and carefully prepared, and contains a complete history of ecclesiastical celibacy, traced through the different centuries and followed through all the changes of temporal government and religious authority. A very full index makes the book valuable and serviceable for reference upon the matters of which it treats.—*Boston Journal.*

THE SEVEN WEEKS' WAR.
Its Antecedents and its Incidents. By H. M. HOZIER, F.C.S., F.G.S., Military Correspondent of the London Times with the Prussian Army during the German Campaign of 1866. Two vols. 8vo. With numerous Maps and Plans. Superfine paper. Extra Cloth. Price $10.00.

. . . All that Mr. Hozier saw of the great events of the war—and he saw a large share of them—he describes in clear and vivid language.—*London Saturday Review.*

LIVES OF BOULTON AND WATT.
Principally from the original Soho MSS. Comprising also a History of the Invention and Introduction of the Steam Engine. By SAMUEL SMILES, author of "Lives of the Engineers," "Self-Help," "Industrial Biography," etc. With a Portrait of Watt and Boulton and numerous other Illustrations. Printed on fine toned paper. One vol. Royal 8vo. Strong Cloth. Price $10.00.

HISTORY OF THE KNIGHTS TEMPLAR OF THE STATE OF PENNSYLVANIA.
Prepared and arranged from Original Papers, together with the Constitution, Decisions, Resolutions, and Forms of the R. E. Grand Commandery of Pennsylvania. By ALFRED CREIGH, LL.D., K. T. 33°. One vol. 12mo. Extra Cloth. Price $2.50.

. . . This work is an invaluable one to the fraternity, giving as it does a complete history of the Knights Templar from 1794 to November, 1866.—*Pittsburg Ev. Chronicle.*

PUBLICATIONS OF J. B. LIPPINCOTT & CO.
Will be sent by Mail on receipt of price.

LIPPINCOTT'S PRONOUNCING GAZETTEER OF THE WORLD,

OR GEOGRAPHICAL DICTIONARY.

Revised Edition, with an Appendix containing nearly ten thousand new notices, and the most recent Statistical Information, according to the latest Census Returns, of the United States and Foreign Countries

Lippincott's Pronouncing Gazetteer gives—

I.—A Descriptive notice of the Countries, Islands, Rivers, Mountains, Cities, Towns, etc., in every part of the Globe, with the most Recent and Authentic Information.

II.—The Names of all Important places, etc., both in their Native and Foreign Languages, with the PRONUNCIATION of the same—a Feature never attempted in any other Work.

III.—The Classical Names of all Ancient Places, so far as they can be accurately ascertained from the best Authorities.

IV.—A Complete Etymological Vocabulary of Geographical Names.

V.—An elaborate Introduction, explanatory of the Principles of Pronunciation of Names in the Danish, Dutch, French, German, Greek, Hungarian, Italian, Norwegian, Polish, Portuguese, Russian, Spanish, Swedish, and Welsh Languages.

Comprised in a volume of over two thousand three hundred imperial octavo pages. Price, $10.00.

FROM THE HON. HORACE MANN, LL.D.,
Late President of Antioch College.

I have had your Pronouncing Gazetteer of the World before me for some weeks. Having long felt the necessity of a work of this kind, I have spent no small amount of time in examining yours. It seems to me so important to have a comprehensive and authentic gazetteer in all our colleges, academies, and schools, that I am induced in this instance to depart from my general rule in regard to giving recommendations. Your work has evidently been prepared with immense labor; and it exhibits proofs from beginning to end that knowledge has presided over its execution. The rising generation will be greatly benefited, both in the accuracy and extent of their information, should your work be kept as a book of reference on the table of every professor and teacher in the country.

COMPLETION OF CHAMBERS'S ENCYCLOPÆDIA!

NOW READY.

THE TENTH AND CONCLUDING VOLUME
OF

CHAMBERS'S ENCYCLOPÆDIA,

A DICTIONARY OF

Universal Knowledge for the People.

ILLUSTRATED

WITH NUMEROUS WOOD ENGRAVINGS.

IN TEN VOLUMES ROYAL OCTAVO.

PRICE PER VOL., CLOTH, $4.50; SHEEP, $5.00; HALF TURKEY, $5.50.

The Publishers have the pleasure of announcing that they have just issued the concluding PART OF CHAMBERS'S ENCYCLOPÆDIA, and that the work is now complete in TEN ROYAL OCTAVO VOLUMES, of over 800 pages each, illustrated with about 4000 engravings, and accompanied by AN ATLAS OF NEARLY FORTY MAPS (sold separately), the whole, it is believed, forming the most complete work of reference extant.

The design of this work, as explained in the Notice prefixed to the first volume, is that of a DICTIONARY OF UNIVERSAL KNOWLEDGE FOR THE PEOPLE—not a mere collection of elaborate treatises in alphabetical order, but a work to be readily consulted as a DICTIONARY on every subject on which people generally require some distinct information. Commenced in 1859, the work is now brought to a close in 1868, and the Editors confidently point to the Ten volumes of which it is composed as forming the most COMPREHENSIVE—as it certainly is the CHEAPEST—ENCYCLOPÆDIA ever issued in the English language.

COPIES OF THE WORK WILL BE SENT TO ANY ADDRESS IN THE UNITED STATES, FREE OF CHARGE, ON RECEIPT OF THE PRICE BY THE PUBLISHERS.

J. B. LIPPINCOTT & CO., Publishers

715 and 717 Market St., Philadelphia

Printed in Dunstable, United Kingdom